THE CINDERELLA TEST: WOULD YOU REALLY WANT THE SHOE TO FIT?

*Subtle Ways Women Are Seduced
and Socialized into Servitude and Stereotypes*

VERA SONJA MAASS

PRAEGER

An Imprint of ABC-CLIO, LLC

A B C ⬥ C L I O

Santa Barbara, California • Denver, Colorado • Oxford, England

Library of Congress Cataloging-in-Publication Data

Maass, Vera Sonja.
   The Cinderella test : would you really want the shoe to fit? : subtle ways women are seduced and socialized into servitude and stereotypes / Vera Sonja Maass.
        p. cm.
   Includes bibliographical references and index.
   ISBN 978-0-313-37924-6 (alk. paper) — ISBN 978-0-313-37925-3 (eBook)
   1. Women—Psychology. 2. Stereotypes (Social psychology) 3. Femininity—United States. 4. Women's studies. I. Title.
   HQ1206.M267 2009
   155.6'33—dc22

                                                                                    2009017549

13 12 11 10 9   1 2 3 4 5

This book is also available on the World Wide Web as an eBook.
Visit www.abc-clio.com for details.

ABC-CLIO, LLC
130 Cremona Drive, P.O. Box 1911
Santa Barbara, California 93116-1911

This book is printed on acid-free paper ∞
Manufactured in the United States of America

Contents

Preface

Cinderella's durability is unmatched. How many generations of young girls have been fascinated by this fairy tale? What accounts for the fascination? The fairy tale is full of promises; it is also full of demands. But the glory of its promises outshines the demands—at least at first sight. The stakes are high: to be chosen by the prince. The criteria for selection are silent beauty, submissiveness, patience, and willingness to work for others without complaint. This combination renders the fairy tale a most efficient vehicle for the socialization of young girls, according to the culture's demands.

In their symbolic forms, fairy tales reinforce self-defeating social and psychological behavior patterns in women's daily lives. Social conditioning—by instilling in women the need for approval and acceptance—continues with modern methods of indoctrination the socialization process begun long ago by fairy tales; and believing in fairy tales makes it easy to believe in other myths. In their search for acceptance as the special one, women are the biggest consumers of advice. Many women spend half a lifetime trying to measure up to someone's formula for perfection.

The fairy tale does not mention Cinderella's life after the wedding ceremony. Perhaps the original storyteller was too lazy to continue, or perhaps the story's impact is so much greater when every girl can indulge her own dreams of what follows the wedding. What follows does not matter much for the merchants involved. The women's shoe industry continuously benefits from the fairy tale's icon, the high-heeled slipper. Merchants who can relate their goods to the fairy tale have ample opportunity to take advantage of it. A good part of a community's economy thrives with the fairy tale's life.

In the fairy tale's traditional version, the story's central icon, the slipper, becomes the critical measure for a girl's fitness to be chosen by the prince. Is her foot small enough to fit into the slipper? Even if it pinches her toes, she will not complain—the reward is worth it, she thinks. But what the girl fails to consider is the fact that if the shoe fits tightly now, there will be no room for growth or expansion of any kind.

The tale's climax is presented in the measuring scene and the likelihood that the girl's foot will fit the shoe in the hand of the prince. This is the important moment, when the girl should carefully examine the slipper's characteristics. Is the shoe large enough or flexible enough to accommodate her goals and desires? Is there space enough for her toes to test different paths and to change directions if she wants to explore other roads? After cautious appraisal, she may come to the conclusion that the slipper is of little value to her and can be refused. She may decide that she does not want to fit the shoe.

The book grew out of many years of psychotherapy work with women of all ages from a variety of backgrounds. The issues discussed in the different chapters of the book are the ones female clients brought to the sessions time and time again; they were integral parts, woven into the tapestry of their lives. These issues were not restricted to women seeking therapy to resolve their difficulties. Women in the community at large expressed very similar concerns, and relevant examples can be found throughout history by studying the stories of notable women. Stories of women in these three areas of life were combined for a balanced presentation of the topics.

The individuals encountered in the pages of this book have not been selected on a random basis. Although they are from various ethnic and cultural backgrounds, the majority of them come from white, middle-class backgrounds. Their names have been changed and their circumstances disguised for reasons of confidentiality. There is no claim that the individuals whose stories have been related are representative of all individuals in the general population.

Acknowledgments

The individuals who agreed to share their stories have become a significant part of this book. Their generosity with their time and information is greatly appreciated. Their enthusiasm about participating was rewarding. To protect the confidentiality of their information, their names have been changed and aspects of their circumstances have been disguised. They know who they are, and my gratitude is extended to every one of them.

Special thanks go to Debbie Carvalko, Senior Acquisitions Editor, Psychology, Health and Social Work, for her suggestions concerning the book's title and her willingness to be available for assistance when needed. To the members of the "Word by Word" writers' group at the Writers' Center of Indiana, I want to express my gratitude for their patience in reading parts of the manuscript and offering feedback and helpful personal discussions. Carole Carlson, Nancee Harrison, Mary McCorkle, Judy Miller, Linda Thornton, Richard Stott, Jim Gamble, and Bob Hall—thank you all.

Part I ──────────────────────────────

Background

Will the "Real" Cinderella Please Stand Up?

> Cinderella and the Prince were soon married. It was Cinderella's dream
> come true. The two brave little mice Jaq and Gus weren't surprised because
> they always knew that if you keep on believing, that's just what dreams do!
> (Disney Enterprises, 1995)

Reports about whirlwind romances in the public media serve to endow the
Cinderella tale with an aura of relevance even in the 21st century. The enduring
power of this fairy tale can be gleaned from the frequency count of its mention in
public communication. Whenever aspects of the tale are compared to some current occurrences, the rest of the story will also resurface—however briefly—in
the minds of the readers or listeners and reinforce its significance and relevance
even to present-day lifestyles.

The story of Cinderella, as one of the most popular fairy tales known, has
impacted the socialization of boys and girls for many generations. Told to us in
childhood, her influence does not end in childhood; it extends through adolescence into young adulthood and is confirmed by the sound of the wedding bells
and the sight of the confectioner's couple on the wedding cake. The Prince has
arrived, and the girlhood dream seems to have come true.

MEET THE ORIGINAL CINDERELLA

How many young women—who have empathized, suffered, and triumphed
with the heroine in the Walt Disney version of the patient, submissive, defenseless, and silently suffering young Cinderella—actually know that Cinderella has

not always been the silent passive girl? How many realize that her transformation from a fighter for justice and truth into the passive and obedient maiden did not occur until the end of the 17th century? The oral tale of Cinderella has been traced back to matrilineal societies in which a female character, such as a dead mother, bestows gifts on the young girl that will enable her to accomplish her goals.

During the course of time the Cinderella-type heroine was changed. Mythologist Jack Zipes, in his 2003 book *The Brothers Grimm: From Enchanted Forests to the Modern World,* traces the change of the Cinderella-type heroine back through a period of four millennia—approximately 7000 B.C. to 3000 B.C. The young, active woman who was expected to pursue her own destiny under the guidance of a wise, gift-bearing dead mother was transformed into a helpless, inactive, pubescent girl, whose major accomplishments are obedience and domestic activities, and who patiently awaits to be rescued by a male hero. In the dominant version of the Cinderella tale in the modern world, the matrilineal tradition has given way to patriarchalization—especially in the literary tradition. In general, the patriarchalization of matrilineal tales led to the replacement of female protagonists and rituals celebrating the moon goddess by heroes and rites emphasizing male superiority and sun worship. The characteristic of submissiveness is not the only aspect that was bestowed upon fairy-tale heroines during the transformation. Silence and general powerlessness completed the picture. Ruth Bottigheimer (1987) described the Cinderella character encountered in the Grimms's tales as follows: "Cinderella, aside from her formulaic incantations, says nothing. Silent at the ball, speechless among the ashes, mute when trying on the tiny slipper"(p. 53).

INTRODUCING THE IMPOSTOR: CINDERELLA ACCORDING TO CHARLES PERRAULT AND THE BROTHERS GRIMM

The Western history of the Cinderella tale is part of the legacy of European peasant tales that in the 15th century, with the rise of the printing press, were transformed from the oral to written versions with an aristocratic audience in mind. As pointed out by Jane Yolen (1977), it was Charles Perrault, the French poet and lawyer, who laid the foundations for a new literary genre—the fairy tale—by adapting old folk tales and remaking them into "moralized," succinct stories. His efforts started the conversion, which paved the way for the Jacob and Wilhelm Grimm's version, as we know it today. Perrault created the most popular version with his *Cendrillon.* He was credited with adding such items as the glass slipper and the pumpkin coach, both instrumental in his version for the smooth process to the wedding so they could live happily ever after. (Or did they?) Thus ends the fairy tale and so does the magic. Life after the wedding seemingly ceases to exist—or, perhaps, it is not worth mentioning.

The two dominant versions of Cinderella persisting in Western Europe and America at the end of the 19th century were those of Perrault and the Brothers

Grimm, and often they were mixed together. An oral tale, once celebrating the ritualistic initiation of a girl entering womanhood within a matrilineal society, had been transformed into a verbal version bearing a literate code that prescribed the domestic requirements in bourgeois Christian society necessary for a young woman to be acceptable for marriage: self-sacrifice, diligence, hard work, silence, humility, and patience. American authors continued the trend of creating dainty and prudish Cinderellas during the 19th and into the 20th century. "The final result of this mass-market development was the Walt Disney film of 1949, which presented Cinderella in her most 'perverted' form—the patient, submissive, defenseless young woman, whose happiness depends on a man who actually defines her life" (Yolen, 1977, p. 7).

What was the need or reason for the creation of the "impostor," a version of the fairy tale heroine that is almost the opposite of the original? Perhaps it was simply a way of managing the turbulent time of growing up, of keeping young girls patient and obedient and preparing them for their marital duties. Today, it would be difficult to insist that the conversion was performed in the best interest of young impressionable girls, and perhaps that was not the purpose then either. Characteristics such as self-sacrifice, hard work, and similar traits can be applied to the advantage of others in a variety of circumstances. However, the reason for Cinderella's conversion is not the main purpose of this book; instead of focusing on the "why," our time is better used investigating the "how" of restoring a version of Cinderella that reflects the competence and self-direction that many of today's women possess and demonstrate.

THE MESSAGE IN THE SLIPPER

A good start might be by examining the message in the crucial scene of matching the maiden's foot to the slipper or shoe. According to Robert Graves (1955), past attempts at linking the Cinderella fairy tale to the Greek myths have interpreted the act of fitting Cinderella's foot into the shoe as symbolizing the marital union within a common sexual allegory, pointing to the Eleusinian Mysteries, which signified the sacred marriage by working a phallic object in a woman's shoe.

In the traditional version of the fairy tale, the girl whose foot fits into the shoe becomes acceptable to the prince. As we know, the two mean-spirited stepsisters failed the test in spite of their willingness to sacrifice their toes (as in the version of the Brothers Grimm). The slipper became the icon for Cinderella's or the woman's role in life; the foot becomes the representation of the whole person, Cinderella's complete being. Keeping in mind that Cinderella seemed to be deprived of speech, her tiny foot might be the only method of communication available to her for presenting herself.

Although it was Cinderella's slipper, given to her by the fairy godmother, the shoe now embodies the restrictions and requirements that the prince and the world place upon her and her role in life. Compliance with the restrictions renders her acceptable to the prince and fit to make the grade of princess. A second— not verbalized but implied message—contains a warning for Cinderella to avoid any changes. As the shoe now fits tightly, there is no room for growth or change. If she grows literally or figuratively, her foot may no longer match the constricting criteria of the slipper.

A recent magazine article called "Cinderella . . . probably lost her slipper because her feet hurt!" can be understood as a warning to that effect of changes. Patricia Kirby reported on a survey conducted by the American Orthopedic Foot and Ankle Society (AOFAS), revealing that 88 percent of women squeeze their feet into shoes that are about a half inch too narrow. Kirby cautioned that when wearing shoes with heels two inches or higher, women's feet will slide forward in the shoe, redistributing the weight and disturbing the body's natural alignment. "Men buy shoes to fit, while we 'Cinderellas' try to make our feet fit our shoes," Kirby pointed out (2008, p. 74).

Looking for guidance about the slipper's inherent message to the assumed original version of the heroine's story, what interpretation of the "slipper" scene would seem reasonable and appropriate in those circumstances? As in the "impostor" version, the foot again is the representation of Cinderella, the person with all her qualities, personality traits, attitudes, beliefs, shortcomings, and so on. The shoe held by the prince then becomes the framework within which Cinderella's goals, dreams, desires, expectations, and ambitions may be realized. In the case that the shoe is sufficient to accommodate Cinderella's goals and wishes, the prince might be regarded as acceptable. If the shoe is too small for Cinderella's goals and expectations, the prince may have to look elsewhere for a bride.

Viewing the slipper as the central icon in the story, Madonna Kolbenschlag interprets it as "a symbol of sexual bondage and imprisonment in a stereotype. Historically, the virulence of its significance is born out in the twisted horrors of Chinese foot binding practices. On another level, the slipper is a symbol of power—with all of its accompanying restrictions and demands for conformity. When the Prince offers Cinderella the lost slipper (originally a gift of the magic bird), he makes his kingdom hers" (1979, p. 75).

A comparison of the two versions as discussed above reveals that the underlying basic assumptions are reversed in meaning: In the traditional version, the shoe is the symbol for the measure applied to the woman for her to be accepted or rejected. In the alternate (and perhaps the older and original) version, the shoe is the representation for what the prince can and is willing to give to be accepted or rejected by Cinderella.

Translated into modern times and stated in an over-simplified way, assuming that Cinderella's primary goal is that of motherhood, she would inspect the shoe held by the prince for the evidence of a sufficient material foundation but also the genes and personality characteristics that make him a good, effective father in addition to being a loving husband. If her expectations were to combine motherhood and a meaningful career for herself, the man, in addition to possessing the attributes of parent and spouse, would have to be willing to share equally in the chores and responsibilities required for the functioning of the family. His ability and willingness to assist her in the realization of her wishes and expectations—in addition to his own—may gain him her love.

Contrary to the opinions of those who think meanings of fairy tales are obsolete, the mere mentioning and alluding to the tales in the popular press proves otherwise. Cinderella's durability can be seen in the attempts to link real-life stories to aspects of the fairy tale. Not long ago, London-based fashion writer and runway reporter Camilla Morton made the connection to Cinderella's slipper with her 2006 book *How to Walk in High Heels: The Girl's Guide to Everything* (featuring a high-heeled women's shoe on the cover), which she dedicated to "aspiring Cinderellas everywhere." As its title promises, it is a "how to" book, offering advice from how to be stylish, to how to deal with affairs of the heart, to how to enjoy your DVR, to how to stay rich and how to travel—although how to find the prince was omitted. But this is not reason for despair; there are ways to catch the prince. As we know from the traditional version of the fairy tale, losing the tiny slipper is one time-honored way; another is strict obedience to *The Rules*, a book by Ellen Fein and Sherrie Schneider, first published in 1997. Ten years later the authors followed up with another edition, *All the Rules: Time-tested Secrets for Capturing the Heart of Mr. Right.*

REFUSALS TO LET CINDERELLA DIE

The fascination with the Cinderella story is so strong and pervasive that it seems to live on forever. Attempts to find Cinderella's counterpart in real life take over people's fantasies and the wishful thinking of young girls. In 1956, Grace Kelly's marriage to Prince Rainier of Monaco was made into a storybook romance that was turned into a glamorous spectacle as it was filmed by MGM. The continued obsessions with finding a new Cinderella to keep everyone's hopeful expectations up have repeatedly focused on Princess Diana, even though—along with Grace Kelly—as Lady Diana Spencer she was not the poor little girl we have met in the fairy-tale books, and her life was not exactly eternal happiness after she met the prince.

What happened to this Cinderella? Did the slipper fit Diana's foot or was it too tight, too loose? Did her foot change in size or shape? Did she know that—if we can believe the tabloid press—the prince's romantic interests were invested in another woman? Is the story of Diana an example of what can happen when Cinderella does not know herself well enough to decide what she wants in her life—except that it should be a prince? Would any prince do, no matter what else he has or does not have?

The answer to the question of whether or not any prince would do seems to be affirmative in some cases, as Mary Jeffery Collier (1961), a female psychology professor who conducted interviews among 32 female students at Kalamazoo College, found out. Asking her students, who had grown up in the forties and fifties, about what had appealed to them most in the fairy tale of Cinderella, she heard that they loved the idea that Cinderella was able to go to the ball and then marry the prince. Obviously, the girls had believed that a prince—any prince—would be the best bridegroom any girl could dream of getting for herself. Those were answers given by young women more than 40 years ago—what might be the answers today?

An American president might in our estimation come as close to being a prince as any man would. How did the princely magic work when Hillary Rodham Clinton made her bid for the presidency? Apparently trying to support his wife in her campaign, former president Bill Clinton had charmed rural voters but at the same time turned off some super-delegates with his imperial assumptions. Reminiscing about his own campaigns, a victory for Hillary in certain states appeared guaranteed in his opinion. A senior campaign adviser admitted that by presenting Hillary as the virtual incumbent who knew the workings of the government, she was initially perceived as running for the third term of Bill Clinton. Those were observations Gail Sheehy (2008) reported from the campaign trail.

Editor Todd Purdum (2008) appears to be in agreement that Bill Clinton was responsible for a string of controversies in Hillary's campaign. According to him, even earlier, in the winter, Bill Clinton "moved with seeming abandon to stain his wife's presidential campaign in the name of saving it, as disclosures about his dubious associates piled up" (p. 78). Former aides apparently thought that Hillary put her career on hold to be with the former president; now it should be her time. But Bill Clinton—it seems—has difficulty being a supporting player.

After the election, when U.S president Barack Obama began his cabinet-building activities, Hillary's name was mentioned again but so were questions about her husband and his past financial dealings and foreign policy involvements—would they pass the scrutiny of the new president's background checks regarding his selection of cabinet members? Even with the announcement of Hillary Clinton as the new Secretary of State, a few questioning voices were heard mentioning former president Bill Clinton's activities while in office and afterward. "Whatever the future holds for Hillary Clinton, her husband is not fading away. He will remain a presence, a force to be reckoned with, as long as he draws breath" (Purdum, 2008, p. 131).

Of course, it is difficult to know what Hillary's life would have been had she not married Bill Clinton. Would she have been as successful on her own or would she have risen even higher? From these events it can be understood that it is not always clear whether marrying a prince will turn out to be an asset or a liability in Cinderella's future.

Even though Hillary Clinton was not successful in her bid for the presidency of the United States, it apparently encouraged the use of additional Cinderella stories. Under the headline "Cinderella vs. the Barracuda" columnist Jonah Goldberg (2008) commented on Caroline Kennedy Schlossberg's interest in occupying

Hillary Clinton's Senate seat, which became vacant when Hillary took the position of Secretary of State. "A multimillionaire from birth, Kennedy has spent most of her life on the charity-benefit and cotillion circuit" (p. E2), Goldberg explains in a patronizing tone, emphasizing Kennedy's apparent political inexperience.

A discussion of whether or not the former president's daughter is qualified for the United States Senate goes beyond the scope of this book. The reason for mentioning this example of "National Voices" here is to point to Cinderella's eternal life in the public opinion. It is also noteworthy that in this case the comparison to Cinderella was neither complimentary nor correct. Charles Perrault, the brothers Grimm, and Walt Disney—who conceived of Cinderella as a poor helpless girl—would turn around in their graves at the thought of a multimillionaire doing all that hard work and enduring the treatment of the mean-spirited stepmother and her daughters until the prince rescued her from this life of drudgery. Such a Cinderella (as Caroline Kennedy) could buy herself any prince; she did not have to wait for him to recognize her royal qualities in her tiny foot. This shoe does not fit.

Cinderella will not die as long as her power persists and can be used for various purposes and causes. Fairy tales are powerful instruments that, like myths, "consciously and subconsciously guide[s] every human being on this planet, for good or ill" explained James N. Frey (2000, p. 11). Myths have an irresistible power that reaches individual human beings on a deep, emotional level, often subconsciously. Myths, fairy tales, and legends have many similar elements as they are repeated in different cultures and at different times. Their widespread use and repetition are what make them so powerful. After all, if everybody knows about them, they must be true. Like rumors, they derive their credibility and mythic powers from repetition. But to remain powerful, they also must conform to and reconfirm the cultural values held for generations.

For instance, heroes have to have certain characteristics; they need to be strong and competent, sexually appealing, rough on the outside but soft on the inside. They can be a little bit naughty but not too much, and they have to be on the side of good. Justice and a fair maiden will be their reward. For female characters, purity of heart can always be rewarded and so can patience, obedience, and willing labor. The trick is to make the reward appear certain, a promise with a 150-percent guaranteed occurrence. Repetitions of the story will accomplish this feat.

Another reason for Cinderella's eternal life is that she is good for business. Merchants love her. Searching the Internet, the list of products that borrow the Cinderella halo is long. The more obvious connection with the makers of female shoes (a handmade satin peep-toe pump will go for $439.00) is joined by merchants for Cinderella hair products, as well as hair removal services, whimsical jewelry, and other accessories—such as handbags, umbrellas, or fans—and slimming underwear. But one can also find Cinderella software, Cinderella pools, Cinderella escort services and modeling agencies, a Cinderella castle for the appropriate honeymoon or other vacations, Rock 'n Roll bands, and many more—all eager to cash in on the magic.

Of course, what is collectively known as the bridal industry reaps the biggest chunk of the Cinderella profit pie with its crowning glory, the wedding gown. When celebrities plan to tie the knot, their preparations are often made known to the public through the media. For instance, *Style* magazine featured five-time Grammy winner Toni Braxton modeling several bridal outfits (Geller, 2001). Her final choice apparently was a "regal cumbersome ensemble inspired by the ultimate fictional bride, Cinderella. An enduring symbol of female redemption in wedlock and a means by which women announce their adherence to traditional marriage ideals, the white dress is the most salient visual object of the modern wedding" (p. 214).

Reality TV shows such as *The Bachelor* do their best to keep the myth of being chosen by the prince alive (Wikipedia, 2008). Contestants for the bachelor daydream about getting married and about their fantasy weddings before they've ever met the groom. One of the women competing for *The Bachelor* reported on the yards of white silk she had already purchased for her wedding gown.

"LIVING HAPPILY EVER AFTER?"

Expectations of a happy and lasting (until death do us part) marriage following the romantic relationship can meet with disappointments. Researchers in the marriage and family field have reported that about 30 percent of divorces occur within the first four years of marriage (Clarke, 1995). This is apparently the amount of time it takes for the two partners to be confronted with the reality of their choices.

Country singer Suzy Bogguss (1993) caught the spirit with her lyrics to the song "Hey Cinderella" in her album *Something Up My Sleeve*. After the veil of illusions is torn to shreds under the impact of reality, the spouses may face each other as the total strangers they really are. To understand the process involving the variables of time and marital satisfaction, researchers gathered information with the use of personality questionnaires from 162 couples at the beginning of their marriage and at different times in follow-up assessments (Bentler & Newcomb 1978). Four years later the still-married couples showed a more homogamous pattern of personality traits than those who divorced. Unlike what fairy tales may attempt to make us believe, in the real world differences between spouses in the areas of personality traits, attitudes, and socioeconomic status seem to be linked to high rates of marital tension and union dissolution (Ruggles, 1997). While waltzing in the dream world of romance, listening to the violins instead of to reason, the young lovers are blind to those differences in their personality characteristics and their attitudes, which a few years later may lead to disillusionment and a parting of their ways.

While studying various aspects of divorce, Joseph Hopper (2001), at the University of Chicago, interviewed individuals who had been the initiators in their divorce. He learned that a significant number of them reformulated their marriages in their own minds into "marriages that never existed." They justified the divorce initiation by symbolically voiding or annulling those marriages.

Because they believed the "happily ever after" myth, the marriage could not have been a real marriage; it must have been some mistake or misunderstanding.

Some of them regarded their marriage as having been bad from the beginning, designating it as a "fake" marriage. Others pointed to insurmountable personality differences in the spouses, claiming that they never really knew the "real" spouse when they made the commitment. Those differences seemed so overwhelming to the divorce initiators that they never seriously contemplated marriage counseling. There was nothing that one could do about this fundamentally flawed marriage other than getting out. It should never have happened to begin with. Denying reality is one way of maintaining the belief in the myth.

Interestingly, very few of the initiators believed that they might have mistakenly elevated their partner and the wedding into an idealized version of marriage. The more frequent explanation for the failure of the marriage was found in the other spouses; they must have been less than truthful in presenting themselves and must have been less committed than the divorce initiators had been at the time. Of course, in many instances this argument was reversed as the noninitiators used it to explain their side of the story. Arguments such as that the other spouse initially misrepresented himself or herself, or that the spouse changed significantly in personality characteristics, are convenient and logical-sounding explanations to cover up for a lack of patience to embark upon a realistic appraisal and to really get to know the person one was committing one's future to.

Almost 30 years ago psychologist Albert Ellis (1979) in his book *The Intelligent Woman's Guide to Dating & Mating* attempted to outline what types of personalities women would be ill-advised to consider as husband material for a long and happy marriage. He warned about the emotionally unstable man, a candidate who can be quite stimulating and fascinating. His moods may change quickly, preventing boredom from setting in, or he may be emotionally needy, obsessively-compulsively seeking love and reassurance. Neither one may make for a good permanent partner. And there is the matter of basic compatibility. People have different interests and passions. While two people don't have to share all their interests to be happy, those that are important take time to come to the surface. Dating partners need to devote space and time for the expression of various personality traits; otherwise, it will not be a happy, long-lasting union.

WAITING FOR THE PRINCE (LADIES-IN-WAITING?)

The power of the fairy tale may keep girls and young women waiting without assigning a goal to their individual lives. In the stories, the heroines are chosen for their beauty and not for anything they do. They apparently just exist passively until the hero discovers them. Their passive waiting will be rewarded when they are finally chosen. Of course, because they don't know much about the prince in their future, they don't know how to prepare themselves for their life after meeting him. Even though out of necessity many young women embark upon a profession or income-producing occupation, they may do so with the thought of marriage and motherhood in mind. If the choice is between a self-fulfilling occupation and one that will accommodate future motherhood, the self-fulfilling path will often be sacrificed.

Marcia decided on a future as dental hygienist, reasoning that she would be able to easily phase into part-time work after the birth of her children. Although she did not know what her future husband would be like, Marcia was certain that she wanted to have children some day. But she also envisioned herself as continuing to work in her profession. When she and Stan started dating seriously, Marcia settled herself into a full-time job as dental hygienist in a busy local dentist practice. Following the births of her two planned children, Marcia transitioned into part-time work.

Everything worked out as she had intended it to be. Why wasn't she happy? Marcia became intellectually bored with her job. As her children grew into school and high school age, she started dreaming about other, more stimulating occupations. Perhaps she could return to school and develop connections to more satisfying work. But she could not afford to resign her well-paid job, which carried with it the health insurance benefits for the whole family; in fact, Stan, who had followed his entrepreneurship tendencies by starting a business venture on his own, expected Marcia to return to full-time work in her field as soon as the children were enrolled in high school.

On the surface, it might appear logical to put one's life on hold and to leave one's mind and spirit open and available to accommodate the future prince's wishes and participate in his plans without reservations. Gina, a "could-be" Cinderella of the late 20th century, subscribed to that surface logic. Gina was intelligent, blessed with many talents, had a good sense of humor, and was well-liked by her friends. With the passage of her 35th birthday she admitted that the arrival of her prince appeared to be delayed. She looked sad and admitted to being bored. When asked why she did not develop any of her seemingly significant talents to relieve the boredom, she responded with the explanation that whatever she did prior to meeting her future husband would be a waste of time and possibly money. She believed that her life would really start when she got married, but because she had not met her future husband yet, she could not predict any of his interests.

On the other hand, Shirley, a young professional woman, did not want to wait. She desperately longed to be married and have children. After a few unsuccessful romantic entanglements, she happened to meet Jeff, a young man who seemed attracted to her. On the rebound from an unhappy relationship, Shirley did not ask many questions about Jeff's past. He had not been married before and she thought he was finally the right man who would commit himself to her and to marriage. Shirley's parents paid for a beautiful wedding for their only child. Shortly after the honeymoon Shirley found out that her husband expected her paycheck to be automatically deposited into their joint account. Shirley made the necessary arrangements. But she did not know that while her monthly checks were used to make the mortgage payments on Jeff's house (Shirley's name was not yet on the deed), he siphoned off funds for his business expenses. Although Shirley's paychecks regularly fueled the tank of the joint account, the gauge constantly displayed a near-empty state.

Money was not the only rare commodity in their marriage; Shirley's husband spent more time with his friends than with her. In her previous relationships Shirley had enjoyed sex, and she had looked forward to regular sexual activities in her marriage. But Jeff's sex drive was not very strong. He had a long list of reasons for not wanting to engage in sex, and many of them pointed to some flaws in Shirley's behaviors. Although finally married, Shirley felt just as lonely as she had before she met her husband. She complained, and Jeff responded by filing for divorce. In spite of Jeff's treatment of her, Shirley pleaded with him to give their marriage "another chance." Jeff told her to move out of his house after he had deducted the mortgage payment for that month from their joint account. This marriage did not have a first chance. Shirley's needs for marriage and motherhood and the haste with which she plunged into this relationship rendered her vulnerable to becoming a victim of Jeff's control strategies. And yet, if Jeff had not taken the final steps of initiating divorce, Shirley would have remained with him, hoping for a change once they had a child or two.

For those who—like Gina above—decide to wait, it can be a long wait, indeed. Helen knew all along what she wanted. She would get married, have a beautiful home, very tastefully decorated, and cook gourmet meals for her husband and their friends and families. Having made that decision, she did not need to think about college. Her plan was to work in an office until she found the right man. The office of a consulting company seemed to be just the right place. Helen was attractive and had no trouble finding dating partners, but somehow there was not a prince among them. Until one day she met a charming man, 15 years her senior. Parker, named after his father, was an executive at a company in a nearby town who had frequent business in Helen's hometown. He took her to expensive restaurants and occasionally insisted on first purchasing a dress for her that would be appropriate for their romantic dinners.

This was the beginning of a beautiful romance; Parker was a reasonably good lover. Helen enjoyed it when she was able to accompany Parker on some of his business trips. This was the life she had dreamed about. There was only one thing wrong with it: Parker was married and had two children. Helen mentioned the possibility of a divorce, and Parker seemed agreeable to that solution but it was too early, his children were still too young to put them through a divorce. In the meantime, he helped Helen with the down payment for a little house. She enjoyed playing hostess and preparing elaborate dinners for Parker and by herself with her family and friends.

It was so exciting to purchase beautiful table linen, silverware, dishes, and wine glasses for her little house. Her floors were covered with deep oriental rugs. Helen felt that her real life was when she visited upscale stores to shop for her house. Here she felt equal to the married and well-to-do women who carefully selected items for their homes. Waiting at the cash register for her items to be rung up, she felt she could compare herself to any of them.

It was unfortunate that she had to maintain her job. She disliked getting up in the morning and leaving her beautiful bedroom, the sanctuary of her Cinderella dreams. Helen had advanced to office manager, not so much by her own desire but by her employers discovering her intelligence and competence in performing much more demanding tasks than what she had been hired for. She was good at writing manuals, as well as proposals and bids to attract prospective customers. The only aspect her employers complained about was Helen's unreliable attendance. Some mornings she just called in sick or came in later than the regular office hours required. Her employers made that the reason for not raising her salary even though they assigned her more complicated responsibilities. Helen did not seem to mind much; the office was not where her real life took place—she thought.

On her salary she could not afford the shopping trips she had become accustomed to, but credit cards seemed to have been invented for just that purpose. Parker was willing to help with the payments, but he was not overly generous because Helen had started dating younger men from time to time, because she still held on to the dream of marriage. However, the men she occasionally dated were not in a position to compete with Parker's assets and could not easily provide the life for Helen that she felt was her destiny. Helen always returned to Parker when these dating relationships dissolved.

Then came the time of Parker's retirement. He was still married and there were not many reasons for him to come to town as frequently as before. Furthermore, there was no expense account, and his wife had unrestricted access to their bank accounts. Helen was left to her own devices. Her credit cards were all charged to the limit, and she could not keep up with the payments. She was barely able to pay the monthly interest charges. Her lifestyle remained unchanged, however. She still did not like to go to the office, even though she needed money desperately. There was no hope for an increase in salary as she was now in her fifties. Career advances were available to younger women, who were more ambitious than Helen. She found out about home equity loans. Real estate had gone up in value, and her house was appraised for much more than the original purchase price.

For a while Helen seemed safe, but real estate values did not remain as high. Her credit cards were again charged to the limit. As with many other people whose mortgage debts exceeded the value of the property, mortgage payments became delinquent but the house could not be sold for a profit to erase the debts, Helen's house was repossessed by the bank. And because she could not pay off the credit card debts, she had to declare bankruptcy. Finally, she had to move in with her older, widowed sister to have a roof over her head and a bed to sleep in, but there was not much space for the possessions she had accumulated in her pretty little house. Now, at almost 58 years old, she was too young for the receipt of social security benefits but not young enough to hope that a prince would come and rescue her.

It is difficult to conceive the reality of Helen's story. Here is a reasonably attractive woman of above-average intelligence steadfastly refusing to accept reality. Back in her teenage and young adult years she had made a choice, to which she apparently felt entitled. At the time, the choice seemed simple enough: become a career woman or a wife. She chose the path of a wife, however, without having the guarantee that a husband, and particularly a husband who met her qualifications, would show up. One would have thought that when she was in her late thirties reality would have asserted itself. But the assistance of her married lover and the promise of credit cards enabled her to continue in her dream-like trance, which was interrupted each day when she went to work but continued as soon as she reentered her home.

Within herself Helen had sufficient resources to prepare herself for a modest but independent lifestyle; instead she chose a fantasy. Helen's story demonstrates that Cinderella cannot afford to wait for the prince to bear the appropriate slipper when he finally calls on her. Even if—unlike Parker—he is not already married, in his boyhood he has been socialized by the same fairy tales, and he may expect to find the stereotyped fairy-tale heroine—the silent, submissive, and powerless beauty who is used to suffering for her final redemption as the chosen one. He does not expect her to look critically at him and his personality traits and offerings. That he approaches her as a prince is sufficient evidence for his value, and he expects a blind commitment from her. No fairy godmother's advice has prepared Cinderella for the task of choosing the prince who is the right one for her. After all, choices were not the ingredients in her basket of goodies.

Fortunately, the Helens are in the minority, and today's Cinderella can exercise her right to choose if she empowers herself to do so. But whether she will be able to recognize the right man is another question. When so much energy and attention are focused on being chosen by the prince, less is available to discern the qualities and characteristics that make him the right one for her or the one to be rejected for her own good.

Or does it even matter? Once married, it is likely that she will change, slowly and almost imperceptibly at first. "Shifts in concern, behavior, and attitude, mark the beginning of an intricate process that unfolds slowly, subtly, and incrementally for many a new wife" is how the process is described by author Dalma Heyn (1997, p. 28) in *Marriage Shock: The Transformation of Women into Wives*. The driving force for this transformation, according to Heyn, is the creation of a "should" voice in the woman's brain that instructs her what she *ought* to do when she contemplates what she would normally *want* to do. Following the instructions of the "should" voice, women may give up part of their identity, the parts they enjoyed about themselves and what their husbands initially liked about them.

MEANING AND FUNCTION OF THE SLIPPER

Returning to the topic of the glass slipper, we can understand it in the fairy tale as the symbolic representation of constraint. As the slipper is pinching Cinderella's toes, impairing her movement and thus preventing her from reaching her goal, it is restricting her self-determination. The very fact that she lost the slipper as she was quietly hurrying away from the ball at midnight implies it was not a comfortable, well-fitting article of her wardrobe that guaranteed her safe movement.

Resisting attempts to make her foot fit into the shoe and instead rejecting the slipper as unfit can be one way of maintaining control over herself and her destiny. And yet, the modern version of the slipper is all around us. High-heeled women's shoes, we are told, are designed to make women's legs look longer, and by increasing the arch of the foot, the whole foot looks smaller and sexier. But they also seem designed to reflect the wearer's helplessness. Those shoes train women to proceed with tiny wobbly steps through life. In comparison, men's shoes are made to stride in when walking and to maintain one's balance when standing. Observing a man with a woman in high-heeled shoes walk side-by-side immediately shows the woman at a disadvantage. While he advances with a self-assured stride, she hobbles along (or rather behind) with her tiny steps that betray an uncertainty of ever reaching the target without assistance.

Of course, the notion of idealizing the smallness of women's feet is not unique to Western culture; the old Chinese custom of bandaging girls' feet so they would not grow to their full size is well-known. Chinese girls and women were not able to walk far after they had been submitted to that procedure. Making the victim believe that the torture is for her own good or to enhance her beauty can be understood as attempts of control at their most sophisticated and successful. If managed well, the victims are only too willing to follow the crippling procedure.

Linking the smallness of women's feet to the concept of beauty introduces the opportunity for another type of constriction, isolation from the comforts of sisterhood, because a focus on beauty introduces competition among and distrust toward other women. After all, only one of them will be chosen at any one time.

The intent of this discussion is not to abolish all high-heeled women's shoes. That would eliminate the element of choice, something that is important to have in all situations. Under some circumstances wearing high-heeled shoes can be amusing—to the wearer as well as to the observer. Being aware of the function of these high-heeled slippers is the important aspect here. A woman who cannot run away, who cannot escape, often becomes an easy target to victimize. Furthermore, because the clicking of the stiletto heels on a hard surface announces the woman's arrival, any perpetrator has prior knowledge of her approach while she is unaware of the presence and intentions of those who may be waiting in the darkness.

It is of interest to note that the National Museum of Women in the Arts in Washington, DC, in their Holiday 2007 brochure describing gifts in the museum's gift shop, included a gallery calendar with the title "Shoes," presenting a high-heeled woman's shoe on its cover. The calendar tempts prospective buyers to "enjoy an entire year of glamorous stilettos, superstar Wellingtons, antique slippers, and tomorrow's opera pumps" (NMWA, 2007). What an ingenious way to keep women's awareness focused on high-heeled shoes throughout every month of the year.

One would not want to go so far as to proclaim that the designers and producers of women's shoes are putting their talents to use in a grand control scheme aimed at increasing women's helplessness. A statement along those lines might qualify for a diagnosis of paranoid schizophrenia. Nevertheless, the transitions in the character of the fairy-tale Cinderella that occurred over long periods of time could pass as control attempts because of the significant modifications that impacted the very personality structures of young women. Furthermore, those modifications did not occur haphazardly in the retelling of the stories; their effect was unilateral and could be traced historically to the discreet attempts of some identifiable forces.

Noted author Judith Viorst (1998) pondered, "Like biological determinists, environmental determinists take a fundamentally fatalist view. Like biological determinists, who see us as the prisoners of our genes, environmental determinists see us as the prisoners of our childhood . . . Is our belief in free will merely an illusion?" (p. 29). Contemplating Viorst's statement, we are confronted with her question, which we may agree with or accept as a challenge. The challenge amounts to exploring and confronting biological and environmental determinisms as to their validity regarding the inevitability of permanent imprisonment by childhood experiences. While biological determinism decides our fate insofar as being a man or a woman, we know of successful attempts to change even that through sex reassignment surgical procedures. It is true, a "reassigned" woman as of yet cannot give birth to a child, but that is a fate for some of the "true" biological women as well.

With regard to environmental determinism, the challenging process can begin with awareness of the symbolic representation of the slipper as an instrument of constraint, limiting women's lives through influences from the past. These influences are affecting women's expression of self through silencing their voices. As their movements are hindered, they wait to be chosen by the prince. Not every girl or woman will be the chosen one; therefore, with beauty holding a high likelihood for being crowned, the beauty contest pits women against each other in competition for the crown, isolating the competitors in the process. In addition, there are many other influences that have shaped women's beliefs and attitudes for generations. Part II of this book will examine in greater detail some of the major influences from the past.

Reaching awareness of the constraining function of the slipper, women can refuse to try on the slipper or they can step out of the slipper later on. They can outgrow the seductions of their childhood by exploring and questioning the reality of the promises in the fairy tales, and they can assume the responsibility and direction for their own destinies. It amounts to women's decisions being guided by their own actions and convictions and to their believing that their values and opinions are meaningful and worthwhile. Women may also decide that being chosen holds less meaning and satisfaction for their lives than making their own choices. As exciting as it may feel to be chosen, it always transpires on the basis of criteria determined by others. Making one's own choices, however, occurs on the basis of criteria determined by the individual woman.

2

Growing Up with Fairy Tales

Barbara Walker (1983) in her book *The Woman's Encyclopedia of Myths and Secrets* tells how—in the traditions of France, Germany, and the British Isles— pagan gods and goddesses, tribal ancestors, and those who worshipped them became "fairies," and the Irish still believe that fairies live in the pagan burial mounds. The Irish and the Welsh called their fairies the Mothers or the Mother's Blessing, and fairyland was the Land of Women. This is an interesting account when one considers how the tales of fairies have been used to render girls silent and powerless in the socialization process of girls and boys.

ROLE MODELS FROM FANTASY AND IMAGINATION

Theologians, educators, literary critics, psychologists, and librarians have debated for centuries about reading fairy tales to children and whether or not children should be exposed to the cruelty and superstition of make-believe worlds, as Zipes (1986) pointed out in the introduction to his book *Don't Bet on the Prince*. Fairy tales play an important role in early socialization, influencing children's perception of the world and their place in it even before they begin to read. In fairy tales the literature of fantasy and imagination can be tied together to create a new view of the world.

In her book *Kiss Sleeping Beauty Good-Bye: Breaking the Spell of Feminine Myths and Models,* Kolbenschlag (1979) attempted to defeat the negative features in the role models of Sleeping Beauty, Snow White, Cinderella, Goldilocks, and other fairy tales. She argued that women are conditioned to internalize rigid spiritual ideas about life, because the teachings of the church provide normative patterns for women that prevent them from realizing their own spiritual and sensual unity, as briefly mentioned in the previous chapter.

In Kolbenschlag's opinion, contemporary crises between men and women are the result of the defeat of the feminine need for ethical autonomy by men and institutions. Cultural education and the socialization process reinforce individuals' capacity for self-realization for men—but not for women. For women the socialization process does not emphasize this aspect. Women often have to seek self-realization in painful and traumatic ways. Fairy tales are symbolic forms, which reinforce self-defeating social and psychological patterns of behavior in women's daily lives.

Similarly, Colette Dowling (1981) does not blame women's dependency on fairy tales but points out that it is important to recognize that fairy tales reflect not only how women are oppressed, but also how they allow themselves to be oppressed. The "personal, psychological dependency—the deep wish to be taken care of by others—is the chief force holding women down today. I call this 'The Cinderella Complex'—a network of largely repressed attitudes and fears that keeps women in a kind of half-light, retreating from the full use of their minds and creativity. Like Cinderella, women today are still waiting for something external to 'transform their lives'" (p. 21).

If fairy tales in their symbolic forms reinforce self-defeating behavior patterns in women's daily lives, as suggested by Kolbenschlag above, could the slipper—the icon for Cinderella's (or the woman's) role in life—have had deterring effects on the past waves of feminism? Regarding feminist issues in the 21st century, women still seem to be suspended between self-affirmation and self-improvement; they view themselves alternately as victims stuck in their traditional roles and as autonomous individuals claiming independence, according to Laura Kipnis (2006). As women persist in the traditional feminine ways, they are complying with men in preserving the male privilege while at the same time resenting men for it.

CINDERELLA AND THE BEAUTY MYTH

"Once upon a time there was a beautiful girl named Cinderella" (Disney Enterprises, Inc., 1995, p. 1). According to feminist writer Naomi Wolf (2002), every generation since 1830 had its version of the beauty myth to contend with. Today, in spite of the efforts of feminism's second wave, the advertisers in the popular women's press censor their readers' intellectual space with the promotion of skin-care products, diet guides, and similar concerns. Their efforts find support in the legacy of our fairy tales where beauty equals goodness and innocence. Cinderella, Snow White, Sleeping Beauty, and others were not only beautiful; they were good in character and spirit as well.

The still-popular Barbie doll, with her slender body, narrow hips, and large breasts, epitomizes the ideal female body in many Western cultures. Synonymous with femininity, "women's breasts are invested with social, cultural, and political meanings . . . Breasts are seen simultaneously as a marker of womanhood, as a visual signifier of female sexualisation" (Millsted & Frith, 2003, p. 455). More than other aspects of women's bodies, breasts are visually presented in the media, and women—as the greater consumers of media—have ample opportunities to compare their own bodies to those they see displayed in television, movies, and magazines (Seifert, 2005). This may lead them to feel dissatisfied with the size and shape of their breasts, perhaps fearing that their romantic partners would prefer women with larger breasts (Harrison, 2003). Studies with college women have demonstrated dissatisfaction with their bodies; most of them desired to have larger breasts (Forbes, Jobe, & Revak, 2006). The growing number of women undergoing surgery to change their breasts is a strong indication of their dissatisfaction.

It has been estimated that in the years prior to 2000 about two million women in the United States had obtained breast implants (Sarwer, Nordmann, & Herbert, 2000). In the period from 2000 to 2006, over one million women received breast implants, and in 2006 women's breast augmentation surgeries (329,000) made this the most popular cosmetic surgery among women (American Society of Plastic Surgeons, 2007).

A team of researchers in California analyzed responses from 52,227 hetero-sexual adults, ages 18 to 65 years, and found that most of the women (70 percent) were dissatisfied with the size and shape of their breasts (Frederick, Peplau, & Lever, 2008). However, most of the men (56 percent) reported satisfaction with their partners' breasts. The dissatisfied women admitted to being hesitant to undress in front of their partners and trying to conceal their breasts from their partners' view during sex.

The end of high-fashion culture presented women's magazines with the need to find a new purpose and advertising hook. The focus shifted from the wrapping to the content, from fashionable clothes to the beautiful body underneath. Thus the door opened to the wide market of cosmetics, diet products, and cosmetic surgery. What represents a beautiful body is determined by cultural trends of the time, and—for a price—there is a whole industry ready to assist women in their efforts to comply with the ideal of the moment.

Although modern women's magazines tackle serious women's issues in their pages much more so than in the past, the degree of the individual magazine's pro-portion of women's issues and the message about the beauty myth is determined by its advertisers. Generations of officially crowned beauty queens have continued in and strengthened the power of the ritual that bestows the apparent promises inherent in women's beauty. By appearing to lend a helping hand to the pursuit of beauty, the advertising departments of beauty-enhancing enterprises pretend to bring the promise within reach of readers of the magazines that carry and get paid for their advertisements. The exploration of the various offers for beauty enhancement requires women's time and energy, leaving less for the investigation of other aspects of their lives.

Authors such as Jessica Valenti, writing about women's issues, confirm that "we are all brought up to feel like there's something wrong with us. We're too fat.

We're dumb" (2007, p. 6). What Kipnis called the *girlfriend industry* encourages women's voluntary servitude to self-improvement. Women's magazines, daytime talk shows, and how-to-fix-something-about-yourself books temporarily alleviate women's anxiety about not measuring up to the popular female model of the time by promising possibilities and opportunities for approaching the desired goals— for a price. The current obsession with thinness and the demand for fitness, among other carefully listed and described problems overshadowing female beauty, require time, energy, and money. "One way or another, women just seem to end up defined by their bodies, or defining themselves by their bodies a source of self-worth, a site of craziness, most likely both" (Kipnis, 2006, p.13).

Perceptions of female attractiveness and desirability as shaped by the media have a particularly strong influence in regard to weight. It is relatively rare to find images of women of normal weight in the media. This trend away from the image of the normal woman has progressed over time. Where in the early 1980s the average model weighed eight percent less than the average American woman, now the difference between them is 23 percent (Daniluk, 1998). Similarly, the weight of Miss Americas has plummeted along with the average weight of Playboy Playmates during the 20 years following the start of the second wave of the women's movement. The average woman, in her frustration to strive for compliance with the current weight trend, comes to hate her own body when she compares her mirror image with the female images in the media. Thus, the admonition of St. Jerome when he established the church's policy on female nakedness that "women should blush in shame at the sight of their own bodies" becomes reality (Muller, 1954, p. 160).

"I have experienced internal and external pressure to be thinner; both rage tyranny on our souls . . . We are plagued with a media-imposed image of beauty, an image that only 1 percent of women even have the genetic predisposition to achieve. Yet we have a whole culture striving to acquire it." Those are the words of Francesca Ferrentelli, a woman who volunteered her story for Cathleen Roundtree's book *On Women Turning 30* (2000, pp. 81–82).

"A cultural fixation on female thinness is not an obsession about female beauty but an obsession about female obedience" (Wolf, 2002, p. 187). Maladies such as anorexia and bulimia are mostly encountered in women. In some ways, the weight-loss cult, with its constraints, is reminiscent of the confining aspects of Cinderella's tiny glass slipper and it appears to function equally well in the maintenance of gender inequality. When are individual Cinderellas ready to decide whether maintaining the constraining influences of the beauty myth is in their own best interest or not?

MODERN METHODS OF INDOCTRINATION

The socialization process begun by fairy tales continues with modern methods of indoctrination. "The biggest consumers of advice are women. They soak it up like sponges: from newspaper columns and women's magazines, from TV commercials and soap operas, from best sellers and talk shows, from ministers and priests, psychiatrists and gynecologists, from beauticians and galloping chefs and auto mechanics, from the housewife next door, from the mail man. Most women spend half a lifetime trying to measure up to someone's formula for the perfect woman . . . The formula is summed up in a motif that repeats frequently in this kind of literature: concentrate on packaging yourself for consumption, but in conversation with men, forget about yourself" (Kolbenschlag, 1979, pp. 14–16).

A flagrant example of this concept has been reflected in the TV program *The Bachelor*, which began with the arrival of 25 women, eager to meet the bachelor and "packaged for consumption," all in glittering evening gowns, more or less revealing or emphasizing what's underneath to assist the bachelor in the selection process. The women's goal was to become the chosen one. This American reality television dating game show started on ABC channels in 2002.

The series quickly gained popularity, with solid ratings being reported throughout the eight completed editions and resulting in an average audience of nearly 10 million viewers. The series had been renewed through the fall of 2007. But something unexpected happened in that season. Brad Womack, Bachelor 11, went through the weeding-out process until there were only two contestants left. When it came time to choose between the two finalists, Deanna and Jenni, Brad could not commit to either one. Thus, on September 24, 2007, the Bachelor remained an uncommitted bachelor. Following that, *The Bachelor's* 12th edition premiered on March 17, 2008.

In light of the fact that many of the couples formed during previous seasons later ended their relationships without the expected commitment to marriage, the premise of finding true love has proven difficult to sustain. Nevertheless, the series lives on and the women enter the competition with the expectation of being chosen by a man they hardly know (Wikipedia, 2008). And the women in the audience join the female applicants on the screen with their hopes and wishes. Just imagine: at least half of the average 10 million viewers sit in weekly suspension, vicariously experiencing the female dream of being chosen—along with the hopes and the tensions and anxieties of envy in the competition with all the other female contenders.

Once a year, one can observe something like a parade of the chosen ones in American culture. On Valentine's Day, February 14, worksites with female employees are the stops on the delivery routes of the local florists for that day. Flower arrangements of all sizes and variations will be deposited at the reception or security guard stations of the worksites or directly at the desks and workplaces of the female recipients. During the day, the flower arrangements are on display and can be compared as to their size, uniqueness, and the meaning of the particular flowers (for instance, red roses symbolizing passionate love). At the end of the workday, the flowers will be paraded out of the worksites by their recipients and transported home. Every one of the young women proudly carries the symbols of being chosen, and the heavier the load, the luckier the recipient. Of course, it would be more convenient to have the flowers delivered to one's home, but then there is no competition; who would see the flowers there? Only the recipient and perhaps the donor—there is nobody around to envy the chosen one. The allure of being chosen and being recognized for it is still difficult to resist. How far have we really come since Cinderella?

Part of the answer to this question can be found in the success of the book *The Rules*, first published in 1997 and followed up with another edition, *All the Rules: Time-tested Secrets for Capturing the Heart of Mr. Right,* 10 years later. The authors, Fein and Schneider, promise their female readers that if they follow *The Rules* strictly, one day a prince will notice them and ask for their hand. The premise for *The Rules*, as stated on page 28 of the 2007 version, is never to make anything happen and to trust in the natural order of things—namely that man pursues woman. Indeed, the authors warn, "by not accepting the concept that the man must pursue the woman, women put themselves in jeopardy of being rejected or ignored" (p. 30). The warning is followed on page 37 with the advice to be quiet and reserved on the occasion of the date itself. In the 2007 version, the authors caution readers several times not to discuss applying *The Rules* to their lives with a therapist because therapists generally encourage their clients to be open and forthright in their interactions.

As the authors repeatedly promise, *The Rules* work for those women whose primary goal it is to be discovered by a man who will marry them. The promise will be fulfilled as long as the women maneuver discreetly within the confines of the traditional, patriarchal, sociocultural framework. The authors do not rattle the constraining cages; they guide their readers in slipping through and between the bars of the cages. By preserving the status quo, they assist their readers in reaching their goal in less direct ways and let their success speak for itself—a smart move in many ways. Is it a good move? Women will need to make that judgment based on the definitions of their own goals.

Looking at modern female psychology, we still see women in a powerless and disadvantaged reflection. Even intrinsically valuable female traits, such as compassion or intuitiveness, which women may have developed out of necessity, are viewed in terms of female "emotionality" and are considered of somewhat lesser value than the typically male "agentic" talents of leadership, decisiveness, and reasoning. Today's women grow up in households where girls are rewarded for submissiveness. It is more likely that girls' rebellion will be punished more readily than their submissiveness. Conditions like those result in girls' possession of certain psychological characteristics. "Traits of naiveté, docility, and conservatism are probably more conditioned than inevitable attributes among modern women. Nevertheless, such traits exist among women and are devalued by men and therefore by women. Furthermore, such traits are intrinsically valueless—whether they appear in women or men" according to Phyllis Chesler (1997, p. 290).

THE PICTURE OF THE SUFFERING BEAUTY (THE BEAUTIFUL VICTIM)

Silence and passivity are not the only significant attributes of stereotyped, fairy-tale heroines. Beauty is the greatest asset of storybook princesses and princesses-to-be. It is the beautiful girl that is being chosen by the prince. Being chosen makes her the special one. She does not need to be witty or resourceful—all she has to do is look beautiful. She waits, ready to be chosen and rewarded for her passive waiting. She never asks for the reasons why she was chosen; she assumes it was for her beauty and "goodness," as a reward for having those characteristics. She never looks critically at the prince and his personality traits. That he is a prince is sufficient evidence for her that he is a good—or at least a compatible—person.

"Allowed no opportunity for discriminating selection, the princess makes a blind commitment to the first prince who happens down the highway, penetrates the thorny barriers, and arrives *deus ex machina* to release her from the charmed captivity of adolescence" (Rowe, 1986, p. 217). Because girls in the fairy tales are being chosen for their beauty, little girls hearing or reading these stories grow up believing that beauty leads to wealth. They learn that "beauty has an obviously commercial advantage" (Lieberman, 1986, p. 190). In her book *The Beauty Myth,* Wolf (2002) confirms this notion when she views beauty as a currency system, similar to the gold standard. "Like any economy, it [beauty] is determined by politics and in the modern age in the West it is the last, best belief system that keeps male dominance intact" (p. 12).

But along with the beauty, there are situations of victimization, such as Rapunzel who had been locked up in an inaccessible tower; Snow White and Sleeping Beauty, who were locked into a deep sleep; and others who were enslaved in various ways—all waiting to be rescued by a passing prince. Thus the beautiful, helplessly suffering maiden became the quintessential heroine of our fairy tales, linking the figures of the victimized girl and the interesting girl in the underlying pattern of the stories. "Because victimized girls like Felicia, the Goose-girl, and Cinderella are invariably rescued and rewarded, indeed glorified, children learn that suffering goodness can afford to remain meek, and need not and perhaps should not strive to defend itself, for if it did so perhaps the fairy godmother would not turn up for once, to set things right at the end" explained Marcia Lieberman (1986, p. 193).

If the victimized maiden refused to remain meek, she might not only lose the fairy godmother's goodwill and kind assistance, she would also run the risk of missing out on the special thrill of persecution, experiencing the combination of self-pity and righteousness. The action described in these stories suggests that submissive, meek, passive female behavior will be rewarded in the end. For many of the girls it is not enough to be just passive; they are frequently victims and even martyrs as well. "The child who dreams of being a Cinderella dreams perforce not only of being chosen and elevated by a prince, but also of being a glamorous sufferer or victim. What these stories convey is that women in distress are interesting. Fairy stories provide children with a concentrated early introduction to the archetype of the suffering heroine" (Lieberman, 1986, p. 194). The notion of the heroine made interesting through her suffering has been carried on from fairy tales into literature, plays, and movies. Although gradually and delicately dying from one disease or another, heroines such as Tolstoi's Anna Karenina, Mimi in La Bohème, and the young woman in the movie *Love Story* seem to live on forever.

The mystery of female silent suffering does not fail to intrigue impression-able men. Randy, a young divorced man, engaged in psychotherapy for several years, repeatedly dated attractive but unhappy-looking women. For him it was always "love at first sight"; it took only one look into her soulfully unhappy eyes to devote his life to her—at least, for the moment. There was no need for words; he understood her misery. When questioned about this attraction for the suffering beauties he explained that he felt he was the special man that could wipe their suf-fering away and make them happy. Like the prince in the fairy tales, Randy would magically lift the veil of suffering from the beautiful maiden. Once happy, the woman would be eternally grateful to him and would never want to leave him. The surprising twist in the process was that as the woman became less unhappy and verbally more active, his fascination wore off. He lost interest in her, and in his disappointment he ended the relationship.

THE PROMISES IN CINDERELLA'S DESTINY

For some, strongly held beliefs in dreams, as pronounced by the little mice Jac and Gus from the Cinderella story mentioned at the beginning of Chapter 1, can be an invitation to future unhappiness. Steadfastly believing in destiny convinced Melinda, an attractive, intelligent, and bold young professional woman, that she had found the man that fate had intended for her when she laid eyes on Mark. At a social gathering following a professional conference, Mark, in his dark hand-someness, looked the part of Melinda's prince. He was actively engaged in con-versation with a mixed group of conference attendees. Feeling strongly drawn to him, Melinda entered the group of people around Mark. After listening for a short time, she emphatically challenged some of Mark's statements. Instead of being annoyed, Mark appeared amused by Melinda's directness and outspokenness.

After the group dispersed, Mark and Melinda decided to continue their discussion over dinner. They enjoyed a lively conversation, which was difficult to end when the waiter disappeared with the now-empty, dirty dishes. At some point during the conversation Mark had mentioned that he had been married before and that his divorce was now final. He did not display any deep sorrow and seemed well-adjusted to this event in his life. Strongly believing that Mark was the man fate had sent her way, Melinda agreed to accompany him to his apartment.

Their lovemaking was fantastic; they could not get enough of each other. In the morning, Melinda barely had time to return to her apartment and change into her workday clothes. After almost four months of passionate dating, Mark and Melinda got married. Melinda had been right all along; life with Mark was her destiny. Five years and two children later they divorced. What went wrong? Where did destiny make a mistake?

Melinda discovered that Mark was addicted to pornography. Their passionate lovemaking of the beginning turned into a sexual nightmare for Melinda. As she filed for divorce, she found out that Mark's addiction had been the reason for the failure of his first marriage. With more time and exploration prior to marrying Mark, Melinda might have been able to learn about what she was going to face. Her staunch belief in destiny had certainly blinded her regarding any possible negative consequences of this hasty but heavy commitment.

Romance grows best in an atmosphere of minimum knowledge of the other person. It is a dream-like relationship that is restricted to the sensation that being around the other person is the most wonderful and exciting experience. In a romantic relationship, often the person does not fall in love with an actual partner but with a dream person who is endowed with all the wonderful traits and qualities that fulfill one's longings. If Cinderella's mind is preoccupied with romance, she may set herself up for a rude awakening, for which one remedy is that of denying that it was "true" love after all—just as found by Joseph Hopper above in his studies.

Dangling the possibility—or perhaps even probability—of catching a prince for a husband would turn many a young girl into a docile and hardworking person. The promised reward is just too great to pass up. Transmitting repeatedly those fairy tales to little girls in the form of bedtime stories is likely to increase the influence on the young brain while it sleeps and dreams. Self-sacrificing, hardworking, and patient women can be an asset to any determined and ambitious man.

How many Cinderellas lovingly shoulder the burden of responsibility for their family's healthcare insurance while their princes follow their dreams of starting and building their own business? When overcome by a combination of exhaustion and professional boredom, Nadine, a married registered nurse with three young children, remembers the excitement she felt while working under contract as part of a research team at the university clinics. So much like Marcia, whose story was mentioned in Chapter 1, Nadine believed she had made a sound decision when, after marrying Ken and planning a family, she left the clinic and started employment as a nurse at a local hospital. Her salary was not much higher than what she had earned as contract worker, but her work schedule was more flexible and the benefits were considerable. With Ken still finishing up his law degree, this seemed like the best option for Nadine. Between the time Ken began to work for a big law firm and the time he decided to start his own law practice, Nadine had kept her employment and—as at the beginning of their marriage—the family's health insurance coverage through her employer was badly needed again.

Laverne, a social worker within a child-welfare agency and mother of a young son, had dreams of returning to graduate study and pursuing a doctorate degree. To accomplish this she had planned on obtaining part-time work on a contractual basis. Unfortunately Julian, her husband, developed an anxiety disorder that made it difficult for him to hold steady employment where he had to interact with coworkers on a daily basis. Julian decided that starting a small business and working from home would be the answer. His anxiety attacks were reduced in frequency and degree of distress while working at home; however, he experienced strong flare-ups when contemplating scheduling visits to prospective customers. Under these circumstances, Laverne saw no option for changing her work schedule and embarking upon graduate studies. Her full-time position provided most of the family finances as well as their healthcare needs. Ironically, although Laverne's benefits would have allowed for Julian to seek therapy for his anxiety disorder, he refused to even consider this option.

After working for more than three decades as office manager of a busy family physician practice, Anne felt worn out. The group of physicians expanded and her responsibilities seemed to increase at a rate comparable to the decrease of her energy. Almost 30 years ago, when Anne and Leo started their family, Leo had lost his job. It did not seem to be much of a tragedy because Leo did not cherish the idea of working for someone else. He decided to start his own business in the insurance field but could not afford to purchase healthcare benefits for his family. Anne's job was a blessing; it provided excellent benefits to take care of the family's needs. Although Leo's business prospered over the years and their children had left the home, Anne remained in her high-stress job. Her suggestions that she work part-time or even stop working while considering other options met with resistance from Leo. Times were unstable, and, as they both grew older, more health problems could be expected to befall them; Anne's secure job and healthcare insurance were needed as much as ever, Leo reasoned.

Looking around in our society, we can observe many employed women for whom the family's healthcare insurance, which can be obtained through the women's employment, is a critical issue. In some cases, such as Marcia's in Chapter 1 and Nadine and Anne's above, husbands are enabled to pursue their goals of establishing their own business without having to worry about providing health insurance for their families. In Laverne's case, her day for pursuing a doctoral degree may never come if Julian's anxiety continues to prevent him from earning a living within the presence of coworkers. Leaving a job that provides these necessities in order to follow their own career dreams would seem impossible to most mothers. How could they jeopardize the lives and safety of their children by considering their own wishes to be as important as those of their husbands? (Maass, 2008) Had they been able to foresee future developments, these Cinderellas might not even have wanted to try on the slipper in the prince's hand.

In earlier times, when a man was known for the size of land he owned in a particular region, the hardworking, submissive wife was a great resource in working the land and extracting the best harvest. In modern times, a man may make his mark with the size of the business he builds. Again, the hardworking wife can function as receptionist/secretary/bookkeeper in the developing business as well as a gracious hostess, entertaining any associates or customers. In the amount of work to be done, the woman becomes an equal partner, at least. When it comes to harvesting the earnings, her role may be less clearly defined.

The value of a woman as a helpmate is clearly reflected in observations made within the academic system (Bellas, 1992). Among male professors, those with non-employed wives received higher salaries than men whose wives worked full-time. Unmarried faculty men earned less, held lower ranks, and published less than married male professors. Considering male professors in the discipline of art history, of those who were married to a less than full-time or not-working wife at the time of their Ph.D. award had an 88 percent chance of tenure, compared to 70 percent of men whose wives were working full time at the time they earned their Ph.D.s. In comparison, single, male Ph.D. recipients have only a 55 percent chance of obtaining tenure. Thus, it seems that marriage in general increases tenure chances for men, and some types of marriage in particular improve men's tenure chances dramatically (Rudd, Morrison, Sadrozinski, Nerad, & Cerny, 2008).

When Mary accepted Walter's marriage proposal, there was no doubt that they would live and work on his parents' farm, which he was expected to inherit after their death. It looked like they were heading for a good future on a sound family ground. Mary did her share of the work while raising two sons and attending to her parents-in-law as their health declined with the passing years. She worked patiently and cheerfully; after all, it was all for the family. Walter's parents died and the farm became his property. Mary's name was nowhere to be found on the deed; but that was just a formality. As their sons grew up, they made it known that they did not see their future in farm-work. Walter gave in grudgingly and they headed for college.

The farm became too much of a responsibility for Walter and Mary to handle as they grew older, and Walter decided to sell the farm and invest the money in his own business. Mary educated herself in bookkeeping and basic computer skills and brushed up on the typing skills she remembered from high school. Through the early years of the slowly developing business, Mary and Walter lived frugally. There was still college tuition to be paid for their sons, and every extra penny went into the business. Both Walter and Mary were active in their church; it was good for the business to be helping members of the congregation. Mary baked pies for church sales and prepared dinner for families who were devastated by the death of a family member. Walter, along with other male members, lent a hand with more masculine tasks to the widows of recently departed male members of the congregation.

One of the newly bereaved widows seemed especially helpless in coping with everyday tasks around her house. Apparently, her husband had been able to fix all kinds of old appliances and tools before his death. Now everything seemed to be breaking down and there was no money for replacements. The poor widow was in desperate need of a helping hand, and Walter responded by coming to the rescue. The widow's main ability to express her gratitude was in preparing delicious meals, which she served to Walter as he was taking care of any of a list of tasks that needed his attention. Mary was not invited to partake in these meals; after all, Walter's presence at the widow's house was primarily to repair broken-down appliances and such. Finally, Mary's patience wore thin. She pointed out to Walter that he was eating more meals at the widow's house than in their home. Walter thought that Mary displayed a rather petty attitude. After all, preparing some food was the only way the widow could reciprocate for the help she received. Accepting the meals was essential in protecting the poor widow's self-esteem.

Mary's mood did not improve. It was as if her life's supply of patience, humility, and silence had been depleted. When her sons came home from college for holidays she complained about Walter's activities at the widow's house. They, in turn, thought that Mary's angry nagging might actually influence their father to spend more time at the widow's. Mary could not win; even in church, people whispered about the bitterness with which she seemed to interact in their congregation. Within a year's time, Walter started spending the nights at the widow's house. He gradually moved his possessions out of their home and discussed with a real estate agent the possibility of selling their house to avoid making the high monthly mortgage payments. The money needed for the business and their sons' college tuition had left very little for a down payment on the house and resulted in the high mortgage payments. Unless Mary would take over the payments, the house had to be sold, Walter informed her.

Of course, Mary could not make those mortgage payments; she had not received an adequate or regular salary for the work she performed in Walter's business. In fact, he suggested that she look for a job elsewhere. His business could not afford paying her anything and the widow had kindly offered to take over for free those responsibilities that previously Mary had performed. Mary and Walter's divorce followed soon after those developments. For the moment, Mary's sons sided with their father. They felt their father was entitled to a harmonious relationship with a friendly and supportive woman after working hard all his life.

With Mary's transformation from the self-sacrificing, hardworking, patient, and submissive wife into a nagging, bitter woman who dared express her anger and dissatisfaction verbally, she had broken the rules and guidelines set up long ago for acceptable behaviors of the "good wife." Mary turned out not to be the "real" Cinderella, after all. She had believed in the just rewards of living in the footsteps of the woman acceptable for marriage to an "honorable" man, apparently without inspecting closely enough the slipper in his hand. What characteristics did he possess that would provide protection when she needed it?

CONTROLLING CINDERELLA'S FATE

The groundwork for Cinderella silently fulfilling her responsibilities and the expectations of others without raising her voice, questioning, or doubting those expectations has been laid for centuries by the forces around her. Those forces can look back on a long history of practice in attempting to control Cinderella's fate. Social conditioning—instilling the need for approval and emotional dependency, along with other influences that we may be unaware of—can function as elements of control, or what is often called brainwashing, preventing us from being self-directed and from developing the human traits that make us less susceptible to subtle influences in our environment (Winn, 2000).

Sadly, those women who cross the gender line of feminine ideals in terms of occupation and personality still face sexual harassment, related Jennifer Bendahl, psychologist and professor of management at the University of Toronto, in an interview. In three studies she found that women with more "masculine" personality traits, such as assertiveness and forcefulness, experienced the most sexual harassment when compared with those women whose list of personality traits included gentleness, warmth, tenderness, and affection (Meyers, 2007). Based on those experiences, women with strong personalities would tend to avoid occupational settings where they would likely encounter significant sexual harassment and would look for more forward-thinking and egalitarian work environments.

In their personal lives, for women who do not embrace traditional gender norms, examining the attitudes of a marriage candidate is equally as important as the attitudes in the workplace. No matter how charming the prospective husband appears to be, if he values conventionally gendered roles, once married, the division of labor in the household will be such that the woman is expected to perform the household tasks normally considered to fall within the female domain, regardless of whether or not she is also a professional working outside the home.

It can be argued that there is nothing to prevent women from liberating themselves from the prescriptions of traditional society and from assuming responsibility for parts of their own destiny. And many women are doing just that. However, there are also those who still operate under the influence of the old fairy tales they heard during their formative years. If Cinderella strongly believes that the good character traits of patience, obedience, hard work, and selfless service to others—with a good measure of physical attractiveness, because Cinderella wouldn't dare not be pretty—will ensure the arrival of the prince who will then take over her life and protect her from all future travails, she will most likely miss the opportunities for self-determination. Steadfastly believing in those occurrences makes planning for one's future life unnecessary; indeed, if we listen to women such as Gina, introduced earlier, it would be a waste of time and effort if not a handicap in preparing for the arrival of the prince. When being chosen is preferred by Cinderella over making her own choices, she places her destiny in the hands of others, and some of those may not have her best interest at heart.

MARRIAGE: THE END OF THE STORY?

As discussed in Chapter 1, the focus of most of our fairy tales rests primarily on courtship, culminating in marriage, indicating that these events are the most important ones in a girl's life. Once she is married, the excitement of courtship ceases and her consent "is no longer sought, she derives her status from her husband, and her personal identity is thus snuffed out. When fairytales show courtship as exciting, and conclude with marriage, and the vague statement that 'they lived happily ever after,' children may develop a deep-seated desire always to be courted, since marriage is literally the end of the story" (Lieberman, 1986, p. 200).

However, in real life, marriage is a major social institution, and as such it functions as a bridge between the worlds of fantasy, as in fairy tales, and reality. The connection between the romantic fiction and the actuality of marriage as a social institution constitutes a significant influence in shaping female expectations. With the impact of the wedding ceremony and the tremendous preparations leading up to it, in the young girl's mind, the connection between fantasy and reality rarely progresses farther into reality than the event of the wedding itself— thereby becoming a parallel process to the fairy tales, which end with the wedding. Cinderella's immersion in the complicated details of the wedding keeps her mind occupied, without leaving much room for thought about the prince's qualities and his demands of her once the extravaganza is over.

In 2005 a survey conducted with the help of over 1,000 brides regarding the average amount of money paid for a wedding revealed a cost of almost $30,000 to cover a one-day event (Wickham, 2008). Considering the still-high divorce rates in this country, what kind of an investment does this wedding-day price amount to? The excitement of an engagement usually envelops the young couple with an emotional veil that protects them from confrontations with reality. Whatever energy is spent on planning efforts for the future seems to focus on the immediate future—the wedding day. Keeping in mind the exaggerated significance of this day, it is not surprising that little energy is left for attending to questions regarding life after the big day, when the exchange of vows and the honeymoon have passed.

As described by Carol Cassell (1984) in her book *Swept Away*, after asking women about their fantasies as little girls about their future roles as grown-ups, most responded with being married. However, the fantasies focused in detail on the wedding itself, such as the number of bridesmaids and the color of their dresses. The girls did not go much beyond the actual ceremony itself in their dreams about the future. As mentioned in Chapter 1, a whole industry depends on the event of the wedding and its preceding courtship period. The engagement period has evolved into a time of shopping and preparation for the big event, the ceremony, the honeymoon, and the portrayal of the wedding as a whole. The garment industry, jewelers, florists, churches, restaurants, caterers, car rentals, and the photographers, as well as many others, derive significant parts of their income from the weddings of Cinderellas and "Cinderella-wannabes."

The advertising industry, similar to other industries mentioned in the previous chapter, also has made use of the Cinderella story in bridal advertising since the beginning of the 20th century, as demonstrated by a Libbey advertisement in 1904 with the headline "The American Cinderella" depicting a bride admiring a large glass vase. "In the second half of the twentieth century, the belief that every bride could be Cinderella became a girlhood fantasy, a democratic right, and *the* central preoccupation of the wedding" (Otnes & Pleck, 2003, p. 54). During the 1950s, the average seven- to ten-year-old American girl was exposed to the bridal fantasy, which culminated during the 1960s in "Barbie," a both sexier and more fashion-conscious bride. Little girls who owned a "Barbie" doll were hoping that the next birthday or other holiday would bring them a "Ken" doll, so they could play out their fantasies about their future wedding.

It is not surprising that girls still see their wedding day as the biggest day in their lives. It is the day when they play "Queen for a Day," a play that is strongly encouraged by—and supports—a whole industry. For a price, the bridal merchants promise and deliver as elaborate a show as the bride's parents can afford. The confectioner's couple on the wedding cake becomes the prescription for the future, even though its sugary construction does little to resemble reality. In some cases it may have taken the parents more years to scrimp on things and save the money for the wedding than the life of the marriage will endure.

THE CASE OF CINDY—NOT A CINDERELLA STORY

Cindy was 11 years old when her mother, an acknowledged beauty, died of cancer. Cindy's father, a professor at a local university, buried himself in grief over the loss of his wife. He was barely able to manage his teaching responsibilities. Cindy remembered the advice from a well-meaning uncle, attempting to distract Cindy from focusing too much on the loss of her mother: he told Cindy to help her father in any way she could by taking on some of her mother's responsibilities. Cindy was a good daughter who made her father's well-being a priority without neglecting her schoolwork. She learned to cook and clean and sort the laundry. Cindy adored her father, and, in order to cheer him up, she tried her hand at writing poetry. But her father's sad smiles when reading her poems did not have the encouraging effect that one would have hoped for.

Less than two years after her mother's death, Cindy's father announced his decision to get married again. Cindy's stepmother-to-be was a widow with two children of her own: a daughter, Lizzie, about Cindy's age, and Lars, a son two years older than Lizzie. They would all be one big happy family, her father promised. The reality presented itself differently, however. Cindy's new stepmother was a loud-spoken woman who believed that Cindy should continue to practice and perfect the domestic skills she had attempted after her mother's death, while Lizzie was allowed to spend her free time taking voice and ballet lessons.

Although not matching the level of her dead mother's beauty, Cindy was very pretty with her dark hair, her fair skin, and her large gray eyes. Eventually she would grow into as attractive a woman as her mother had been, people said. Her stepmother convinced Cindy's father that it was important to keep Cindy "protected"—a term that turned out to be closer to isolation than protection. Cindy was a good student, and when it came time for college considerations, the decision was easy—she would enroll in the same private, residential girls' college that her mother and her grandmother before her had attended. Originally, it was planned that Lizzie would attend the same college as Cindy. But when Lizzie's grades did not make her eligible for acceptance at the same college; she decided to attend a college in her hometown.

Cindy and her roommate Anita became close friends, something that Cindy was desperately in need of. Her stepmother's isolation tactics had been successful in distancing Cindy emotionally from her father and also in preventing opportunities for developing meaningful friendships in their community. Cindy was happy to have someone to trust and to confide in. Anita's parents were just as delighted with their daughter's friendship and included Cindy in many of their family gatherings. For Thanksgiving holidays it seemed more efficient and convenient to accompany Anita to her home, which was closer to the college, than to travel to the more distant location of Cindy's home. Her father did not seem to mind, Cindy observed sadly.

With the passing of the college years, Cindy became more and more estranged from her family. Although she was grateful to Anita's parents for making her part of their family, she missed the relationship with her father. After graduation Cindy found a career-start near her friend's hometown; she never moved back into the home of her childhood for any significant period of time. In her new environment she dated several young men without experiencing the deep emotional involvement she was longing for—until she met Derek, who was tall, blond, and handsome, with bright-blue eyes that seemed to look into the bottom of her soul. Derek's voice and physical appearance bore some resemblance to her father's, a fact Cindy had not been consciously aware of. It was a beautiful wedding; everybody said so. Cindy was happy; she had found her prince, her protector, who would not abandon her as her father had done. Derek would always be there for her.

With the addition of a baby girl life went on smoothly within their little family. Derek's job required more frequent travel now and the times between sexual activities increased. But Cindy's involvement with her baby daughter kept her busy, initiating in her the transition from lover and wife to mother. Then suddenly, her world seemed to collapse. It was a warm and gentle Wednesday evening, an evening following a day filled with promises of a splendid spring to come; Cindy would remember it for the rest of her life. In a long-distance telephone call from the area of Derek's more frequent business trips, a woman's voice informed Cindy that Derek was involved in a sexual relationship with the woman's husband. The husband was considering leaving his wife and three young children to devote more time to his relationship with Derek. The woman had followed her husband to the hotel and found out her husband's lover's name and address. Disbelieving the woman's account, Cindy called Derek, but there was no answer from his room.

Derek returned home late the next day. Hoping that it was all a misunderstanding, Cindy told him about the disturbing telephone call. Derek appeared shocked but admitted that it was true; he was involved with the woman's husband. Derek confessed that he had struggled with his sexual interest in men for some time and had acted on it in his early youth. But he knew that his parents would never accept their son's homosexual or bisexual tendencies. He could not disgrace them by acknowledging his sexual orientation. Upon meeting Cindy he had been genuinely attracted to her, and he had hoped that by marrying her he could overcome his sexual desire for other men. For a while it seemed that he had made the right choice, but, more recently, his sexual desire for men had increased again. The woman's husband was the first man he had been involved with sexually since their marriage, although there had been temptations earlier, which he had been able to resist.

Responding to Cindy's question, Derek admitted that this affair had been going on for almost six months, and, yes, the men's feelings for each other had grown stronger over this period. Was Derek planning to leave his family just like the other man apparently considered doing? Derek seemed to be at a loss for an answer; he asked Cindy for help and understanding.

How could she understand what was happening to him when she could not even understand what was happening to her? How could she have been so deceived? This was Derek, her husband, her protector. True, their sexual life had not quite been what she expected, especially while they were still in the honeymoon phase of their marriage. Derek's sexual desire did not seem strong enough to support lovemaking more than once or twice a week. While he was not an ardent lover, he was gentle and considerate—just not very passionate. Cindy did not have a basis for comparison; she had no sexual experiences prior to meeting Derek. Remembering her psychology classes in college, she even wondered if Derek might have repressed his sexuality for some dark reason. Although she would have preferred more frequent sexual activities, she did not want to hurt Derek's feelings by asking for more and it had been sufficient to start her on the path to motherhood.

Thinking back, she remembered that when she told Derek the news about being pregnant he seemed surprised, perhaps even confused—not quite what she had expected, but she explained it away to herself, thinking that he was probably overwhelmed with the awesome responsibility of parenthood. Derek was a man who took his responsibilities seriously—unlike her father, who had deserted her emotionally.

Where could Cindy go for help now? Her only close friend was Anita. Should she burden her with this problem? How could she explain her own ignorance about Derek's true feelings? The explanations she had used to quiet even the tiniest questions or doubts she had experienced in the past did not work anymore. Should she, or could she, continue with the silence—now heavier than ever—in order to protect Derek, her daughter, and herself from shame? If she remained silent to avoid the shame, she would be emotionally isolated again, more painfully so than during the isolation of her youth. If she revealed the truth, would people judge her to be incompetent in her judgment of people and character? And what would her daughter ask when she began to understand the nature of her parents' marriage? Would she blame Cindy for giving her a father who defied the rules of natural family constellations by turning to another man for his sexual fulfillment? Would her daughter accuse her of not making sure that she had chosen an honest, responsible man worthy of parenthood, a man to protect and guide his child through the stormy periods of childhood and - adolescence and prepare her for adulthood?

CINDERELLA'S AWAKENING

Melanie, a 25-year-old married woman and mother of a one-year-old daughter, felt anxious and depressed but could not put her finger on what the reason for her negative feelings could be. After all, she had been an independent young professional, with a brand-new career, who married the man she loved and gave birth to a beautiful baby girl. Admittedly, the first job in her new career had been disappointing and she decided to quit working prior to the birth of her daughter, but she and her husband were excited about their new family. To gain more insight into the reasons for her unexplainable lack of happiness, Melanie decided to seek the help of a psychotherapist.

It was during her third therapy session that lightening struck: Very slowly, since her marriage to Brad, she had let him pamper her more and more. After her years of independent living it seemed so nice to have someone taking over some of the mundane day-to-day hassles for her. This trend had intensified during the months of her pregnancy and even more so after the birth of her daughter. Although working full-time, Brad was willing to take on additional chores—at least, in the beginning. When his enthusiasm over the assignment of extra tasks cooled, he voiced a few complaints. After all, Melanie had the whole day to herself and the baby; surely she could manage to perform the regular, everyday household chores. Initially, Melanie thought Brad had changed; he was not the wonderful man she had married. She felt unfairly criticized instead of loved and adored, and, in turn, that took a toll on her sexual desire for him.

After some soul-searching, Melanie realized that she little-by-little had become less active and less independent in her daily life. In the past, she had been so proud of her own independence; now she had even developed a dislike for performing some errands and for tackling the duties of ordinary life. Almost in a trance-like state she murmured that all the fairy tales she remembered from childhood ended with the marriage between the prince and the young maiden. The most popular ones, such as Cinderella and Sleeping Beauty, did not go on beyond the wedding. There was nothing following the climax of being wed to the prince. Life ceased to exist—or was it just not important anymore?

Melanie knew her own value as a human being, and she had looked around until she found the prince who could give her what she was worth—sincere love, respect, and commitment. It had been worth waiting and finding him. But without being consciously aware of it, she had slowed down, reduced her activities, and decreased her responsibilities. It was as if an important part of her had fallen asleep. But she was not happy in her sleep either. There was a sense of boredom that was tiring as well as depressing to her. Now she was waking up to the realization that it had been a crippling sleep, not a restful slumber. Cinderella had been crippling herself in her sleep.

If in the past anyone had asked Melanie if she believed that fairy tales come true in real life, she would have laughed. Fairy tales were for children; well-educated professional young women of today did not take them seriously. Yet

Melanie, a highly intelligent woman who had spent years of hard work and studying in preparation for a professional career, had subconsciously incorporated the old messages that are embedded in fairy tales into her being and transferred them into her real life of today. Such is the power of fairy tales as transmitters of messages from the past.

A few days after her 43rd birthday, author Frederica Mathewes-Green (2002) realized that she had not received a Cinderella watch packaged in a tiny clear-plastic slipper, as had come her way on birthdays during years past. Frederica was one of generations of little girls whose idea of female beauty had been shaped by the women of Disney. Her intentions for the future had been to become a grown-up lady who would wear a long fancy dress and a crown. While everything about her body would grow her feet would get smaller and smaller until she could fit into Cinderella's tiny shoes.

The realization of the missing birthday package prompted her to sit down with her teenage daughter to review the lessons of the Disney fairy tales. *Snow White,* a beautiful young princess, is required by her wicked stepmother to dress in rags and scrub the floors; apparently killed by the jealous stepmother, she comes to life again at the prince's first kiss. Similarly, *Sleeping Beauty* comes back to life from her long sleep through "true love's kiss." *Cinderella,* another young beauty, compelled by her wicked stepmother to scrub the floors and dress in rags, is chosen by the prince as her ugly stepsisters unsuccessfully compete for his attention. Cinderella, in the 1950 Disney movie, has "got the simple goodness of the young Donna Reed, till she gets wrapped in that fabulous white ball gown and, with upswept hair, turns into Grace Kelly" (Mathewes-Green, 2002, p. 87).

In all three tales, beauty is a prerequisite for the happy ending. And the ending of all three stories comes within minutes of the rescue. Nobody has to or wants to worry about life after the "happy ending"—those are the lessons. Although the author likes Cinderella best of all the heroines, she is resigned that it will probably be too late for her to look like Cinderella. Looking into her mirror, the author thinks that the fairy godmother—with the figure of an old pillow, a multiple chin, white hair, and a kind smile on her round face—may be the image reflected in a few years. Finally, the shoe fits.

Part II _____

Past Influences—Usable or Refuseable?

3

The Silencing of Cinderella's Voice

Cinderella—does she have a voice and does she have a choice in using it? Not if we adhere to the accounts of the French poet Charles Perrault and the German fairy tale recorders Wilhelm and Ludwig Emil Grimm, who transformed Cinderella into the domesticated young woman possessing the virtues of self-denial, obedience, and industriousness that make her suitable and acceptable as a wife within the framework of middle-class, Protestant ethics.

Cinderella's silence, as described by Bottigheimer (1987), did not originate as part of an overt curse that condemned her to silence; it was "the pattern of discourse in the Grimm's tales that discriminates against 'good' girls and produces functionally silent heroines" (p. 53). Using "Cinderella" as an example, Bottigheimer shows how silence and powerlessness are combined in the description of the title figure.

Women's silence still occupies a central position in much of recent literary research, demonstrating a concern with sex differences in human speech and the question of who speaks in given situations. Speech can be understood and used as a form of domination, and as such speech serves as a key indicator of social values and the distribution of power within a society. Bottigheimer (1987), in her analysis of Grimm's fairy tales, discussed Heinrich Vigilis von Weissenburg's 1497 declarations "Von dem Heilgen Swygenhaltten" (Of the Holy Maintenance of Silence) about the reasons why women should be silent and defenseless.

It was the first woman, Eve in paradise, who was deceived and led astray by the serpent. She was considered to be the introducer of sin, whereas Adam's transgression was viewed to be of a lesser degree; he succumbed not to a serpent's temptations, but rather he followed Eve's example. Adam was bound with natural love to Eve who was part of him, having been created of his body, whereas Eve was led astray by a creature to which she had no relationship and no love. That Eve was made of Adam's rib, not he from hers, was another reason for her to be quiet. Upon closer examination, the logic of this list of reasons may not seem all that convincing now, but it worked for a long time. And even today, there are vestiges to be found in our cultural institutions.

SILENCE AND POWERLESSNESS

Taking a historical view of fairy tales leads to the conclusion that hardship or deprivation can be translated into an account in which silence stands for the domestic, political, and social experience of the poor. Girls and women deprived of language exemplify the relationship between language and autonomy. In several other well-known Grimm's fairy tales, the narrative language used in telling the stories provides images of muted females. For instance, in the "Frog King" the reader encounters the princess's many compliant reactions to the frog's imperious commands, such as, "Be quiet" (*sei still*). Similarly, in "Hansel and Gretel," in addition to Hansel's greater frequency of speech, he tells Gretel "quiet, Gretel" (*still, Gretel*) on one of the few occasions that she utters some words to express her fears.

Of additional interest is the role of the biological mother that is outlined in the narrative of most of these tales. Snow White's mother reportedly thinks to herself but never speaks a word. Finally, when her daughter is born, she dies as silently as she had lived. In similar fashion, Cinderella's mother dies after having recommended her daughter to be good and pious. In "The Twelve Brothers," the mother speaks only once before she disappears from the rest of the tale, and the children's biological mother in "Hansel and Gretel" is completely absent and has been replaced by a stepmother when the story begins.

In her analysis, Bottigheimer (1987) based her argument on a detailed examination of the editorial history of one particular tale, "Our Lady's Child," when she pointed to the effectiveness of depriving a girl of speech in the process of breaking her will. "This completes the equation of speech with individual power and autonomy. It is precisely the deprivation and transformation of power that seems to motivate the shifts evident in the transformation of individual folk and fairy tale heroines during the Early Modern period in European history" (p. 76).

As pointed out by Bottigheimer, it is within a Christian framework that we find a stringent silencing of women, such as the prohibitions against women's speech in the New Testament epistles expressed in Paul's letter to the Corinthians: "As in all congregations of God's people, women should not address the meeting. They have no license to speak, but should keep their place as the law directs. If there is something they want to know, they can ask their own husbands at home. It is a shocking thing that a woman should address the congregation" (I Cor. 14:34-35).

This is, of course, congruent with the declaration of the *Catholic Encyclopedia,* that in some respects the female sex is inferior to the male sex, regarding both body and soul. Those sentiments are echoed by a 19th-century Anglican churchman when he proclaimed that women are "intrinsically inferior in mind, and imperfect and infirm in character." When Clement of Alexandria quoted the words of Christ from the Gospel According to the Egyptians, "Women are not worthy of life," he provided a strong recommendation to women: "Every woman ought to be filled with shame at the thought that she is a woman" (Lederer, 1968, p. 162). Experiencing shame just for existing is a fate that would leave anyone in a state of hopelessness and helplessness, as well as depression, because the only solution to overcoming shame in this instance is death, the end of existing. Although the church ostensibly declared war on the devil, in reality the church made war on women. "Woman was the Church's rival, the temptress, the distraction, the obstacle to holiness, the Devil's decoy" (Tuchman, 1978, p. 211).

Despite the openly announced inferior status of women, many women are religious and pious, giving rise to the question of how they have been conditioned to internalize those rigid spiritual ideas that mark them as inferior beings. How have women come to accept the teachings of religions and churches and their normative patterns for women, which prevent them from realizing their own spiritual and sensual unity? (Kolbenschlag, 1979) It is not only within religions and churches that we find the silence of the powerless. Even today, many women in the context of marital conflict silence themselves. Perhaps out of fear of their husbands' reactions, these women remain silent and keep their anger bottled up inside during arguments. But marital conflict and stress are associated with heart disease and mortality; as a longitudinal study demonstrated, women who "self-silence" were four times more likely to die than women who expressed themselves and their feelings (Webber, 2008).

ARE WOMEN SILENCING THEMSELVES?

Anger is not all women keep bottled up; many do equally well with keeping their wishes unexpressed. It was Christy's 35th birthday. "Half-way between 30 and 40" was her first thought when she woke up. Ambivalent about how she should feel on this day, she got up to prepare breakfast for the family. Soon enough her two children would come tumbling down the stairs. Robert, her husband, must have already started his morning routine in the bathroom. Mornings were a hectic time in their house; everybody needed to get ready for work or school. Among the hugs and congratulations, Christy had her hands full getting breakfast on the table. As soon as she was able to sit down she opened the gifts from her children. They were always eager to see the expression on her face— was the gift suitable? She left Robert's gift for later—just in case.

Christy's thoughts strayed to the past and to birthdays she remembered in her teenage years. As soon as everybody had left Christy went back to the bedroom with Robert's gifts. Opening one package revealed a colorful shawl and a pair of sand-colored leather gloves. The smaller box contained a beautiful Murano glass dish, small enough to fit on her dressing table. And yes, the little gold citrine-and-diamond butterfly brooch she had mentioned a few times over the past several months was there.

How different her birthday was from the ones she remembered her mother having. Her mother always pretended to be grateful but Christy had observed tears on her mother's face on some of her birthdays. Her mother never opened the gifts from Christy's father in the presence of anyone around. Christy had asked her if she was disappointed but her mother avoided giving a direct answer. "Women don't ask for what they want. Their husbands, if they love them and care about them, know what their wives want," her mother told her. Christy's mother had died several years back. Once she asked her father about her mother's happiness. He thought Christy's mother was happy. "She never complained," he added. That's when Christy realized why her mother did not open the gifts from her father unless she was alone; she needed the time to overcome her disappointment and put on a thankful appearance to the rest of the world.

Not saying what they want in the way of a gift, with the assumption that if the man loves her and cares about her, he will know what she would like, is the surest way for women to not get what they want. And—turning it around—if the woman doesn't get what she wants, it must mean that the man does not love her. So the woman will be disappointed on two counts: first she does not get what she desired, and second, she begins to doubt that the man really loves her. Applying this type of thought process is a guaranteed recipe for unhappiness.

Who trained women to think the way Christy's mother thought? Was it part of the overall silencing scheme, or did it have other reasons? Christy learned and applied a valuable lesson from observing her mother. Her decision to express her wishes to her husband prevented disappointment to cloud their relationship. Sadly, there are still young women out there who accept Christy's mother (or their own mother) as a model for their lives.

"Women are not by nature silent; they have been silenced. Women do not lack a voice; their words are unwelcome" insisted Heyn in her book *The Erotic Silence of the American Wife* (1992, p. 18). She was referring to the punishment of female passion outside marriage, as described in the literature. Women, reading these stories in books or seeing them on the stage or TV, got the message that it was dangerous to talk about passion and they decided to remain silent. In her interviews with women who admittedly had engaged in sexual encounters with men other than their husbands, Heyn learned that the women felt freer to explore and enjoy their own sexuality with these men than with their husbands. Many of them loved their husbands but allowed themselves to be sensuous and passionate only with their lovers.

There are various reasons to explain this phenomenon. Some women may have decided to marry a certain man less for sexual experiences than for marriage and motherhood. With those grounds for marriage, sexuality and sensuality may not have entered their minds in connection with their husbands. Or they may have had this image of themselves as "good women" at the time of transition to wife that the notion of sexuality did not seem to fit. Perhaps they thought their husbands would disapprove of them if they expressed their desire for sex or would become suspicious about their wives' past sexual history. They may have married a man who resented a woman's expression of her desires and did not dare to speak up.

"I will never forget the shame and embarrassment I felt when my husband criticized me for expressing a wish of where and how I wanted to be touched" Arlene explained in a low voice. After years of silent lovemaking, always initiated by her husband, Arlene—attempting to overcome her low sexual desire— had, with the help of books and educational videotapes, explored her own sensuality. Her hesitant approach to express her wishes elicited an angry response from her husband. "The way he talked to me made me feel like a whore," Arlene continued her story. "Since then, every time we had sex it came back into my mind and my body stiffened. Perhaps there would have been better ways to deal with it than what I ended up doing; it's too late now."

Following this experience, for a while Arlene realized her ambivalence: she longed for some tenderness and at the same time was consumed by fears of being degraded and rejected ever again. Although divorced from her husband, it took several years for Arlene to even think about entering another intimate relationship. She had tried to fit into a shoe that didn't fit and paid with years of pain for it.

More often than not, where once there was passion at the beginning of the marital relationship, the process of ordinary daily life had managed to extinguish it. If the change had occurred suddenly, the women might have noticed it and reacted against it. However, in a slow-moving process, the change is so subtle that it passes unnoticed, until one can hardly remember it having been different at some time in the past. Whatever the reason for the missing passion and sensuality in the marital relationships, it seems the women did not communicate the loss of it. Perhaps they were not fully aware of anything special missing, or they thought this was a natural development. But if they did not assert their right to their sexuality, then one could say they silenced their voices about it.

THE SILENCING EFFECTS OF PHYSICAL LIMITATIONS

Professor Edward Shorter (1982) in his scholarly endeavors of exploring the history of medicine, addressed the fact that women in the 17th century and prior to 1900 did not demand to be able to vote or attend a university. In comparison to men, Shorter explained, women faced an overwhelming physical disadvantage. They were burdened with many unwanted children, were generally less well-fed than men, and were further weakened by diseases not afflicting men, such as anemia and infections connected to childbirth, among others. These conditions did not leave them the energy to insist on equal standing and personal authority.

In addition, subjectively women "accepted their disadvantaged status as part of the normal order. They concurred in society's judgment that they were poisonous, diseased, and inferior" (Shorter, 1982, p. 285). The women's belief in their own inferiority prevented them from demanding equality between men and women until there were opportunities for feminism to develop.

It is not the purpose of this book to point the finger at institutions or individuals in efforts to blame them for the status of women today. Generations of women have lived and struggled with this issue. Now, it is too late for blame. We can't afford to waste more time and energy on blaming. Rather, the goal is to explain the past as a basis for understanding the present and for influencing the future.

LISTEN TO ME!

Lois, a quietly attractive woman in her early 30s, had joined an ongoing workshop designed to assist people with taking control of their lives. She had made her decision to join as soon as she found out about it, even though that meant that she would be late for the first meeting. Lois arrived after most of the participants had already introduced themselves. Embarrassed about being late, she did not offer much about her own history. She had been married for about two years and was a nurse by profession. When asked about her goals in this workshop Lois stated that she wanted to be listened to. Blushing, as she saw the questioning expression on some of the participants' faces, she added, "When I have something important to say."

Lois grew up as the only girl in a family with two older brothers. When she was about four years old her maternal grandfather had moved in with them because he needed someone to prepare his meals and do the maintenance chores after his wife had died. Lois did not remember much of her grandmother; she had been ill most of the time, and her mother spent several hours a week at the grandparents' house, taking care of them. Now it seemed more reasonable to have the grandfather live with the family.

Lois felt uncomfortable around her grandfather; he often came into the kitchen when nobody else was around. He tried to play with her and put her on his lap. When he did so he touched her between her legs to lift her up to him or he put his hands on her chest, slightly rubbing her breasts, to keep her from sliding down from his lap. Somehow Lois felt that his touches were not right, not appropriate. She had a difficult time explaining it to her mother, who told her that the grandfather was a kind old man who would not harm anybody. How could Lois even think of him doing anything wrong? That was the end of the discussion. Lois got the impression that her mother meant that there was something evil about her thoughts. Lois felt unprotected, unimportant, and bad. After having been rejected by her mother when she tried to confide in her, she did not even think about talking to her father, who was more involved with her older brothers and their activities.

Nothing changed. Lois tried to avoid being alone with her grandfather as much as she could. But there were situations when he got a hold of her struggling little body and touched her inappropriately. Once he even put her hand on his penis after having opened his pants, telling her that this was a toy for her to play with. Lois made one more unsuccessful attempt to talk to her mother. Soon thereafter her grandfather died. At the funeral she thought her mother looked at her accusingly. She may have misinterpreted her mother's sadness over her father's death, but Lois never had a close relationship with her mother or with anyone else in the family. The situation with her mother and her grandfather taught Lois that what happened to her was not important enough for anybody to listen.

Her belief was confirmed when she married Ralph a little over two years ago. She did not realize it at first, because she was not very talkative in her interactions with others, but for the past year Lois had noticed that Ralph listened to one opinion only—his. Even if he seemed to listen to her views, his actions were usually based on his arguments without further discussion of her statements. Lois responded to these situations with quiet but smoldering anger. More recently Ralph introduced the topic of starting a family. Lois was in favor of having children, but she was concerned that Ralph would not listen to her ideas of how to bring up children. Before making the commitment to parenthood, she wanted to learn how to express her opinions more effectively than she had in the past. That was her reason for joining the workshop.

One of the men in the group appeared stunned by Lois's statement. In his opinion, parenting was the primary purpose for marriage, and because Lois had already married Ralph, she might as well go along with starting a family. Two of the female members, however, thought that Lois was realistically cautious. Apparently, the women had married men holding traditional viewpoints and now they found it difficult to assert their opinions. Being mothers, they felt they could not express themselves as openly and directly as they would want to because disagreements would create family conflicts, something they wanted to spare their children. Pamela, the older of the two women, expressed her support openly with her statement that if she had realized earlier the difference in her husband's and her own views on marriage, she might not have made the commitment to marriage and motherhood with him.

Encouraged by the support, Lois decided to disclose more of her marital situation. She blushed and her voice trembled as she mentioned that her opinion was not the only thing her husband did not listen to. He was similarly uncommunicative about their sexual relationship. He wanted sex his way. He did not want her to initiate sex—that was his job. But he wanted her to be ready and willing to be available to him. He did not ask her what she wanted; in fact, he did not like it when she said anything at all during their lovemaking. Without much foreplay and talking, it was difficult for Lois to become aroused, and vaginal lubrication became a problem.

Much like Arlene above, Lois decided to take some action to overcome this difficulty. Lois tried to prepare herself by reading some erotic literature and initiate sex when she felt aroused. That's when she learned that Ted did not want her to start sexual activities. He could not get an erection that evening. "I finally realized that he objectifies me, he is having sex with himself—I am just an object to be used. And one does not listen to objects."

Lois continued by explaining how this realization had shocked her, especially in view of the childhood experiences with her grandfather and her mother's refusal to listen to her. Her husband's lack of listening was devastating. "How did I get myself into this situation?" Lois continued, "by choosing my husband I am in a way reinstating my mother!" Lois had reached a significant conclusion that might aid her awareness about her own role in the situation. Apparently, Lois's husband was sexually not attending to her as a person. The anger Lois was experiencing when this happened most likely had a blaming component to it—either blaming her mother, her husband, or herself—as her statement indicated.

"What are you going to do?" asked Pamela. "Refill my prescription for birth control pills" was Lois's quick answer, "until I have learned a way to express myself successfully, and if Ralph will listen to me, we might consider marital counseling." Hesitating for a moment as she looked at the male group member who had criticized her earlier remarks and then turning to Pamela and the rest of the group, Lois continued in a low voice, "The next several months will be difficult for me. Discussing this issue with you has strengthened my determination to be cautious about what type of parents my children will have. Perhaps I will be too old to have children by the time I find the right other parent. But that is not as much a tragedy as having children that one or both parents are unable to raise in a healthy environment because of the parents' own problems."

The above story demonstrates how frustrated and powerless a person feels when her voice is being silenced, in this case first by her mother and then by her husband through their lack of listening to her needs. When Lois decided to join an interactive group workshop she found an audience willing to listen and respond to her thoughts and ideas. Instead of continuing the struggle in frustrating isolation, she reached out to strangers that were welcoming the expression of her opinions and ready to bond with her within the parameters of the group process.

SILENCE AND ISOLATION

In the Grimm's tales, silence and isolation became associated with females, as Wilhelm Grimm edited female isolation into many of the tales that had previously reflected different and more sociable aspects of women. During a period of editorial reworking from 1812 to 1857, Grimm consecutively removed direct speech from women and gave it to male figures. The history of the illustration process of the Grimm's tales provides vivid visual confirmation about the femaleness of isolation and its converse, the isolation of femaleness. "In Ludwig Emil Grimm's illustrations, done under Wilhelm's careful supervision, a conscious pattern of isolating heroines emerges. Girls, but not boys, are routinely shown with downcast eyes and demure demeanor, which effectively inhibits them from seeing their own surroundings and thus represents a form of personal isolation" (Bottigheimer, 1987, p. 111).

As can be observed in various settings in today's world, individuals who stare down at the ground they are standing on rather than openly looking at others around them are less likely to be included in conversation or activities by those others. Elevators in buildings provide an excellent laboratory for such observations and experiments in social isolation versus social interaction. When entering the confining space of an elevator that already includes one or more individuals, in the absence of an available corner, people usually try to find a space within an imaginary bubble to surround them. They fixedly stare at a point on the wall or down on the ground, trying hard to avoid eye contact with any of the strangers. Their unspoken message is not lost; none of the other passengers in the elevator will dare penetrate the "bubble" with a smile or a word.

On the other hand, entering an elevator with a friendly greeting, appropriate to the time of day, or welcoming a new passenger with a smile, opens doors to a brief friendly conversation, which one can conclude and leave at one's floor of destination with the warm feeling of having been in contact with a well-meaning, fellow human being. Thus, the brief bond between strangers may leave each of them with an experience of reduced existential isolation.

Returning to the discussion of fairy tales, isolation of the heroine is further facilitated and completed by another aspect described in the stories. No other girls with similar or different qualities ever befriend her or help her. Healthy female friendships do not exist in fairy tales.

In their psychological separation from other women, they may go so far as to say that they prefer the company of men because men are more interesting and honest than women are, and that relationships between women are characteristically trivial and insincere. Thus distancing themselves from their peers, "women are trapped into functioning as individual support systems for male enterprises and networks. They are needed, tolerated, used, much like batboys or mascots on professional teams. The 'groupie' image is symbolic of the female predicament: One establishes ephemeral female relationships in order to follow the rock star or team heroes. When female relationships are inconsequential, women are all the more vulnerable to male exploitation" (Gilbert, 1987, p. 41). The link in these relationships—a group of isolated individual females—is not a bond of sisterhood; rather, it is held together with the goal of increasing the aggrandizement of the hero or the team.

"Groupie" formations can also be found in certain family constellations, such as in families where several daughters compete for the attention of the father, the only male figure in the family. Variations of this theme can be easily construed and adapted according to the needs of a particular family system, as Martha found out when she married Donald, the younger of two brothers. Donald's parents insisted on their sons' presence on family holidays. The family meal served to instruct the participants on their rules. Reginald, the older son, usually sat between his parents, while the seat on the father's other side was occupied by the father's younger brother, who had never married. Donald's place was on the other side of his mother. There were two aunts, widowed by now, who settled near the father's brother. The two young daughters-in-law (Reginald's and Donald's wives) were placed farther down the table.

The dinner conversation was directed seemingly by the father. But Martha noticed that whenever she or Liz, Reginald's wife, made mention of something that happened in their families, their mother-in-law responded not to either one of them but directed comments or questions regarding the topic to the son, the husband of the young woman who spoke. The mother-in-law usually finished her comments or questions with a statement directed to or involving her husband. As it happened repeatedly, Martha was able to detect what she thought was her mother-in-law's strategic silencing of her daughters-in-law and—by turning the conversation to her husband, confirming the notion that it was the men's place to talk. Liz seemed to either not notice or mind when the conversation was directed away from her in this manner. Martha waited for a sign from Liz that might indicate Liz's opinion in this situation, but her facial expression was difficult to read.

BENEVOLENT SEXISM'S SILENCING AND ISOLATING FUNCTION

Marianne and her two friends from college, Susan and Anita, had established the ritual of meeting once a month ever since their graduation. The three of them had taken many of their classes together and had formed a strong bond. They were going to make an impact on the world around them. Susan and Anita went on to law school, while Marianne devoted herself to environmental studies and literature. She used her literary talents to express her concerns about human abuse of the environment. Marianne was the first to get married, with Susan and Anita by her side as her bridesmaids.

She had met Patrick at a sports event when he rescued her from the unwanted attention of two other male spectators. The two men whistled as she entered the row of her seat. Marianne tried to ignore the young men's attempts at conversation when Patrick rose from his seat down the row and moved next to Marianne, politely asking for her permission to occupy the seat next to her. Marianne's first impulse was to deny his request, but Patrick seemed so sincere and courteous in his protective behavior that she agreed. At the end of the event Patrick calmly offered to escort her to her car to make sure that the two men would not follow her. He did not ask for her name or telephone number but stated he would like it if they could meet for coffee the next day.

Thus started a beautiful romance. Patrick maintained his chivalrous behavior. In his opinion, it was unsafe for a young woman to go out alone at night and he insisted on escorting Marianne to her outings. Of course, many of her evenings were spent on dates with Patrick. After their wedding Patrick maintained his protective attitude but with a change in his behaviors; instead of escorting her, he persuaded Marianne to stay at home with him in the evenings. Instead of venturing out in the dark, Patrick wanted Marianne to be with him, so he could pamper her with affection. How could Marianne object to his loving protectiveness? It seemed more important to spend her evenings with the man she had committed herself to than to go out on her own to meet with her friends or to pursue other activities and interests of her own. Susan and Anita were disappointed that Marianne missed their monthly meetings. Patrick had succeeded in isolating her from the friends that had been such an important part of her young adulthood.

Considered as a subjectively favorable form of chivalrous ideology, benevolent sexism is an expression of protection and affection for women who comply with traditional female roles. On the other hand, women who seem to be striving for control through feminist ideology or sexuality are considered within the concept of hostile sexism, an adversarial view of gender relations (Glick & Fiske, 2001).

Although just as constraining to women as hostile sexism, benevolent sexism, with its disarming appearance, aims to pacify women's resistance to societal gender inequality. By casting women in a favorable light, along with promises of advantages to those who align themselves with a male protector, benevolent sexism reduces women's resistance to patriarchy. Some women may even interpret this male "protection" as being cherishing rather than constraining actions. There is no need to speak out against the man's seemingly chivalrous actions, and while they appear to be the chosen and "protected" women, they become isolated from other, less-protected women who may, through their outspokenness, become the targets of hostile sexism.

THE SILENCING FUNCTION OF LANGUAGE

Considering the use of language as a social strategy, one can conceive of different categories for the application of language in the persuasion of people to do things or to say things, to remain silent as well as to command people's attention, or to get them to maintain social relationships with the speaker (Guerin, 2003). Thus, language itself, in the form of discourse, can function as a structure of domination, influencing other people to respond or to remain speechless in fear, intimidation, or admiration.

According to Susan A. Speer (2005), language can also be understood in terms of the *form* of language (how gender is represented *in* the language) and the *function* of language (how language is *used* by men and women). Considering the question of how gender is presented *in* the language leads to the observation that language reflects and perpetuates sexist as well as heterosexist versions of reality. Taking, for example, the asymmetry of traditional address terms for men ("Mr.") and women ("Mrs."/"Miss"), men are defined in their own right, whereas women are classified in terms of their relationship to a man. The more recent use of the address term "Ms." for women can be seen as an attempt to neutralize previously sexist language.

How do language users *produce* speakers as male and female? Research about linguistic differences between males and females can be interpreted in three different ways. The "deficit" framework focuses on evidence for women's powerlessness and subordination when contrasted with men. Examples of male dominance and control in language fall into the "dominance" framework, and views stressing men and women's different but equally valid communication styles would be found in the "difference" framework. A detailed discussion about gendered language goes beyond the scope of this book (see Speer, 2005, for in-depth discussion of this topic); however, some aspects of language of the "dominance" framework are relevant here as far as they function in a silencing capacity during communication. The use of questions and interruptions is often intended to prevent women from talking and to gain control of the discussion in what Dale Spender (1980) called "man made language."

For centuries, language has provided subtle but powerful strategies for "putting women in their place," dominating them, and confusing them. Some of the linguistic attacks are difficult to recognize. Often the offense is expressed by attaching trivializing appellations to women, such as including the word "dear" when addressing a woman.

Another tactic is to strike by way of a compliment. For instance, complimenting a woman on her appearance instead of on her ideas and verbal content at a professional presentation is a form of trivializing. For professional women, the awareness and recognition of this type of control attempt is important because their manner of response will determine the nature of future verbal and behavioral exchanges. If the woman responds to the emphasis on her appearance, the content of her professional presentation is interrupted and perhaps even prematurely ended, thus silencing her professional voice. Women "must learn to delve beneath the surface of the linguistic hypocrisy that is often characteristic of communications between men and women. They must learn to detect offenses and not let them go by unanswered. For each time an insult passes unremarked, it only leads to more of the same. Failure to respond to linguistic attacks constitutes a tacit acceptance of them" (Shainess, 1984, p. 225).

While engaged in discussion, speaking in an inexpressive manner often conveys the notion of control, or what Sarah Myers McGinty (2001), an expert in the field of linguistics, calls the *affect of control*. Several elements characterize the affect of control, such as the speaker's straight posture, maintaining eye contact with the audience, controlling facial expressions, and brevity of speech. Pronouncing decisions or suggestions in an impersonal and inexpressive way lends an aura of autonomy and "correctness" to the speaker's position, because the verbalizations seem to be the result of pure logic and unemotional rationality. It functions to reaffirm the person's dominance through logic and rationality vis-à-vis emotionally expressive verbalizations. This approach works particularly well within male-female verbal interactions (Sattel, 1983).

Refusing to respond verbally is another "silencing" tactic. Nancy and Jane were married to two brothers, Alex and Fred. Both women experienced some unhappiness in their marriages. Their husbands gave them the "silent treatment" whenever things did not go their way or when the wives asked for something the husbands did not want to discuss. Alex simply stopped talking to Jane when she raised topics he did not want to address, whereas Fred at times went so far as to leave the room to avoid responding to Nancy's emotional outbursts—as he called her verbalizations. Discussing their frustration, the two sisters-in-law guessed that their husbands might have learned this approach of avoiding issues they did not like as they were growing up in their family of origin.

As the two women continued to confide in each other, Jane admitted to becoming very anxious upon Alex's verbal withdrawal, whereas Nancy responded with feelings of anger and disgust. Jane's anxiety was based in the fear that Alex would leave her and she would be abandoned. Nancy's anger originated in her belief that Fred did not respect her opinion on issues she brought up for discussion. She wanted him to listen to her side of the argument instead of withdrawing. The two women realized that the message in Alex's behavior was very much like the one in Fred's behavior, but the women's responses arose from different emotional conditions. Nancy's anger prompted her refusal to engage in sexual activities with Fred. Sometimes it took months before she reluctantly agreed to have sex with him. Jane, on the other hand, in her fear of abandonment, tried to fulfill Alex's every wish, hoping that he would decide to talk to her again. Refusing sex was not something she dared to consider. However, her fear of saying or doing something wrong turned her into a very quiet and passive participant in their sexual encounters.

In their discussions, Nancy and Jane recognized the sadness that there were four people who did not get what they wanted, yet they had started out loving each other enough to spend the rest of their lives together. Prior to making the commitment to marry Fred and Alex, neither Nancy nor Jane had negotiated their expectations for the marriage. Now, after having been married for several years, the request for changes in their husbands' behaviors would have to convince the men that there was something to gain for them. However, anger, disgust, and passive-aggressiveness were not likely ingredients to achieve this. Of course, there was always the option of divorce, but neither woman wanted to consider this option at the time.

Nancy and Jane decided to calmly bring up to their husbands what they would be willing to give to get the attention they wanted. They would also explain that their giving would be a result of changed feelings about their husbands. By inquiring what it would take to have their husbands communicate with them in a respectful and loving way, they also indicated that the husbands were in control of getting what they wanted. If Alex and Fred were refusing to listen to them, the women would use another approach, perhaps by writing it down for the husbands to read at a time convenient to them.

The two women progressed well in their pursuits of improving their marriages. A main reason for their progress was that they worked together. They were not isolated within their own marriages but dealt with the common difficulties, reminding and reinforcing each other. For instance, if Jane was about to give up and assume her old compliant behaviors out of fear of being abandoned by Alex, Nancy was there to remind her of their goals and encourage her not to abandon herself. Similarly, Jane had occasions to persuade Nancy not to act on an angry impulse and thus undermine her chances for success. Not persisting in isolation, the sisters-in-law had found a way to re-establish their voices in communication with their husbands.

According to psychologist S. A. Shields (2005), behavior characterizations from the 19th century based on reason and logic are currently rejuvenated in modern considerations of the reason-emotion dichotomy. This characterization claims the existence of different, gender-based emotional styles, where the male-oriented emotion is judged as superior to the female-oriented emotionality. Emphasizing in an inexpressive manner a woman's emotionally expressive verbalizations can result in repression of further responses on the part of the sensitive female.

This raises the question of whether we really need to consider behaviors and expressions along a "dichotomy"—a generally exclusionary path. When does an utterance qualify for an expression of emotion, and when does it become "emotionality"—by looking at the sex of the speaker? Does the experience of emotions automatically exclude logic and reasoning and does reasoning close the door on emotions? A person's tear-filled eyes due to experiencing sadness may briefly blur the person's vision, but does it of necessity also "blur" the person's reasoning abilities? And if we were to assume that emotions interfere with individuals' reasoning capacity, what would we expect of the effects from a person feeling anger, an emotion with conceivably the strongest impact on one's thinking and behavior? Anger, one of the few emotions men in our culture can allow themselves to feel and express?

Trying to explain various phenomena (and people) on the basis of dichotomies or their differences entails the risk of emphasizing gaps and turning them into hurdles that may become insurmountable. It is reminiscent of the proclamation years ago within popular psychology that men and women come from different planets. Distancing approaches like those do not only lend themselves to the creation of stereotypes, they can also turn partners in intimate relationships into strangers who have nothing in common because they concentrate so hard on the differences between them.

A WOMAN'S SPACE

Jody, a young woman engaged in group therapy, admitted that she felt insecure and insignificant. When she was younger she had fleeting dreams of writing or painting—there was some evidence for talent in both areas—but she never followed through on either (Maass, 2002/2006). As it turned out, Jody did not have a space of her own where she could concentrate on her creative attempts and where she could leave her work safely when she needed to interrupt it. With four lively children in the house, the only sacred space was her husband's study.

Jody had approached her husband with the suggestion to have their twin sons share a bedroom instead of occupying separate rooms. After all, their two daughters who were five years apart in age shared a bedroom. Her husband's reaction surprised Jody. In his opinion, it was important for the twin boys to form their independent identity and separate rooms would help in accomplishing that. Besides, Jody had the whole house to herself most of the day, he added. Jody responded with silence; what could she say? Apparently, she was asking for too much already.

What and where is a woman's space? Traditionally we picture her in the kitchen of a house, the couple's bedroom, or even the family room. In the average family home there are bedrooms for the children and there may be a study for the husband—if there is another room available. Rarely does the family dwelling accommodate a separate room for the woman of the house. Ironically, when she was a child at her parents' home she may have had a bedroom all to herself, but now that she is an adult she has lost that luxury. It seems that for women, as a right of passage, they lose their privacy—after all, the young woman's mother probably did not have a room of her own either.

Today there are women who have spacious offices or laboratories at their workplaces. University professors, human resource directors, editors, and many other female professionals are used to working in rooms that have their names on the doors. These same professional women often have to wait until their children have moved out of the house in order to find a space for themselves. Depriving an individual of personal space can be as effective as depriving him or her of a voice. About 80 years ago English writer Virginia Woolf wrote the story *A Room of One's Own,* describing an author's needs for creating her works. Since Virginia declared, "a woman must have money and a room of her own if she is to write fiction," how far have we come? (1929, p. 4).

YESTERDAY'S VOICES AND THE LEGACY FOR TOMORROW

In the histories of art, science, literature, and music, records of women's contributions seem to be rare. What are the reasons for the absence of women's voices in these areas? Is it a general lack of talent, or are women's talents and skills of a lower degree or quality than those of men? Do women lack the desire or the time to create the meaningful masterpieces that will make their places on the pages of history? Robert Southey, one of the most eminent literary men of his time, seemed to have the answer to this question when he advised writer Charlotte Brontë, "literature cannot be the business of a woman's life and it ought not to be. The more she is engaged in proper duties, the less leisure she will have for it, even as an accomplishment and a recreation" (Robert Southey, quoted in Margot Peters, 1977, p. 54).

Then, in contrast to women, men's "proper duties" did not keep them from engaging in artistic pursuits if they were so inclined. In addition, Southey's statement placed women's writings in the category of recreational activities engaged in during leisure times, not to be compared with the "serious" writing efforts of men. One way of deterring women from engaging in artistic pursuits is to reduce or eliminate leisure times for them by increasing their proper duties.

While growing up, the American writer Louisa May Alcott was kept busy with household chores, leaving her very little time for reading, writing, or thinking. Her father, though unable to earn a living for his wife and children, frowned upon female self-consciousness and criticized it as being selfish and narcissistic. The daughters were helping to support the family, and, notwithstanding his censorship of Louisa's need to explore her own feelings, he did not seem to hesitate in letting her provide for him to the end of his life (Showalter, 1988).

As with literature, "the history of art is peopled with men, not women. The male artist is the hero; the female artist is invisible. The woman is present only as the object of the artist's gaze, to be consumed, to be frozen and framed, to be possessed" (Ussher, 1991, p. 280). Is it then that the images of women as objects, rather than as creating artists or scientists, determine women's place on the periphery and keep their voices from being heard?

In the early part of the 20th century, Marjorie Organ Henri's transition from painter to her husband's "muse" serves as example of a female artist silencing her own voice. After she married the prominent Ash Can School painter, Robert Henri, she devoted most of her time to posing for him (Gaze, 1997). To questions about her own work she responded with not having "the extra grain of ego she needed" to persevere (Rubinstein, 1982, p. 168). She indicated that her husband's ego was sufficient for the two of them and that her art was not as important as his. Her statements reflect a lack of happiness—even if it was her choice to make her husband the source of significance in her life. The transformation from an active participant with her own artwork to the stationary position of muse would be expected to have an impact on her personality and her emotional state, as she restrained her abilities for a public acknowledgment of her husband's greater talent.

In a similar vein, the Russian artist Sonia Terk was a wealthy young woman when she became Robert Delaunay's wife, which enabled him to devote himself to his talents and develop the foundations for his future greatness. When Sonia's financial resources in Russia dried up, she channeled her talents into decorative arts for an income. She explained that it was out of a desire to put her husband's career first. According to her, she played second fiddle from the beginning of their relationship, and it was not until the 1950s that she put herself first (Chadwick, 1990).

It would be incorrect to say that the past silencing has been completely successful, just as it would be wrong to say that all men consciously oppress women. There are accounts of women who individually have assumed the right to be self-determining and have been able to express themselves through their endeavors in art, literature, politics, medicine, science, and other fields. We can all recite lists of eminent women whose accomplishments have left their mark throughout history. There also have been men who have encouraged and supported women's strivings in the roles of father, husband, mentor, and friend. Perhaps the existence of these "special cases" has given the general oppression a subtle appearance and therefore made it more difficult to detect and to confront.

History also has recorded women speaking out collectively for the advancement of women. The consciousness-raising communications of early feminist activists, and the writings of more recent authors of the women's movement, have paved the way for women's awakening and have furthered understanding among women and society. They have laid the foundation on which today's women can proceed in their own journey to self-discovery and self-determination. And a rather private journey it will be, as Chesler (2005) has argued that feminism has lost its power to improve the lives of women. Has Cinderella really drowned and outlasted the voices of feminists?

The legacy given to women is a mixed and complicated one. How to proceed now is a question to be answered by the individual woman. The early feminists of the 18th century and beyond, women such as Mary Wollstonecraft, Elizabeth Cady Stanton, and Susan B. Anthony, based their demands for equal rights before the law on the principles of individual justice. Their brand of humanistic feminism gradually changed with the rise of what has been called the "second wave" of feminism, a perhaps more radical sex/gender-focused approach. The liberal version of consciousness-raising efforts of Betty Friedan and Germaine Greer, intended to awaken women's minds to opportunities of individual self-fulfillment, gave way to a focus on the political dimensions of their lives, as demonstrated in the writings of Kate Millet, Alison Jaggar, and others (Sommers, 1994).

It is not the intention of this book to provide a thorough history of the development of feminism, but only to highlight some aspects of it, as they are relevant to the topics discussed in some of the chapters. There are many meaningful and valuable works available on this topic, produced by a variety of writers, covering different angles of the issue. However, clashes of "old" and "new" versions of feminism do not serve the strengthening of women's voices; divisions that lead to confusion result in a weakening of the cause. If, as described in 1926 by the British feminist and novelist Winifred Holtby (1992), the movement's premise of the importance of the human being is changed to emphasizing the importance of women's point of view and taking an adversarial stance toward men, the risk of alienating men and isolating women into various opposing camps is real. Teaching and demonstrating how men (and women) can benefit from supporting each other would seem to be a more successful strategy.

The window of awareness of women's plight was opened slightly for a time, and the voices could be heard. How do we keep those voices alive during new periods of silencing that may just be coming upon us? Our world's concentration will frequently be focused on other things. Headlines debating the state of the economy, financial scandals in business and industry, acts of terrorism, and—not least of all—military actions reported in many parts of the world will continue to affect us all, not just women. There are so many issues that call for attention; the quandary of women is but one piece of it.

In comparison with those bigger issues, how easy will it be to draw the curtain over the window of awareness of women's interests? How much effort will it take to keep the window open to the sound of the voices of today's women, and who will see to it that the window remains open? We could apply here the words of Rick Pitino from his book *Success Is a Choice:* "that window of opportunity may be open only a crack, getting people to believe that it is indeed open is so important. You let them know they have a long way to go. You let them know how difficult it's going to be. But you also let them know that the opportunity is there. It's not an unrealistic hope. There is a window there; and the more you work, the wider that window opens" (1997, p. 35). That window could accommodate the voices of women and men on equal terms.

The voices in this book belong to a variety of women. There are women from the community at large who volunteered their stories, and there are those who are struggling to find answers through therapy. The lives of female artists, writers, and scientists constitute another segment of the female population. Learning about their lives helps us understand how difficult it is for women to make decisions that give meaning to their lives and define their identities in one way or another.

Customarily we think of individuals who possess great talents, and who have earned recognition for these talents, as persons of determination, drive, and direction. Those characteristics, in turn, are expected to impact and facilitate the person's search for meaning and significance. But for every celebrated artist or scientist there are several who did not succeed despite their talents. Not all are truly arriving at their anticipated level of significance. For various reasons, this seems to be especially true for females. The story of Marjorie Organ Henri, related earlier, is just one such example. Then, if these talented women experienced difficulties in the struggle to decide between the parts of the self they wanted to devote to others and the parts they needed to keep for themselves, how can we expect the rest of us, who do not possess a great talent as a guiding light, to resolve this conflict without pain?

What are the factors that determine whether or not an individual will achieve significance or self-actualization? What are the variables that weigh even heavier on women involved in the process of self-actualizing or self-determining? Psychologists, who hold the humanistic view, propose that becoming authentic and self-actualizing requires increased self-awareness and exercising choices. The examination of past influences, and determination regarding their usefulness in today's life situations, makes up this part of the book with the expectation that it will facilitate individuals' search for self-awareness. Understanding the origins and developments of some of these influences will shed light on the nature of one's own beliefs and attitudes. By illuminating the purpose and meaning behind some of those influences, their reflection will be less imposing, and thus more open to questioning and amenable to modification.

For instance, the designation of a certain day for doing all the family's laundry made sense in the days when women had to go down to the river to do the washing, or when apartment buildings in big cities had a community laundry facility that had to be scheduled and reserved for each of the inhabitants. With the occurrence of individual washing machines and dryers for each apartment, such scheduling is no longer required, and a family's laundry can be taken care of in bits and pieces at any time of day or night, depending on the individual's preference. In a world of constant change, established traditions become obsolete and ripe for replacement by different ways that make sense in their application to new situations.

Holding on to old traditions just for the sake of it would seem ridiculous in this simple "wash-day" example. However, its presentation here serves the function of analyzing influences from the past and breaking them down into simple elements to facilitate making the decision regarding their current usefulness. Returning to the suggestions of humanistic psychologists, selecting among the many influences that impact us is an important part in the journey to self-actualization. To be able to choose wisely among the cultural influences that one wants to integrate or internalize on a personal level, the individual needs to apply "dialectical" thinking, a way of perceptually "framing" the meaning of events in opposite terms. Using internal narrative dialog, individuals can facilitate the selection process about which influences to incorporate into their being (Jenkins, 2000).

Perhaps women need special encouragement and assistance for developing the dialogical self within themselves, because women have been programmed to silently listen to the voices of others rather than to their own. After all, they have been taught that their voices and messages are not important enough for others to listen to, so why should they pay attention to their own voices? And even though women's growth and progress are individual responsibilities, it is worth remembering that Cinderella's silence and isolation are factors that promote and maintain her own helplessness. They may prevent her from expressing her goals when she applies the test to see if she wants the shoe to fit.

As Speaker of the House, Nancy Pelosi, in her book *Know Your Power,* quoted her late colleague Tom Lantos: "the struggle is a long one and we must have faith that we will succeed—and insist that our voices be heard" (2008, p. 98).

4

Examining Influences from the Past

"One is not born, but rather becomes a woman" Simone de Beauvoir proclaimed more than half a century ago (1952) in her book *The Second Sex*. Her words find an echo in the views of humanistic psychologists, who suggest that human beings in a conscious state represent a process of becoming (DeCarvalho, 2000). It is a process that generally occurs on two levels. On the environmental or cultural level, it is a nonreflective process of self-engagement in daily activities according to the goals and traditions of a particular culture. In this nonreflective form, becoming proceeds as a product of identification with the culture and internalizing its values.

The second level, or the "authentic" process of becoming, requires individuals' ability to reflect and contemplate the choices offered by the culture. Persons being engaged in self-reflection and contemplation of the process of becoming develop or evolve into what they prefer to become. They pick and choose from the menu of cultural influences what they find useful, and discard or refuse to attend to what is of no value in their individual processes of becoming.

It is important to understand that without selecting among the alternatives, individuals become what their culture or someone in their lives will decide for them. Especially for women, this has been the course of events for generations, initiated by their parents, continued by teachers and religious mentors, and finally confirmed by husbands. But, as pointed out in the previous chapter, women can select between those influences from the past that are useful for current application and those that appear less valuable and therefore can be refused.

GENDER-BASED ASSUMPTIONS

Cultural traditions determine the roles of men and women, and as such, gender is cultural in origin. According to those traditions, many societies practice differentiation between women and men based on a pattern of inequality and varying degrees of male domination (Kimmel, 2000). As society's cultural configuration is largely determined by its economic, political, and social variables, the determining factor regarding the status of women is embedded in the division of labor around childcare. In societies where men become involved in childcare to a greater degree, women are less tied down to childcare labor, and their status tends to be higher.

In other words, the more involved in childcare a woman is, the fewer are her opportunities to engage in activities for her own benefit. Prior to whispering "I do," many brides forget to seriously consider this fact. Is she accepting the ring of a man who believes in equal involvement with childcare, or will she be shouldering the sole responsibility for their future children? Again, after all, it comes down to the question: "does she really want the shoe to fit?"

If we consider the possibility that gender has a cultural character, as suggested by some writers over the years (Lieberman, 1986; Kimmel, 2000), it would facilitate our understanding of acculturation's processes and goals if we examined the channels of acculturation. This examination is a requirement for reaching the second level, the "authentic" part in the process of becoming, as outlined by humanistic psychologists. Generations of women—in forming their self-concepts—have followed the guidelines of behavioral expectations as taught to them and rewarded by the agents of their society. Now is the time for examining the channels of acculturation used by society.

THE MYTH OF WOMEN BEING "CRAZIER" THAN MEN

According to professionals in the psychology and counseling field, in the popular culture, women have historically been regarded as suffering more from mental illnesses than men (Eriksen & Kress, 2008). And, according to Karen Eriksen's experience, this myth has not been laid to rest despite contradictory research results. There has been concern about the possibility of clinicians to bias diagnoses based on their client's gender. Because of their independence, assertiveness, and goal-directed activities, men are considered to be healthy adults, while women—due to their lower degree of independence and aggression, their submissiveness, and greater excitability in minor crises—are viewed as psychologically unhealthy. Submissiveness, absence of aggression, and dependence, among other traits, are the characteristics women have been encouraged for generations to incorporate into their personality structure, but once achieved, it makes them eligible for a mental illness diagnosis.

Women's intrinsically valuable traits, such as intuitiveness or compassion, have probably developed because of male-imposed necessity rather than because of biological disposition or due to free choice (Chesler, 1997). These female emotional characteristics have come at a price. "It is illogical and dangerous to romanticize traits that one purchases with one's freedom and dignity—even if they are 'nice' traits; even if they make one's slavery more bearable; even if they charm and soothe the oppressor's rage and sorrow, staying his hand, or leave-taking for one more day" (p. 288).

To be considered psychologically healthy adults, women's behaviors should be similar to that of men. But as demonstrated in Bendahl's study, discussed in Chapter 2, compared with women exhibiting traditional behaviors, women with more "masculine" traits experienced sexual harassment in the workplace.

Women have been socialized to put the needs of others ahead of their own, and this training, in incorporating the "good wife syndrome," may in turn qualify them for a personality disorder (Caplan, 1992). Diagnoses of personality disorders have been found to reflect sex bias. Antisocial, paranoid, compulsive, and passive-aggressive personality disorders are predominantly found in men. Borderline, dependent, and histrionic personality disorders, on the other hand, are more prevalent in women. The criteria for the disorders in which women predominate could be seen as exaggerations of socially prescribed feminine characteristics inherent in many cultural beliefs and practices (Horsfall, 2001).

DISCOUNTED BY OTHERS AND GIVING UP ON SELF

The world of art may hold the illusion of gender equality in the recognition of talented men and women, but, as briefly discussed in Chapter 3, this sphere of life is just as much inhabited by gender-based assumptions as any other life-sphere. An ironic, gender-based differentiation between women can be found in the French painter Pierre-Auguste Renoir's opinion on the matter. Renoir, a leading painter of the impressionistic style and celebrator of beauty and feminine sensuality, regarded female professionals, such as writers, lawyers, and politicians, as bores and monsters, whereas female artists were simply ridiculous—despite his friendship to Berthe Morisot, an acknowledged impressionist painter of the time. His view of female singers and dancers was more sympathetic because they were working-class women who employed their talents for the entertainment of men (Higonnet, 1992). In other words, if women's skills and talents were not used for the entertainment or aggrandizement of men, they were considered to be worthless, or boring, or even monstrous.

The painter Kay Sage considered herself a loner and did not identify with other women. One might say that she met at least one of the prerequisites of fairy tales' heroines. Although showing early signs of artistic talents, her potential remained untapped until she moved to Paris in 1937, where she met Ives Tanguy, a surrealist painter (Suther, 1993). Both had come to the end of unhappy marriages. Through an inheritance from her father, Sage was financially in a position to help Tanguy with the divorce from and settlement for his first wife, as well as financing their move to America. They were married in Reno in 1940.

Although Sage had developed her painting style independently and considered herself one of the surrealist painters, she was not accepted or endorsed by them. Instead, the works of Sage and Tanguy were treated in the traditional gender arrangement of disciple and master, despite the difference of their painting styles. Consequently, Sage's paintings were regarded as lesser versions of Tanguy's.

The gender-based assumptions operated just as strongly in the sphere of their private lives. Sage accommodated to Tanguy's perceived superiority with self-denial to the point of complete identification with Tanguy and the abandonment of her own work. She quietly endured his violent behaviors that resulted from excessive alcohol intake. After his sudden death of a cerebral hemorrhage in January 1955, she engaged herself in two memorial projects involving Tanguy's work. Even after his death, she continued with her self-abandonment in the area of her artistic being, and finally in her physical being, when she shot herself in January 1963 after an earlier, unsuccessful suicide attempt in April of 1959. Only then, ironically or perhaps fittingly, did she receive acceptance and respect from those who had known both Sage and Tanguy; but the acceptance was for the surrealist widow, not the surrealist artist. The lesson of Sage's story can be understood as "abandonment of the self is an open invitation for abandonment by others."

According to the prevailing norms of the time, Tanguy—as a man—expected more validation, and he received it. Apparently, Sage expected less and her expectations were also met. "Most women have not interpreted the culture's messages as extremely or irreversibly as Sage did, and most men have recognized the potential damage to themselves in the formulas for masculinity that circumscribed Tanguy. Yet the basic elements of Sage and Tanguy's story are neither idiosyncratic nor obsolete. They are still dangerously familiar" (Suther, 1993, p. 153).

If Sage had identified with other women instead of isolating herself from them, would she have received support and advice from them to the effect of applying her financial resources to her own work and person, rather than supporting a man who mistreated her and apparently took advantage of her? Would she have been recognized as an artist in her own right? We don't have the answer to those questions, but her path could hardly have been more troubled than it was. Perhaps the support and encouragement through sisterhood with other women would have reduced the likelihood of such a tragic ending.

Abstract expressionism, another art style, was developed by American artists after World War II; it contains its own examples of the influencing power of gender assumptions on the lives and works of female artists. The celebrated masters of abstract expressionism were men, such as Willem de Kooning, Jackson Pollock, Mark Rothko, and David Smith. The works of female practitioners of the style, such as Lee Krasner, Elaine de Kooning, and Dorothy Dehner, though just as talented and important in their expression, were treated as less serious than the works produced by their more celebrated husbands (Sterling, 1995).

What prompted Lee Krasner to pour her energy into furthering Pollock's efforts at the expense of her own work, although her teacher Hans Hofmann had exclaimed, "This is so good, you would not know it was painted by a woman" (Sterling, 1995, p. 193)? Presumably, that was meant to be a compliment, but it was also a comment on the gender attitudes prevailing at the time. Somehow her own work seemed insignificant to her, as Pollock became the important one. In their 1949 exhibition titled "Artists: Man and Wife" Krasner's role was defined by the title as dependent and subsidiary. Discouraged, Krasner destroyed most of her works from that period, and it was not until after Pollock's death that her pre-Pollock productivity reemerged (Wagner, 1993).

Of course, there are other examples of female artists who remained devoted in their efforts toward their own work despite their relationships with creative men. Lillian Hellman, one of America's most popular playwrights, continued with her work and lifestyle during her 30-year relationship with Dashiell Hammett—even when her lover suffered from severe writing block (Benstock, 1993). Similarly, Georgia O'Keeffe, America's most popular woman artist and best-known American modernist of the first two decades of the 20th century, continued to paint throughout her life. For about 20 years she gave time and energy to the work of her husband, Alfred Stieglitz, posing for more than 500 photographs. But after initially supporting her work, Stieglitz became increasingly resistant to her independence (Konau, 1999). The struggle O'Keeffe experienced with the tension of her public and private roles is reflected in her statement "I am divided between my man and a life with him . . . I have to get along with my divided self the best way I can" (Slatkin, 1993, p. 227).

Both Lillian Hellman and Georgia O'Keeffe managed to keep the integrity of their individual person parts and their artist parts intact in their struggle to maintain their independence. They refused to capitulate and abandon their selves for the aggrandizement of others.

The ideas of what they should and should not accomplish have been communicated to women by way of models and examples, starting in early childhood with the transmission of fairy tales. In the fairy tales, behaviors valued by the culture generally find great rewards, and those behaviors deemed unsuitable for girls in a given society are responded to with harsh punishment. Girls' self-abandonment for the sake of others is hardly considered unsuitable behavior for girls in most fairy tales. When, through the vehicle of fairy tales, the dreams and hopes of little girls are pointed in the culturally desired direction, the girls are ready to enter the larger community, where the indoctrination process continues in schools and other social institutions.

ACKNOWLEDGMENT OR CRITICISM?

"Roughly four decades after the development of the modern women's rights movement in this country, women have secured top positions with Fortune 500 companies. But when it comes to jobs with the highest-profile arts groups in

Indianapolis, men are still leading the pack." With those words Whitney Smith described in the Indianapolis Star/INDY Sunday of February 10, 2008, the current arts scene of that town. Although an increase in the number of women occupying management positions has been observed since the 1960s and 1970s, the writer continues, in the first decade of the 21st century, even the most experienced women artistic or managing directors are relegated to working for small- or mid-sized organizations. The top-level arts groups, such as the Indianapolis Symphony Orchestra or the Indianapolis Museum of Art, are still headed by male leaders.

The writer of this article does not distinguish whether the described situation is a consequence of gender-based assumptions at work, or whether these accomplished women have abandoned the pursuit of higher accomplishments for other personal reasons from which they may derive greater satisfaction or happiness. What may have been meant as a wake-up call about gender bias still operating in the city of Indianapolis can also be interpreted as criticism for the women's achievements. Acknowledgment or criticism remains the question of this newspaper article.

Whether or not a woman has the capability of following the humanistic psychologists' suggestion for entering the process of becoming in an "authentic" manner depends largely on how successful her society's acculturation has been. Courageous is the girl who retains the capacity to question rather than to blindly absorb and follow her culture's gender-based assumptions. It's a beginning, but it is not enough yet. Gender-based assumptions belong in the category of past influences that are still operating today in some areas. Women experience the impact on their lives, but recognizing these influences and acknowledging them for what they are does not mean that every young woman has to adopt them for her own life.

Similarly, sacrificing one's own skills and talents, or putting them into the service of others instead of using them on the behalf of oneself, is a decision for the individual woman to make—hopefully after exploring and comprehending the consequences. Cinderella has a choice here about what to use and what to reject.

MEANING IN WOMEN'S LIVES

A search for meaning in life is closely connected to and impacted by gender-based assumptions because of cultural prescriptions that the search be different for men and women. The concept of femininity stresses the notion of being fragile and of not acting as a powerful agent on one's behalf. As described in the section on benevolent sexism in Chapter 3, feminine characteristics will be rewarded by certain parts of society in order to persuade women to both relinquish attempts toward self-determination and to refrain from searching for women's meaning in life outside the parameters supplied by the society's culture.

In fact, in cultural communications, the word "meaning" is more often used in terms of "purpose" when focusing on women. Words such as "meaning," "purpose," and "significance" carry slightly different connotations, even though in everyday usage relating to existential questions, they are often applied interchangeably.

According to existential psychiatrist Irvin D. Yalom (1980), "meaning" is a general term referring to sense or coherence, whereas "purpose" refers to intention or function, such as what is its role or function? "Significance" is another, closely related term that in some instances has the same implication as "meaning" but in other instances is also used to refer to "importance" or "consequence." The term significance is entangled with a sense of personal power. Seldom do we hear a woman described in terms of significance. Her achievements are of a more mundane nature; motherhood and being a helpmate to her husband are the areas where she is generally expected to find the meaning of her life. This use of "meaning" is very close to Yalom's definition of "purpose"—the function being in the roles of wife and mother, whereas the intention might be found in those around her who intend for her to function in a certain capacity.

Women are also valued as agents for keeping their society's economy afloat. For instance, in commerce, women play roles on both sides of the table: selling goods either directly, by serving their customers in stores, or in a more removed capacity, as advertising adornment, while at the same time functioning in the role of consumer. Additionally, women's purchasing activities have supplied comedians with materials for their routines for a long time. Portraying women's shopping activities within a framework of exaggeration is bound to bring a round of laughter and applause from certain segments of the audience. Again, as appreciated as these activities may be by some parts of society, they do not approach the level of "significance" that might be applied to the lives of some representatives of the male population.

Historically though, women have been encouraged to search for the meaning in their lives within the biosocial context of motherhood. Another life purpose could be found in the realm of helpers and companions to men. But there have been changes over generations, and teenage girls have learned that being on the mommy track can cost them dearly (Langer, 1996). They have come to realize that postponing or interrupting a promising career to have children can amount to a career regression. When they return from motherhood duties, they are faced with having to start paying their dues all over gain. Their seniority on the job has dwindled as peers have passed them by on the career ladder. Most likely, their skills are outdated and their support networks disrupted.

On the other hand, women who direct their early energies toward a meaningful career and planning on delaying romantic pursuits until a future point may end up equally disappointed. As outlined by Barbara Dafoe Whitehead (2003) in her book *Why There Are No Good Men Left,* those single women have departed from the earlier courtship system without perhaps fully realizing it. This courtship system was functioning well for college women who married in their early 20s. But for many others, graduation day opened the career doors, while at the same time closing the gates of the playing field for mate selection. During the purposeful preparation for a meaningful career, marriage was a nebulously defined given in the minds of the young women. They knew that they wanted to get married some day and have a family, but, while focusing on aspects of their careers, somewhat reminiscent of the old fairy tales, they might have thought the right man would come along naturally at the right time. As things did not work out so naturally, they might have to explore other resources and dating systems.

Then there are those who perceived their situation as offering them no choice. "Most girls with only brothers as siblings are being treated in special ways; my family treated me like an unwanted stepchild," Lynn, the divorced mother of two young children related her experiences while growing-up. "My mother focused all her attention on my two brothers. I was just good enough to perform the household chores she assigned me to do. My good grades from school were not rewarded—they were unimportant. My brothers were the ones my parents expected great achievements from. My brothers needed to excel in careers or professions, because they would have to support families later on and they were the ones to bring recognition to my family."

"As soon as I was old enough to help out at the local grocery store after school or during summer vacations, my mother saw to it that I was spending the time she did not need me at home for chores working at the store," Lynn continued her sad story. "Actually, I was proud of the trust the storeowners put in me. I still remember how excited I was running home with my first earned money in my hand. The excitement did not last long though; my mother took all the money and put it away. When I asked her about it she said it was going to be part of a college fund. 'For me?' I asked. 'No, you don't need to worry about college; it will be used for your brothers' tuition' my mother responded. My cry of 'but that's not fair!' my mother countered with 'your parents decide what's fair in this family. Now go and tend to your chores.'

Both my brothers entered college. Martin, my oldest brother, left college after almost two years. Libby, his girlfriend, got pregnant, and he had to get a job to support his new family. My younger brother Billy dropped out of college at the end of his second semester. He was on academic probation for his poor grades and had lost all interest in studying. The college fund was depleted by then," Lynn continued, "and all that was available to me was to go to secretarial school—if I had money for the tuition—or to get married."

This partial account of Lynn's life accompanied her application for a college scholarship years later. With the help of the local librarian she had studied hard to prepare herself for the Scholastic Aptitude Test (SAT), which she took as an adult along with the high school girls and boys in their small town. Lynn achieved high scores that would be an asset in her attempts to finally embark upon her dreams of going to college.

THE MYTH OF WOMEN'S NEED FOR ATTACHMENT

More than 20 years ago, psychologist Paula Caplan cautioned that the myth of women's masochism "serves two purposes: It leads both women and men to believe that women are deeply, inevitably pathological—for is it not sick to enjoy misery?—and it is a powerful block against social action that could help women.

Because of the myth, women's problems can be attributed to our deep-seated psychological needs, not to the social institutions that really are the primary causes of the trouble" (1985, p. 10).

Substituting the words "need for attachment" for "masochism" makes the connection with yet another myth. It explains in part the power of the belief in this female "need." Women who strongly identify with the culture in which they live come to believe that connectedness within relationships is a basic ingredient of their feminine identity. If the guiding principle for women has been defined as establishing and maintaining close relationships, the fear of losing that connectedness through separation may be so overwhelming that it overshadows the danger of becoming submerged in another's life. And in intimate competition with the man, fear makes some women step back from the competition.

It would be incorrect to imply that *all* women truly believe in this need for attachment; many women in their paths have experienced the need for self-sufficiency and have come to enjoy this state once they got accustomed to it. On the other hand, there are still many young women who have not achieved the strength required to create their own self-actualizing goals and pursue them with determination. While growing up, many girls have not been trained to seek solitude, which is so crucial to getting to know oneself and one's wishes and desires. Solitude without loneliness provides the foundation for the development of a capable, strong, self-directed individual—man or woman.

The belief in the need for (and attachment to) another, a significant person, inhibits women's capacity to work productively—to be creative, energetic, and committed. The myth that women's salvation is to be found in attachment to others carries with it the hidden—and perhaps seductive—corollary that women will not have to be responsible for their own existence forever; eventually, someone will arrive who is willing to take over and provide support financially, physically, and emotionally.

Leonora Carrington, the beautiful and rebellious daughter of a wealthy English industrialist, was 20 years old when she met the 46-year old, handsome, and brilliant Max Ernst. He was a famous artist and a renowned ladies' man in his second marriage. Leonora, whose work showed great imagination in the best surrealist style, became Ernst's pupil and fell deeply and hopelessly in love with him. They lived together for a while but were separated by the forces of history that placed Max Ernst in a detention camp. Leonora was devastated and collapsed into mental illness (Suleiman, 1993).

Years later they met again and Max Ernst pleaded with Leonora to return to him. Leonora refused; her life with him had come to a close because she felt she could not be his slave, which would be the only possible life with him. Leonora became a well-established painter and writer in Mexico City, married to the Hungarian photographer Csiki Weisz and giving birth to two sons. She summarized her understanding of dependency in a statement she made in 1990: "There is always a dependency involved in a love relationship. I think if you are dependent, it can be extremely painful . . . I think that a lot of women (people, but I say women because it is nearly always women on the dependent side of the bargain) certainly were cramped, dwarfed sometimes, by that dependency. I mean not only the physical dependency of being supported, but emotional dependency and opinion dependency" (Suleiman, 1993, p. 115). In the end, Leonora chose independence and meaning for herself; she refused to become dwarfed by dependency and feel her foot pinched by the tiny slipper.

FEAR OF ABANDONMENT

An intimate sister to the need for attachment with resulting dependency is the fear of abandonment. They are linked like Siamese twins—where one goes, the other must follow. The woman who seriously believes that it is essential for her happiness to be part of a couple or a family will do everything in her power to please those around her and keep them from leaving her. For some women, the fear of abandonment is so crippling that they become victims of those who have agreed to assume control over them. The need for attachment opens the doors to submergence in another's existence, or it may invite victimization and martyrdom.

Examples of a woman's life submerged in the man's existence can be taken from the lives of artists such as Marjorie Organ Henri, Lee Krasner, and Kay Sage, already discussed in earlier parts of this book. A striking example of submerging the self in another is reflected in the life of Oona O'Neill Chaplin, the daughter of writer and playwright Eugene O'Neill and widow of actor Charlie Chaplin. According to Jane Scovell's (1998) biography, appropriately titled *Oona: Living in the Shadows,* Oona was two years old when her father abandoned the family for another woman—an actress, Carolotta Monterey—who made it her single-minded goal to nurture O'Neill's genius, a proposition that O'Neill, in his need for admiration and being totally cared for, could not resist.

Despite the disappointment in her father, Oona grew into an attractive, intelligent young girl, who apparently aspired to become a movie actress. In Hollywood at 17 years of age, she met her Prince Charming. At the wedding Oona was 18 and Charlie Chaplin was 53 years old; he was her prince and a father substitute.

Oona's role in life was first and foremost to be a wife, then a mother. There was no career to interfere with those roles. She seemed to feel that she did not possess any talents except as wife and mother, although others thought she could be a good writer. It is doubtful however, that Charlie would have encouraged her if she had developed a natural talent. Nothing was to take her attention away from him. After Charlie Chaplin's death, Oona seemed unable to go on without him. Even before his death she had sought solace in alcohol, and this continued to provide a handy escape. Although allegedly she became romantically involved with several men, nothing lasted. Her world became distorted by alcohol, leading to outbursts of anger—anger against men and anger against herself: What had she done with her life?

Oona's biographer drew an interesting comparison with another woman who had lived a century earlier than Oona but had been in a similar situation. Cosima Wagner, the daughter of genius Franz Liszt, became the wife of another genius, Richard Wagner. When Richard Wagner died, Cosima went through a period of intense grieving. But unlike Oona, when Cosima emerged from mourning she took over the Bayreuth music festival and brought it to greater success than Wagner, the composer, had been able to do. In answer to a question about why she had not managed the festival during her husband's lifetime, Cosima's response was "Because then, I served."

Perhaps the fear of abandonment accounted for the difference in the two women's responses to the death of their husbands. Where Oona's father had abandoned his children after the divorce from their mother, Franz Liszt never severed the connection with his daughter Cosima, even after he had walked out on his family. Where Cosima's self-esteem had not been destroyed through her father's leaving, Oona's had. "Charlie's death, his *involuntary* leave-taking, reactivated somber memories of her father's *deliberate* abandonment, and Oona was overpowered by grief. Unlike Cosima Wagner, she could not move past mourning" (Scovell, 1998, p. 283) and she seemed to have nothing to move toward.

The threat of abandonment works as a particularly powerful agent because of its socializing function through the telling of fairy tales, such as "Hänsel and Gretel" by the Brothers Grimm. "From early antiquity to the present, abandonment has been accepted as a 'sensible' if not legal mode of dealing with children when they become problems" (Zipes, 1997, p. 60). Furthermore, the happy ending in the fairy tale signifies that the father, who—with urging from the stepmother—abandoned the children in the dark woods, was not to blame. The situation forced, and sanctioned, his actions. If anything, the children's existence in troublesome times was the problem. This line of reasoning invites the conclusion that the abandoned are to blame for their abandonment. And this makes the fear all the more powerful, because the victim becomes the culprit. Thus, for the abandoned, the first inquiry becomes "what have I done to cause this?"

One is reminded of the case of Cindy in Chapter 2. The first abandonment in her life occurred with the death of her mother, to be followed by her father's shift in attention from Cindy to his new wife and her children. The final blow was struck with the discovery of her husband Derek's sexual attraction to another man. Was she to blame for the three occasions of abandonment in her life?

THE INTIMATE COMPETITION

Oona's biography includes hints of a literary talent, which would not be surprising, considering the fact that she was the daughter of a famous playwright. However, neither Eugene O'Neill nor Charlie Chaplin would have tolerated any artistic ambitions in their wives or even daughters. And when the possibility of abandonment looms large, those who fear it cannot afford to enter the intimate competition.

Mary Shepherd Greene was the second American woman artist (Mary Cassatt was the first) to win medals in the famous Paris Salon d'Automne in 1900 and 1902. Mary married Ernest Leonard Blumenschein, although her parents were not in favor of her marrying a "mere illustrator" (Henning, 1978). For a few years Mary and Ernest shared a studio in Paris and supported themselves through illustration commissions for American magazines. In 1909 they returned to New York and later made their home in Taos. Mary somewhat reluctantly left the comforts of New York to follow Ernest. Ernest was a highly competitive man and a perfectionist. To avoid competing with him in painting, Mary put down the brushes and paints and instead worked at jewelry-making. In Taos she filled her days with being a wife and mother and providing a beautiful home for her family and friends—all in a house that did not have running water until shortly after 1931.

Mary explained that when she was painting, she had to have completely uninterrupted time to concentrate on her work, but with jewelry, she could pick it up or leave it, according to her schedule. Her explanation indicates that she suppressed her talents as a painter in order to stay away from competitive conflicts with her husband and to provide for her family while conducting a smoothly running household. In other words, she did not allow herself the freedom to take the time required for continuing with the work she had been successful in as a single young woman, the time Ernest undoubtedly allocated to his own work. Visiting with Mary's portrait of Louisa Fletcher in the Indianapolis Museum of Art—done in 1912—one cannot help but consider her decision a sacrifice.

The discussion of the histories of famous people here is not with the intention of characterizing men such as Eugene O'Neill, Charlie Chaplin, or Leonard Blumenschein as oppressors of their wives' talents or personality, but because details of the women's lives are available to the public in various reports and writings to form an opinion about their capabilities. The purpose is not to chastise the men but to understand the circumstances and reasons for the women's decisions about their own lives, how they apparently accepted some influences from the past that other women decided to refuse.

THE MANDATORY CHOICE BETWEEN TWO OPTIONS (CAREER OR MARRIAGE)

As has been found, many women who delay marriage in order to establish themselves in a career first find it difficult to meet acceptable prospective husbands in time to start a family before the biological clock shuts down. However, what appears to be a forced choice between two options is not necessarily a true picture of reality. Starting at the beginning would suggest starting with a correct definition of the options. When choosing a career, does that mean it will be impossible to get married and become a mother? It might be more complicated, but most people would agree that it is not impossible.

Selecting the marriage-motherhood track instead of embarking on a professional path, will that guarantee a blissful marriage and happy family life?

Of course not, most people would say, and reality proves them right (Maass, 2002/2006). For those women who have discarded the career path, what will they have to look forward to if their husbands leave them, or if they themselves wanted to end the marriage, or even if the marriage remains intact but they are not free to determine their activities and interests? Just as success in a rewarding career does not render women incapable of forming and maintaining intimate relationships, so financial dependence and weaker self-images do not promote true emotional closeness and bonding to another person. Submissiveness and serfdom rarely facilitate intimacy-building; more often they result in fear and anxiety on the part of the dependent and submissive person, as discussed above.

Exploring the question of choice between career and marriage on a deeper level, it appears to be just another myth, one that—for today's young women—may not be worth accepting and following. Actually, the choice would be more appropriately considered as options in lifestyles, choosing between an autonomous and a deferential lifestyle. Within this framework of options, the woman would select for a husband a man subscribing to egalitarian values or one holding traditional values, who in his authoritarian philosophy is invested with the marital power. In other words, Cinderella selects the prince who presents the shoe that fits her desired lifestyle. If she has not determined yet what would be the appropriate lifestyle for her, she better not rush into commitments to any prince.

In 1963 Maria Goeppert-Mayer received the Nobel Prize (Dash, 1988). She grew up in Germany, studying mathematics and physics. In those days few role models were available for young women entering the field of science. Maria met and married the American chemist Joseph Mayer, who believed that there were places for women in science. They moved to the United States. After the birth of their two children, Joseph Mayer strongly supported Maria's return to her work in research—even though she had to do it as an unpaid faculty wife. He took great pleasure in observing her career flourish and was proud of her achievements.

Maria's parents had provided early encouragement. Her father, a pediatrician, had seen many women immersing themselves in raising their children without indulging in any interests of their own. He did not want that to happen to his daughter, and he praised Maria for her curiosity. Maria's mother did not discourage her. The values, beliefs, and attitudes a person is exposed to during childhood play significant roles in the life of the adult. In the case of Maria Goeppert-Mayer—as in many other cases—there were obviously parental influences at work. Did those parental influences prepare her for the task of choosing the right husband for herself? Would Maria have become a scientist without the parental encouragement? Would she have remained actively involved in her work with a different, less egalitarian husband, one who could not tolerate any competition from his wife? There are no answers to those questions, but it would seem that when Maria received the Nobel Prize, it was the confirmation of her earlier choice: the shoe held by Joseph Mayer was the one she wanted to fit.

Even earlier, in the second half of the 19th century at the Sorbonne in Paris, Marie, supported by her sister Bronya, nearly starved to death keeping up with her studies. Following her first romantic disappointment, Marie was determined never to marry. But she met physicist Pierre Curie and recognized his potential to fulfill her great intellectual and emotional desires. Although Pierre was a renowned scientist in the field of crystallography, he wholeheartedly supported Marie in her doctoral research investigating the newly discovered phenomenon of emissions from certain minerals (later named radiation). The couple received the highest awards of the scientific community, including the Nobel Prize. From available records it is clear that Marie Curie had found a way to be an excellent, devoted mother to their two children while continuing her established level of intensity in her work (Kerr, 1994).

When Pierre suddenly died in a traffic accident in 1906, Marie lost not only her husband, but also her companion in the intellectual quests she thrived on. However, she continued with her work as a professor at the Sorbonne and also devoted herself to mentoring her daughter, Irene Curie, and her son-in-law, Frederic Joliot, passing on to them all her knowledge about radioactivity and x-rays. The three of them created the first artificial radioactive material in 1934, the year Marie died. As the story of Marie Curie demonstrates, women may lose their prince through death or desertion. If a good part of life's meaning remained in their own person and identity then, although saddened by their loss, they are able to continue on their path. Losing a significant life-partner is a tremendous misfortune, losing oneself or one's significance is a far greater tragedy.

From those two accounts (Maria Goeppert-Mayer and Marie Curie), it can be understood that somehow, determined women were capable of connectedness in relationships without giving up their own identities and goals as professionals. It appears that they resolved the problem of confluence of these life areas by the time they began their life's work. Shouldn't this be sufficient evidence that the insistence on a decision between career and motherhood is little more than a myth that women can dispose of if they want to do so?

More recently, Nora, a professional woman, told how she had met her husband in her first semester of graduate study—in a statistics class. Nora was there on a modest assistantship that covered most of her tuition but did not leave money to live on. Ray was not much better off. After about a year, Ray told Nora that he had just enough money for two Ph.D.s if they lived very frugally. Nora said she had never heard a more convincing declaration of love. Ray had realized that her doctoral degree was just as important to their relationship as his own. Nora recognized that Ray offered the acceptable shoe—it fit. They both received their doctoral degrees on the same day and maintained their personal and professional association from then on. After more than 35 years, the shoe still fits.

Exploration of career-path data from a national sample of 508 art historians who received their Ph.D.s in the time period from 1985 to 1991—also discussed in Chapter 1—revealed that 71 percent of the male professionals achieved tenure, as compared with only 44 percent of the female professionals. However, an even more significant finding was that, although single men and women have about equal tenure odds, among married professionals the male professors married to nonworking or part-time employed wives had a significantly greater chance at achieving tenure than married female professionals. Even those female professionals who were married to men holding part-time employment had about the same chances for tenure as single female professionals. These results demonstrate that men gain more than women do by being married to a partner with low career engagement, even in a discipline in which women earn most of the Ph.D.s (Rudd, et al., 2008).

Choices in career and mate selection may not include all the same variables, but the above study shows that they are not as independent of one another as one might think from a superficial point of view. In reality, the variables are interconnected, as shown in the study and in the cases of Nora above, Maria Goeppert-Mayer, and Marie Curie. To select the individually right choices, it is necessary to define each option correctly and in detail. Working from correct definitions of a given situation facilitates the exploration for available solutions. The women chose to "integrate myriad tasks in their lives stemming from their roles as leaders in their field, as wives, as mothers, and as companions. Most of the mothers made use of nurses, governesses, and household help, as one would expect. Yet the evidence suggests that the eminent women who were also mothers were as committed to parenting as they were to their work" (Kerr, 1994, p. 89).

The importance of defining options correctly is reflected in Marlene's story. Just recently Marlene, a 32-year-old, attractive, single woman, decided to enter psychotherapy for her depression. What seemed to be at the root of her depression? She responded with a stream of tears while mumbling, "I make very bad decisions." One of her most recent "bad" decisions was becoming romantically involved with a married man. Marlene is aware of a long history of bad decisions, each one carefully pointed out by her parents with questions such as, "Why did you do that? It's wrong, it's bad, it's ridiculous."

As she was growing up, Marlene did not care much for school and had no aspirations of going to college. But she always liked to be around children and thought marriage and starting a family would be a reasonable outlet for that. Her friends knew that they would get married and have children some day; it was just a matter of time to wait for the appropriate partner to appear. Until that time would come, Marlene worked as secretary with a chance to advance to administrative assistant some day. She dated some young men, but the expected prince did not appear on the scene. Instead a married man at her workplace pursued her with wonderful-sounding promises.

Feeling lonely, she gave in to his advances. With the aid of reliable birth-control methods, Marlene enjoyed the initial stages of their sexual relationship. Being pursued by this man made her feel special, not only because of his courting behavior; the fact that it was a secret they shared increased the romantic flavor of their alliance—at least in the beginning. Marlene created little reasons for visiting his office, just to see a quick smile on his face or to exchange a few words with him. As time progressed, Marlene experienced a more profound loneliness than she had in the past; nearly every holiday was spent in solitude, unless a friend or relative invited her. The life of the "other woman" lost a lot of its luster as she found herself more and more without her lover's company. Her requests for more time with him made her appear less desirable in his eyes; in fact, he became bored with her nagging and tried to end the relationship.

Marlene was not that easy to push aside, however. She visited him in his office and made what could be described as a "scene"—loud enough to be heard in the adjacent office. As result she was called into the office of the company's human resources person, who had already been in a meeting with Marlene's lover. Marlene, being a lower-ranking employee than her lover and a single woman who did not have responsibilities for feeding a family, was dismissed under some vaguely described employee rule. There was a hint, not a threat, expressed by her now ex-lover, that if she were to sue the company, future employment somewhere else might be difficult to obtain. Marlene did not have the money to consider pursuing legal action, and she was too ashamed about the affair to have it become public knowledge beyond the company she had worked for. Even without any intention of legal involvement, finding new employment was more difficult than Marlene had imagined. Assistant administrator positions generally required a college degree, and unfilled secretarial positions were not that plentiful.

Marlene found it necessary to move to a larger city to obtain employment, a situation that brought financial hardship; her new job paid slightly less than her previous position, and housing in the city was generally more expensive than in her hometown. In addition, she did not yet know any people in her new environment, and her loneliness increased, as it had with her previous "bad" decisions. Marlene paid dearly for this most recent bad decision, and it had been one more occasion for her parents to remind her of her lack of competence in making decisions wisely, a task they did not teach her to improve. They did not realize that criticism alone was not sufficient for improvement to occur. Furthermore, while Marlene admitted that her involvement with a married man was a mistake, she saw no need in changing her approach toward her future—to wait for the man to get married to.

Fifteen years earlier in her life, Marlene thought she had a choice between two options: independence and having a family. Because she opted for having a family, she did not go to college and work on developing a career for herself. But her basic premise was flawed; one of the options she perceived as part of the choice situation was not in her control. The prince she counted on was not a given—he was an unknown entity that might never materialize. What she believed to be a choice might have led her walking on a dead-end street.

TAKING A CLOSER LOOK AT MYTHS

As we examine these influences from the past, we may come to wonder about their durability. What makes them so powerful over such a long time? Generations of people, and particularly women, hold on to these old beliefs and myths in the face of the great changes our world has experienced. The answer is in the very cleverly designed formula: the myths are interconnected and *seem* to follow one another in a logical sequence. They involve the basic elements of beliefs, feelings, and behavior. And what is even more important, they reinforce one another's existence.

For instance, if we start with the meaning in women's lives, it is implied to be in relation to another: a man, a child, or some other person to care for. Without the other there is no meaning to the woman's life. As stated earlier, for women, meaning is closer to the idea of purpose than to that of significance. With that purposeful meaning established, the need for attachment becomes a basic requirement; there has to be the "someone" to care for. It is also noteworthy to observe the increased sense of urgency in these statements: from the meaning it progresses to a *need*—not just a wish or desire. If indeed it is a need, how can we survive without its fulfillment?

Very appropriately, fear follows, for if our needs remain unfulfilled due to the significant person's abandonment of us, what is to become of us? To prevent the abandonment, we have to be on our best behavior. For instance, we cannot enter into competition with the significant other, and if we want to earn money, it has to be a choice between marriage and career. There is nothing wrong with contributing a little money through one's work, but it cannot interfere with the care of the significant one. If the work activities become more important, or, even worse, if the woman develops a skill or talent as great as the man's, then it will take on the flavor of competition. Intimate competitions apparently ruin the relationship and abandonment becomes a distinct possibility.

The woman's "correct" behavior of not competing—she hopes—will prevent his displeasure and the potential of him leaving her. So, as long as she is not abandoned, her actions are being reinforced. She is doing it right! Or is she? There are stories of several known women in this book who followed the myths, but how happy were they? There are also some examples of women who determined their own meaning in life and followed their career goals even while being married. Their biographies did not disclose significant unhappiness, except for natural grieving when a person close to them died.

LOVE MAKES EVERYTHING ALRIGHT

It would be neglectful to omit this statement, which has functioned as justification for all kinds of choices and decisions for generations. Love is the great redeemer. In the name of love everything is possible and all is forgiven. This unwavering belief in love seems to affect in particularly tragic ways the very young. As psychotherapist Jill Murray described in her book *But I Love Him* (2000), so many young girls—still in high school and with a promising future—become involved in abusive intimate relationships. As a therapist at a battered women and children's shelter in Southern California, the author worked with the girls, helping many in realizing that they did not have to continue in this abusive lifestyle, but also witnessing some returning to their abusers.

The parents and teachers of girls involved in abusive dating relationships often have difficulty understanding why the girls remain in these relationships. Some of them have witnessed abusive behaviors at home within their families, but that is not an explanation for all those unhappy girls. For some of the girls it is the attention they receive from their boyfriends. Even if it is a negative, punishing attention, the girls may regard that as preferable to getting no attention. For others it is the unwritten rule that without a boyfriend the girl is nothing. If she has managed to attract the attention of a boy, she has a certain status within her group, and she is willing to endure a lot in order to prevent being abandoned by the boy.

It seems that the myth of the need for attachment is still alive and well. These unfortunate girls learn early that what they call "love" is a painful condition. Abusive boys at that age can be quite possessive. The girls are possessions rather than individuals to experience tender emotions with.

Recently, 16-year-old Jennifer appeared to have become accident-prone. When she had broken her arm she told her mother that she had stumbled and fallen against a low brick wall. Her mother remembered that not too long ago Jennifer had twisted and sprained her left wrist. Now there was a letter from Jennifer's school. The Physical Education teacher had noted that Jennifer had used physical problems, such as cramps, stomach pains, and similar complaints, to excuse her from participating in the class. These complaints had not been expressed every week, but they were frequent enough to give rise to concerns about Jennifer's physical health.

Reading the letter, Jennifer's mother remembered some fleeting thoughts she had about Jennifer's personality. Her daughter had always been so vivacious. People used to comment that Jennifer did not meet any strangers; people took to her immediately because of her big smile, being ready to greet everybody. Lately though, Jennifer seemed a lot more withdrawn and less likely to smile. Her lovely young face displayed a more brooding expression. Even her girlfriends called on Jennifer less often than they had in the past. It all seemed to coincide with the arrival of Greg, her boyfriend, in Jennifer's life. They were on the telephone frequently and for long periods of time. Her mother had already doubted the soundness of the parents' decision to supply Jennifer with her own cell phone.

In her parents' mind, the phone was a reward for Jennifer's good behavior, a means of protection should she be stranded somewhere, and an encouragement toward her developing independence. It also introduced an opportunity for hiding parts of Jennifer's life from her parents. When her mother confronted her with the letter from school, Jennifer at first became defensive but then admitted that she had to avoid gym class from time to time because of some bruises. Where were the bruises on her body, her mother questioned. On her upper arms and thighs, Jennifer responded, adding that Greg and she sometimes wrestled in playing around and she seemed to bruise easily. Her mother wanted to know if Jennifer had shown Greg the bruises and asked him to be less rough; surely, he would not want to hurt her on purpose. That's when Jennifer broke down in tears and told her mother the whole ugly story about Greg's domination of her and his threats to break up with her if she did not comply with his requests and his behavior.

Her mother could not believe her ears; their beautiful and bright young daughter, mistreated by a boyfriend! That only happened to other, less privileged and less intelligent girls. But the mother managed to remain quiet, just holding Jennifer in her arms until the sobbing subsided. Instead of questioning Jennifer—although she very much wanted to—the mother calmly declared that they would make an appointment with a therapist to whom Jennifer could talk confidentially. Her parents were there to listen to her, the mother continued, but they also wanted Jennifer to have the opportunity to sort things out with someone who would approach the situation perhaps more objectively than her parents could. In return, the mother asked Jennifer to discontinue communication with Greg but to refer any of his calls to her parents.

As could be expected, Jennifer hesitated to promise not to be in contact with Greg. After all, she had so much invested in this relationship and she still loved him. Perhaps if Greg could believe that she was not going to leave him, he would not be so angry most of the time and would treat her better. A lot of his anger stemmed from being jealous. What would her friends say if she and Greg broke up? Jennifer's mother expressed sadness over her daughter's willingness to be mistreated in the name of love. She encouraged Jennifer to discuss her feelings with her parents and the therapist, but for the moment she insisted on a "no contact with Greg" rule until they all would have a clearer understanding of the situation. If Jennifer violated the rule, her parents—in their responsibility to her—would have no other choice than to pursue legal actions against Greg and his parents. The mother hoped it would not come to that, but that would be Jennifer's decision.

It took great self-discipline on the mother's part not to reproach Jennifer and argue with her about her boyfriend's character and behavior. As much as she was hurting over her daughter's mistreatment, she realized that Jennifer was in even greater emotional pain. In the mother's opinion, there was also a need for a physical examination by the family's physician regarding any injuries. And as a first step in her life without Greg, Jennifer could reorganize her time to increase her efforts in her schoolwork. Jennifer's grades had dropped noticeably within the last several months, and she would need some uninterrupted blocks of time for studying.

Jennifer is not an isolated case. As it was difficult for her mother to comprehend how their smart and pretty daughter could be trapped in an abusive relationship, so it is difficult for many other middle-class mothers to understand when it happens to their daughters. Abused or battered women do not come from such a privileged background, people believe. Those poor, battered women are in that situation because they have nowhere to go. They don't have loving and caring families they can turn to. And perhaps they believe they don't deserve any better, serves as another explanation. Then do the girls from middle class families believe the same of themselves? Self-esteem—or the lack of it—is, indeed, a major part of the problem.

Murray pointed to the importance of self-esteem when she exclaimed: "positive self-esteem is one of the most precious gifts we can give our children ... It is a parent's responsibility to tell and show her daughter that she is the finest creature on earth; that she is loved for the very fact of her being, not for her achievements" (2000, p. 165). The words sound easy; parents, just pack up some self-esteem into a pretty package, tie a ribbon around it, and hand it to your daughter. What is wrong with this picture? For one, self-esteem cannot be given to another person. Several decades ago, teachers in schools were instructed to make sure that the pupils had their share of self-esteem. It did not work then and does not work now. Only the individual person can decide what factors make her or him feel good about the self. Each girl (or boy) has to determine the criteria for her (or his) self-esteem; the most loving parents (or fairy godmother) cannot prescribe the criteria for them, nor can they give it to them.

The other fallacy is that telling the young girl that she is loved just for existing in this case gives the daughter the argument for continuing to love her abusive boyfriend. If she wants to still love him because he exists, then she had better do so from a distance to avoid the bruises and broken bones. No matter how loveable his existence may be, in reality, his abusive behavior makes him unlovable. The author suggested a loving statement coming from a loving parent, but it does not hold up in real life. In real life, our behaviors have something to do with the way people regard us and treat us. In fact, teaching the young girl that she is loveable for her mere existence may extinguish any attempts on her part to know more about herself and to be aware of her own wishes and goals as well as her behaviors—it is not necessary. No wonder there are still Cinderellas waiting for the prince without awareness of themselves or the kind of prince that would suit their wishes and goals for the future.

Differentiating a person from his or her behavior has been a topic for discussion in psychology for a long time. The eminent humanistic psychologist Albert Ellis tried to make that distinction when he stated that "a basic tenet for rational living is that people not rate themselves in terms of any of their performances, but instead fully accept themselves in terms of their being, their existence. Otherwise, they tend to be severely self-deprecating and insecure, and as a consequence they function ineffectively" (Ellis, 1973, p. 17). Instead of rating themselves, individuals could just accept the fact that they exist and that it is better to enjoy life than to be in pain. To this end, they may assess their traits, characteristics, and performances, Dr. Ellis suggested.

In everyday life, however, it is difficult to make the distinction between person and behavior because—as mentioned earlier—our behaviors are the major elements in interactions with others. Our behaviors will influence others to a great degree and determine whether they want to be with us or shy away from us. For their own safety, Jennifer and other young girls in similar circumstances would do better to observe their boyfriends' behaviors than blindly believe in the goodness or value of their existence.

Thus, the myth that love makes everything right, and the beliefs that self-esteem can be given to others and that we are loved just for our existence, may be items for further scrutiny before deciding whether or not they can be of use to us at all now and in the future. They, like the myths discussed earlier, need to be seriously challenged regarding their validity and utility instead of adhered to blindly.

The list of influences from the past is by no means complete. The examples discussed here and in the previous chapter are just a few illustrations of the vast impact customs and attitudes of past generations might have on the lives of women of today and tomorrow. Arguments may be raised pointing out that women are capable of making their own decisions and designing their own paths. And that is certainly true; many women are doing that—as they have been doing all along, which is demonstrated by the stories of women from previous generations told in the different chapters of this book. Admittedly, those may have been exceptions then, and there are many more of them now. But for every woman succeeding on the path she chose for herself, there are others who are still struggling with the notion of self-determination.

Part III

Effects of Past Influences on Women's Life Areas

Cinderella's Sexuality

CHICAGO, Illinois (AP)—At least one in four teenage girls nationwide has a sexually transmitted disease or more than 3 million teens, according to the first study of its kind in this age group . . . About half of the girls acknowledged having sex; among them, the rate was 40 percent. While some teens define sex as only intercourse, other types of intimate behavior including oral sex can spread some infections. (CNN.com/health/2008)

Compared to many other parts of the world, the rates of teen pregnancy, childbearing, and sexually transmitted disease (STD) in the United States are very high (Kirby, 2007). Data from the Centers for Disease Control and Prevention (2007) reveal that chlamydia and gonorrhea rates have increased for teenage boys and girls, but for women age 15 to 19 the increases are now the highest compared to any other age/sex group. Women in the 20 to 24-year-old age bracket show the second highest rates for chlamydia and gonorrhea, as in past years. For the period from 2004 to 2007, syphilis rates have shown an annual increase in women age 15 to 19 and have been highest each year in women in the 20 to 24 year old age group. Recent estimates indicate that while 15 to 24 year olds represent 25 percent of the sexually active population, they acquire almost half of all new STDs. Equally disturbing are reports regarding sexual aggression in adolescent dating relationships, leading to the first National Teen Dating Violence Awareness Week in 2006. According to the Liz Claiborne Inc. study (2008), 62 percent of tweens (age 11–14 years) reported having friends who had been verbally abused by their boyfriends or girlfriends and one in five 13–14 year olds in relationships said they know friends who have been struck in anger or kicked, slapped, or punched by a boyfriend or girlfriend (Liz Claiborn Inc., 2008).

About one hundred years ago, the superintendent of the Chicago public school system decided to introduce a series of "sex talks" into the high school curriculum. Ella Flagg-Young, the courageous superintendent, was concerned about the epidemic of venereal diseases in Chicago and arranged for speakers to visit and talk to the older students about the dangers and consequences of premarital sexual intercourse (Moran, 2000). However, due to strong criticism, the program did not survive the school year. The debates over sex education in the United States have not changed much since then.

"Over the last decade, abstinence-only sex education became more common in the U.S., largely as a result of federal government funding initiatives. Through direct funding and matching grant incentives, the U.S. government steered more than a billion dollars to abstinence-only education programs between 1996 and 2006" (SIECUS, 2005). Despite recent declines, the teen pregnancy rate in the United States still remains high. More than 30 percent of girls become pregnant at least once before they reach the age of 20 (National Campaign to Prevent Teen Pregnancy, 2006). About 82 percent of teen pregnancies in 2001 were unintended (Finer & Henshaw, 2006).

According to Valenti (2007), women's sexuality is often treated like a commodity, a joke, or a sin. Abstinence-only education during the day conveys the message that sex before marriage is bad, but *Girls Gone Wild* commercials at night promote the idea that to be popular during spring break, it's time to start making out for the camera. Although these two messages appear to be contradicting, they are promoting the same idea that young women are not able to make their own decisions about sex. Cultural forces of the day will provide the messages. And what is the message popular culture transmits to young girls today? Sexiness ranks higher than intelligence and character; sexiness has become the measuring stick for determining a girl's value in the public eye (Liebau, 2007).

Considering the reports mentioned above, as they describe the current situation regarding young people's sexuality, what can we conclude about the state of Cinderella's sexuality? *Confusion!*

We can be sure that the fairy-tale Cinderella was a virgin until the prince found her. With all the work the wicked stepmother and her mean daughters piled on Cinderella, she would have had neither time nor energy to engage in sexual activities. How did she ever learn about sex? Did she know how it should and could feel for her? Not much is known about sex education in those days. Perhaps the level and amount of knowledge about sex and sexuality passed on then was similar to what has been included in the federal programs designed to promote abstinence-only sex education in the United State only with less money. Like the fairy tales, abstinence-only programs end with the notion of the wedding; it is the climax beyond which the participants live happily ever after—presumably without the need for abstinence.

HISTORICAL DEVELOPMENTS

Historically, the development of female sexuality has been impacted by sociocultural influences of the various periods. Even the most cursory examination of history reveals constraining influences on human sexuality in general and on women's sexuality in particular. In answer to questions regarding the purpose of sexual pleasure, Albertus Magnus, a German cleric of the 13th century, suggested that men's powerful release in intercourse and the emission of semen during ejaculation were the spark of life that was men's contribution to the reproductive process. Women's pleasure, on the other hand, was considered to be merely a byproduct of the man's significant donation to the creation of new life as a child was conceived (Hull, 2008).

Throughout the Middle Ages the demand for women's subservience to men remained strong; it defined women's place in society, as well as men's attitudes toward women. The New Testament's prescription for love within marriage describes the relationship in a hierarchical manner, as the often-quoted passage from Ephesians 5: 22-28 shows: "Wives submit to your husbands as to the Lord. For the husband is the head of the wife as Christ is the head of the church, his body, of which he is the Savior. Now as the church submits to Christ, so also wives should submit to their husbands in everything."

Despite the brief moment of enlightenment during the 18th century, when Mary Wollstonecraft of England wrote the book *The Vindication of the Rights of Women* (1792), which proclaimed that sexual satisfaction was as equally important to women as to men, the Victorian era—with the notion of women as asexual beings—soon buried the progressive views of the Enlightenment period. It then left the world with the so-called sexual double standard that is still alive and well in many cultures.

In his book *A History of Women's Bodies* (1982), Shorter, Professor of the History of Medicine, asked the question "Did Women Enjoy Sex before 1900?" Approaching the question from two opposing viewpoints, Shorter came to the conclusion that traditional men saw women as "raging volcanos of desire" (p. 12). And he quoted Jacques Solé as mentioning that, after the late Middle Ages, the Catholic Church expressed mistrust of women, 'the most dangerous of all the serpents.' Interestingly, this notion of female sexuality still seems to be expressed in the music videos of today. The notion of women's insatiable sexual hunger that could and would swallow up men's spiritual being if not broken and controlled still prevails in some circles.

Shifting to the women's view of sexual enjoyment, Shorter cautioned that evidence from middle-class and aristocratic women on this subject started to become known during the 18th and early 19th centuries, a time when more advanced attitudes about family life and emotional expressiveness developed. Therefore, this evidence can hardly be accepted as relevant regarding married women from the popular classes before that time. For those women, sex was a burden to be dutifully—and quite frequently resentfully—performed, rather than a joyful activity (Ladurie, 1979).

This assumption can hardly be surprising when considering that most men of those times were quite indifferent to their wives' suffering, much unlike 'modern' family sentiment. There is little evidence that women derived much enjoyment from sex, as intercourse in the traditional family was brief and brutal. "The main characteristic of the sexuality of traditional men is its ruthless impetuosity . . .

Impetuousness appears in men's refusal to abstain from intercourse during the mother's lying-in period. Stories abound of husbands mounting their wives just after they had delivered, heedless of the doctor's pleas" (Shorter, 1982, p. 9). Before the medical advances that brought women safer childbirth conditions and the availability of reliable methods of contraception, women hardly had any reason to expect enjoyment during sexual intercourse.

During the 19th century, the culture in the United States was full of sexual contradictions, as women's sexuality was described in terms of opposing images of Madonna and whore. The 20th century saw some psychological progress in the views of Sigmund Freud, who reasoned that sexuality was as innate in women as it was in men, and in the writings of Havelock Ellis, stressing the importance of "the love rights of women" in his 1920 book *On Life and Sex*. The media of the 1950s presented the American public with a two-sided concept of sexuality. In television programs, married couples were shown in separate beds divided by a gap of at least one foot between them, while almost at the same time the first issue of *Playboy* magazine made its appearance, focusing on the recreational aspects of sex. Women searching for their own sexual identity did so "within the confusing dichotomy of the 'pajama-packaged' wife and the scantily clad sex kitten" (Maass, 2007, p. 7).

And even more recently Paula Kamen, author of *Her Way: Young Women Remake the Sexual Revolution* (2000), is telling a familiar story about the old female sexual inhibition. When interviewing young women around the country, she found many women who have difficulty telling men what they want in bed because they are afraid of scaring the guy away. Despite the well-known assertion that penetration is an inefficient way of producing orgasm for many women, it is still the primary sex act in the minds of people of our culture. And most females live in fear that if they step outside the approved circle, abandonment and loss of love will be the consequences (Hooks, 2002).

IMPLICATIONS OF WOMEN'S RAPE FANTASIES

Women's sexual fantasies, and especially those that involve rape scenes, have intrigued researchers within the framework of female sexuality studies from time to time. It seems so incongruous that any woman would fantasize about being raped; being overpowered and terrorized, having pain and humiliation inflicted upon oneself, would seem the last thing women would fantasize about. Opinions about the reasons for erotic rape fantasies are divided, some offering an explanation by relating it to women's innate masochism (Deutsch, 1944; Freud, 1933/1965) while others found no evidence for masochism in the surveys with women (Bond & Mosher, 1986; Laumann, Gagnon, Michael, & Michaels, 1994).

Although our culture is infused with depictions of male, conquering, sexual heroes dominating women and placing them into the role of sex object, there are men who fantasize of submitting sexually to strong and willful women (Sue, 1979). On the other hand, research has revealed that apparently some women who subscribe to feminist beliefs may also engage in fantasies of forced sex, even though this might present an ideological conflict for them. "Feminist women, therefore, may not differ from women as a general group" (Shulman & Horne, 2006, p. 370).

Attempting to develop a path model of women's fantasies about forced sex, Shulman and Horne (2006) conducted an online survey of 261 adult women. Analysis of the participants' responses indicated the existence of a direct path between childhood sexual abuse and forceful sexual fantasies. But another direct path from sex guilt to forceful sexual fantasy, mediated by erotophilia also emerged. The combination of low-level sex guilt and high levels of erotophilia was predictive for sexual fantasies including force. Low sexual guilt and greater erotophilia, interpreted as a general openness to sexuality, appear to be associated with more forceful sexual fantasies. The investigators explained their findings on the basis of an openness-to-sexuality theory, such that "lower sexual guilt may allow women greater erotophilic pleasure, which may increase the usage of forceful sexual fantasies among women" (p. 373).

Those who view sexual behaviors from a biological background point to the males' display of dominance and pursuit vis-à-vis the females' display of submission and surrender as the basic pattern in the animal world. Carrying this observation over to human sexual behavior would suggest that human females might have a natural predisposition to surrender to a dominant male. If that were the case, women may transfer this biologically based mating ritual into their fantasies (Fisher, 1999).

Another suggested explanation for women's erotic rape fantasies involves the avoidance of blame or responsibility for expressing sexuality. Being forced into sexual activity would eliminate the emergence of self-blame and guilt feelings, which would inhibit sexual gratification (Deutsch, 1944; Knafo & Jaffe, 1984). But here again, research studies have produced conflicting results. An extensive research of the literature on women's rape fantasies indicated that 31 percent to 57 percent of women reported having had rape fantasies, either on a frequent basis or as a favorite fantasy (Critelli & Bivona, 2008).

Still another explanation for women's rape fantasies involves the woman's sense of attractiveness and desirability. Confronted with the woman's beauty, the man loses control and discards all expectations of civil decency in order to have her (Knafo & Jaffe, 1984). In this type of fantasy, it is the woman's sexual power that instigates the rape. Thus the beautiful woman, just by existing, arouses the male's rape instinct, and in a passive way, she assumes the responsibility (or blame?) for his behavior. Additional questions for investigation might be to explore whether women who feel insecure about their attractiveness to men are more or less inclined to have rape fantasies than others. And among women who do fantasize about rape situations, do those with greater insecurity regarding their desirability engage in these fantasies more often than other, less-insecure women? (Critelli & Bivona, 2008)

Except for her mother and her physician, nobody knew about Irene's physical deformity. Her outward appearance was beautiful, and her general disposition appeared to be gentle and friendly. In accordance with research findings (Schooler, Ward, Merriwether, & Caruthers, 2005) that shame about body image is linked to lower levels of sexual assertiveness and less sexual experience, Irene's dating history was brief. She married the first young man who proposed to her. During their marriage, she never enjoyed sex because she could not relax sufficiently to concentrate on any physical pleasure associated with sexual activities. Her husband's professional success and improved medical technology allowed corrective surgery for Irene's deformity. The surgery had been successful, but Irene's self-concept did not improve. The scar—a leftover from the surgery—still reminded her of her imperfection.

Irene's lack of sexual desire and absence of orgasm distressed her husband. Upon his suggestion, they embarked upon several unsuccessful therapy experiences, with divorce as the final outcome. Although single by now with her children away at college, Irene decided to try one more therapy approach. Irene had never masturbated, and mentioning the concept of self-pleasuring gave insight to Irene's mental and emotional reluctance to conceive of herself as a sexual being. Following a period of intensive therapy, Irene appeared at her therapist's office, exclaiming that she had experienced her very first orgasm. Although excited about her achievement, she was embarrassed to relate the details. A particular fantasy that involved a rape scene had been helpful.

Upon questioning, Irene hesitatingly revealed that being raped relieved her of responsibility for the sex act. In view of her conservative upbringing, this seemed to be a reasonable explanation. But it was only a part of the explanation. The primary reason was rooted in her physical deformity. In order to feel sexual—and perhaps even seductive—one had to be flawlessly beautiful, she reasoned. Women with physical defects had no choices; they were barely worth the attention of a rapist. This case history is described in greater detail in a different book, but a shortened version of it is appropriate here for the discussion of this topic (Maass, 2007).

A woman's hesitation in admitting the existence of rape fantasies—even to her therapist—is understandable when considering the belief that women use token resistance in response to sexual attention from men. The concept of token resistance defines a situation where a woman says "no" to sexual advances when in reality she truly wishes for the perpetrator to continue. It may be thought that the woman displays resisting behaviors to avoid negative judgment about being too interested in the sexual attention (Osman, 2007). It is not surprising then that men and women may have different perceptions of what amounts to sexual harassment, except for the most severe type of harassment.

Examining individuals' perceptions of sexual harassment provided the focus of a study involving 541 undergraduate psychology students between the ages of 18 and 22 (Osman, 2007). Participants were requested to respond to vignettes depicting situations of verbal and physical sexual harassment. Participants holding a strong belief in token resistance did not perceive a harassment situation when the woman in the vignettes said "no" to the unwanted sexual advances. Their perception was essentially the same as when the woman offered no resistance. Even in the situation where the woman displayed physical resistance, the same participants did not perceive the situation as one of sexual harassment. Only the combination of simultaneously expressed verbal and physical resisting behaviors resulted in a perception of harassment in the individuals with strong beliefs in token resistance. Those participants who held a weaker belief in women's use of token resistance perceived harassment when the victim offered verbal and/or physical resistance.

While the belief in women's use of token resistance to sexual advances is still prevalent in our society, in those who hold onto that belief, perception is clouded about what constitutes rape and what might be judged a stalling tactic in the traditional feminine role of finally giving in or going along with the man's advances. Strongly held beliefs are often more powerful than reality, because they can impact perception to the degree where, in the believer's mind, the conviction becomes reality, and the female victim becomes the teasing seducer. Unfortunately, women admitting rape fantasies would only strengthen those beliefs and undermine their own credibility.

In their review Critelli and Bivona (2008) extended their investigation to include romance novels, and particularly historical romance novels that frequently include the rape of the main female character. In romance novels, male heroes must be handsome and muscular, but can also be sexually bold, not sensitive and gentle, and have the physical and mental characteristics of warriors (Salmon & Symons, 2003). The female lead character in romance novels may encounter a dominant, sexually aggressive male who violates her.

The rape scene in the novel increases excitement and dramatic tension in the reader—will her purity transform his cruelty into love and a lifetime commitment to her? If the heroine fails to conquer his heart and transform his evil nature into something less violent, but without reducing his masculinity, what's wrong with her? This argument sounds like a variation on the theme "how many ways can a woman be blamed for her own rape?" Even Cinderella's fairy godmother did not mention any such powers to supply Cinderella with for meeting the challenge of the hero's transformation.

THE QUESTION OF STIFLING FEMALE SEXUALITY

The decades of the 1960s and 1970s saw the feminist movement and the "sexual revolution" that followed the accessibility of oral contraceptives (OCs) on the market. The sex norms of earlier times were confronted, as women's fear of unwanted pregnancies could be alleviated and the freedom to pursue sexual pleasures, which previously had been men's prerogative, could be experienced. But the increasingly tolerant public atmosphere regarding sex came to a rude awakening with the diagnosis of the first AIDS cases in the early 1980s.

Apparently disregarding the freeing powers of effective birth control measures, the rise in female sexuality in the path of the "sexual revolution" was interpreted by some as evidence that in the past female sexuality had been restricted by social and cultural suppression. Were the suppression efforts exerted mainly by men or by women? Psychologists Baumeister and Twenge (2002) explored this question. Although there were arguments in support of each gender exerting control over female sexual drives, the authors found stronger evidence for the conclusion that the proximal causes of the suppression are mostly seen in females. In other words, although institutional attempts to stifle female sexuality may be male in origin, the agents carrying out the stifling efforts seem to be mostly female (such as mothers warning daughters and women being more judgmental regarding other women's sexual indiscretions).

If women are suppressing each other's sexuality, are they doing it out of altruistic motives, because of the risks connected with sexual activities (sexually transmitted diseases, unwanted pregnancies, etc.), or is the goal to influence the sexual marketplace so that they can avoid having sex without being afraid that other women will supply it to their boyfriends or husbands? Supporting arguments for this view have cited social exchange theory, which examines behavior in terms of rewards and costs. Within this theoretical framework, sex could be regarded as a resource that women have and men want. In order to obtain sex from women, men must offer them things they desire, such as commitment or physical and financial security (Baumeister & Tice, 2000).

Thus, sex takes on the characteristics of something that can be traded, but limiting its availability ensures that the price men would have to pay in exchange for it remains high. Unlimited availability of sex, on the other hand, would reduce the value women could hope to exchange it for. In a sexually competitive society, wives and girlfriends might be apprehensive about losing their men to other women who are willing to supply sexual favors. A provider of easily available sex would thus become a threat to other women and would run the risk of encountering criticism or punishment from them. "[W]omen may feel that they can be sexually unresponsive without risk of losing their male partners as long as the men cannot find other, more satisfying partners, and so suppressing other women's sexuality is vital" (Baumeister & Twenge, 2002, p. 199).

A study involving a sample of highly sexual women seemed to support the female control of the suppression hypothesis. In contrast to women with the relatively rare diagnosis of persistent sexual syndrome (PSAS), who experience excessive and unrelenting sexual arousal without feeling any sexual desire (Mahoney & Zarate, 2007), these highly sexual women reported desiring sex at least seven times a week. They also expressed their concern about experiencing significant difficulties in their relationships with other women. Apparently, they had been subjected to pressure to reduce their sexual activity. Reportedly, they felt more comfortable and accepted by men than by women (Blumberg, 2003).

On the other hand, if men were responsible for the suppression of female sexuality, was the goal to withhold sexual pleasure from women, perhaps to ensure women's fidelity to their husbands or to eliminate paternity-related doubts? Or did men feel threatened due to their physical sexual limitations, such as men's refractory period, inability to have multiple orgasms, or the visible nature of their arousal or lack thereof? (Hyde & DeLamater, 1997) On the other hand, feminists would likely interpret men's efforts to stifle female sexuality as control and victimization methods (Travis & White, 2000).

THE FEMINIST MOVEMENT AND THE "SEXUAL REVOLUTION"

One of the women's liberation movement's early fundamental goals was to advance women's sexual pleasure and satisfaction. The first public expression of this goal was in the form of a mimeographed pamphlet of an essay with the title "the Myth of Vaginal Orgasm" written by Anne Koedt, a comrade of Susan Brownmiller's at New York Radical Women. The group distributed their writings in 1968 under the title *Notes from the First Year* and sold it to women for fifty cents and to men for a dollar (Chancer, 1998).

In retrospect, as cultural critic and feminist theorist Bell Hooks (2002) admits, the women who decided to freely give blow jobs and sleep with men ultimately lost the war in the bedroom. Men appreciated women's sexual liberation as long as it meant willingness to experiment with sex, no strings attached, but when it meant that women took the right to say no to sex as well as saying yes, men revolted.

The question of how to represent sex—even the question of how to *have* sex—became the dividing line within the women's liberation movement. In the late seventies, Susan Brownmiller, a founder of the New York chapters of Women Against Pornography, Gloria Steinem, Shere Hite, Robin Morgan, the poet Adrienne Rich, and the writers Grace Paley and Audre Lorde, formed a splinter group with the focus on fighting pornography. "Pornography is the theory, rape is the practice," was one of their slogans, coined by Robin Morgan (Chancer, 1998).

One of the most powerful determining factors regarding the use of sexual materials had been gender; men were always more likely than women to watch sexually explicit material (Malamuth, 1996; Janssen, Carpenter, & Graham, 2003; Lo & Wei, 2002). The traditional version of pornography for women had been the romance novel. Both genres seem intent on reorganizing aspects of gender. As indicated earlier in the discussion on rape fantasies, in romance novels, "it's men who undergo the gender transformation. The reconfigurations in the romance genre are psychological rather than anatomical: imbuing men with sensitivity and insight into female needs, like really handsome girlfriends with penises" (Kipnis, 2006, p. 67). On the other hand, the way female sexuality is represented in music videos clearly demonstrates the durability of sexual stereotypes. Females in these videotapes are shown in a constant state of sexual arousal, eagerly waiting and ready to serve irresistible but aggressive males. Both men and women seem to fantasize about radically transforming the other sex.

In a more recent study attempting to identify motivational factors for Internet pornography use, the results showed that men, more so than women, engaged in Internet pornography use for relationship-building and for mood maintenance. Men were also more likely than women to use pornography habitually. As had been predicted, overall, males demonstrated stronger motivation for Internet pornography consumption than females (Paul & Shim, 2008). An interesting connection between pornography use and sexual attitude was suggested, with the explanation that men's pattern of sexually explicit material consumption is a reflection of their preference for short-term sexual liaisons, an explanation that is often downplayed in general discussions of pornography use (Malamuth, 1996).

Returning to the events within the feminist movement, it was the issue of pornography that split the sisterhood into two distinct and passionately oppositional factions. There were the antiporn feminists, represented by Catharine MacKinnon and Andrea Dworkin, and earlier associated with the group Women Against Pornography (WAP). The other faction was made up of women who thought that if feminism was about freedom for women, women should be free to look at pornography, or even to participate in pornographic representations; it also included those identifying with New York State ACLU president Nadine Strossen's position of defending pornography within the framework of free speech, sex, and the fight for women's rights. Still others, stressing civil liberties, came from an anticensorship perspective associated with the Feminist Anti-Censorship Task Force (FACT), such as writers Carol Vance, Ann Snitow, and Ellen Willis (Chancer, 1998). Sadly, according to Brownmiller, the antiporn initiative was the last expression of radical feminism. No future issue was pursued with a level of passion comparable to that of pornography. Many of the old conflicts within the women's movement and the sexual revolution remained unresolved. What is left is a residue of confusion.

RAUNCH FEMINISM

A group with the name CAKE (because "cake" is a slang term for female genitalia) might count for an expression of that confusion, stemming from ignoring the contradictions of the past and producing a patchwork of different, conflicting ideologies that combine into one incoherent brand of raunch feminism (Levy, 2005). Apparently, CAKE's fame is based on its parties, which range from "Striptease-a-thons" to porn parties in theme. Porn movies are frequently projected on the walls at those parties. According to founders Emily Kramer and Melinda Gallagher, who consider Hugh Hefner a hero, CAKE's goal is to change public perceptions about female sexuality and to redefine its current boundaries.

But "raunch culture isn't about opening our minds to the possibilities and mysteries of sexuality. It's about endlessly reiterating one particular—and particularly commercial—shorthand for sexiness" (Levy, 2005, p. 30). Traditionally, raunch is something that has appealed to men and was offensive to women. Now participating in it is an opportunity for women to appear "cool" and tougher, to be different from other women and more like a man (or what Ariel Levy called a "female chauvinistic pig"), and to have sex like a man. As stated on the inside cover of the book, "Female chauvinist pigs are making sex objects of other women—and of themselves."

An issue that has been raised repeatedly in sex research is that of sexual compliance or consenting to unwanted sex. Although men participate in unwanted sex at times, it is generally more likely that women engage in sexual activities in spite of not wanting to do so. Various explanations for this occurrence have been offered, such as the influence of traditional gender roles, with women feeling required to satisfy a partner's needs in order to maintain intimacy (Impett & Peplau, 2002; O'Sullivan & Allgeier, 1998), or women's beliefs about "uncontrollable" male sexuality, as if the man is too aroused to stop (Gilbert & Walker, 1999); while other researchers have tried to find answers within the framework of exchange theory (Lawrence & Byers, 1995) to promote intimacy, to receive approval from one's partner, or to impress peers (Impett & Peplau, 2003).

Another explanation comes from the notion that young women reject feminism because they see the movement's critique of social injustice as offensive to young women who regard themselves as rational and self-determining (Rich, 2005). Whereas the conventional "Pleasing Woman" is expected to be "actively selfless" in fulfilling men's sexual needs, the notion of the modern "Together Woman" incorporates a pseudo-empowerment idea and the assumption of complete control over her own life (Phillips, 2000). "Together Women" do not conceive of themselves as victims of perpetrators; if anything, they may agree to have been victims of their own poor judgment.

Young women's alienation from collective feminism, and their rejection of being victimized, may be linked to the permeation of "neoliberal" dialogue, which expresses such values as free choice, self-determination, and personal responsibility (Rich, 2005). It has been argued that neoliberalism erodes social resources required for the safeguarding of young women's sexual well-being; instead it offers a rhetoric of self-determination and personal responsibility that leads to women's self-blaming for any sexual victimization they may experience (Fine & McClelland, 2007).

In a study with 22 female undergraduate students from an elite private school, the participants reported having experienced unwanted sex with a total of 30 different male partners. In addition, six of the participants also admitted to having been sexually assaulted (Bay-Cheng & Eliseo-Arras, 2009). An analysis of the participants' responses in the interviews indicated that the combination of the roles of gendered norms and neoliberal norms—used by the young women to help make sense of their experiences afterward—produced women's participation in unwanted sex. In other words, the young women acted according to conventional gender norms of satisfying their male partners' wants, but they either made themselves believe that these situations could be learning experiences, which would therefore be beneficial to them, or they blamed themselves for having exercised poor judgment.

Blaming the victim for his or her victimization has been done before, but to convince the victim that she is to blame takes this scenario a step further. What are the factors that brought about this development in women's sexual attitudes? Did it occur as an outgrowth of misinterpreted or misunderstood aspects of the women's movement? When feminists talked about women's liberation and empowerment, they meant tearing off the boundaries and limitations that had been imposed upon women. They were talking about equal rights for women, not just the freedom to be sexually provocative or to observe and participate in pornography or to have sex like a man or to blind themselves with misinterpretations of personal responsibility and self-determination. But, as discussed previously, the striving for equality, freedom, and power—in sex as in any other area of life—has become an individual one, an option and responsibility for each individual woman.

For today's Cinderellas, the questions Wolf asked are still relevant: Does a woman "have the right to sexual pleasure and self-esteem because she's a person, or must she earn that right through 'beauty,' as she used to through marriage? What is female sexuality—what does it look like? Does it bear any relationship to the way in which commercial images represent it? Is it something women need to buy like a product? What really draws men and women together?" (2002, p. 271).

SEXUAL STEREOTYPES AND THE POWER DIFFERENTIAL

Parallel to—and more or less independent of—the developments contributing to women's sexuality described in the previous section, throughout the 20th century, and beyond, gender-role socialization has provided a persistent attitudinal framework for men's and women's behavior and their notion of sexuality. The traditionally stereotyped versions of the independent and aggressive male and the equally stereotyped dependent and submissive female are still alive and well. The lingering cultural stereotypes impose their enduring, lifelong effects on both male and female sexuality, overshadowing at times the impacts of the efforts and actions of the women's movement.

There is still a tendency for women to be drawn to powerful men. Is it due to a wish to please the "father," or is it a case of what psychiatrist Natalie Shainess (1984) termed "borrowed power," situations where women believe that they can overcome their helplessness by attaching themselves to a powerful male? Or is it because attention and admiration increase women's self-esteem and make them feel important—even more so if the admirer is a powerful man? As Barbara Amiel, former political columnist for the *Sunday Times* and wife of Conrad Black, member of England's House of Lords since 2001, explained in a *Chatelaine* article with the title "Why Women Marry Up," power is sexy in its own right; but, in addition, the power owner's self-confidence inspires a shiver of subservience in those who approach him (McDonald, 2004).

If, indeed, a "shiver of subservience" can be said to function as a mechanism for sexual arousal in women, the efforts of the women's movements must seem to have been in vain, because the traditional Cinderella apparently is here to stay. As unfortunate as this observation is, it might help explain why many women have been the target of sexual misconduct by clergy or health professionals. Females represent the overwhelming majority among the victims of abuse by mental health professionals. Information from the Therapy Exploitation Link Line network shows that more than 3,500 women and only 18 men have contacted their services since 1989 (Wohlberg, 1999).

Therapists working with female clients who in the past had been targets of violations of professional ethics codes by clergy or therapists may find that the victims, while affirming their current privilege for confidentiality, refuse to take steps to penalize the previous perpetrator. Furthermore, some of the women involved in a sexual relationship during their past treatment—where the sexual relationship was terminated by the treating professional—admitted that, given the opportunity, they would have continued the sexual involvement and that they were silently jealous of other patients who became recipients of the professional's sexual attentions. Such tragic disclosures indicate the degree of influence the powerful male therapists still had over their female clients (or were given by them).

The female quest for authority figures and men's desire for young women represent what Polhemus (2005) called the "Lot complex," referring to the biblical text describing the critical relationship between Lot and his daughters, which has haunted the imagination and has wrought history and influenced behavior from biblical times to the present.

Despite such developments as the raunch feminism and sexual, neoliberal norms, general contemporary sexual norms still reflect the sexual double standard (Kimmel, 2000). Conventional wisdom—reinforcing the old double standard—still tells us that women continue to associate sex with love, whereas men have very little difficulty enjoying sexual intercourse for pleasure and physical release without being bothered by emotional commitments. Linking sex with love places a heavier commitment on women who are engaged in sexual activities than the recreational type of sex that is generally understood and accepted for men. The parameters of pleasure—a sensual experience—can be changed from day to day and from hour to hour, whereas "love," as a deeper emotional experience, is expected to occur in an individual's life only a certain number of times.

It is not difficult to see that this double-standard concept of sex that links sex to love for females opens the door to criticism toward women who "love too much," or who fall in and out of love too often when changing partners. Frequent partner change is more readily accepted in sex-for-pleasure situations.

DEGREES OF COMMITMENT AND POWER

A significant factor in the relational dynamics between romantic or sexual partners has been recognized in the distribution of power as discussed earlier. The uneven distribution of power within a relationship may lead to exploitation of the less powerful partner by the partner with the greater resources, usually the man. The level of commitment toward a relationship bestows differential levels of power to the involved partners, with the less-committed individual usually enjoying a greater degree of power than the more committed one. Among other characteristics, the power differential is played out repeatedly in the sexual arena of life. The powerful partner can demand sex; the powerless one provides it.

Linking the notion of power differential in relationships to attachment theory, the nature of women's attachment style is thought to result in their greater commitment to a partner, because they see themselves as having expended great personal investment in the relationship and fear losing their partner. Research concerned with the dynamics of female victimization at the relational level has revealed associations of women's level of commitment to the relationship with participation in unwanted sex (Impett & Peplau, 2002). The women's investment in a particular relationship may lead them to consent to unwanted sexual activities. This observation supports the *Principle of Least Interest,* and points to the less committed partner as the one who holds power over the more committed one, whose behavior is designed to minimize the probability of dissolving the relationship.

Women who strongly believe in the "beauty myth" would seem especially vulnerable to the dynamics of the principle of least interest; with increasing age their beauty fades, and so does the interest of their partner. The women's investment in the relationship has taken a substantial part of their resources, and they perceive the threat of losing that investment. The tolerance of sexual coercion is just one of the characteristics women may accept in order to protect the perceived investment (Katz, Kuffel, & Brown, 2006).

An aspect of power can be viewed as operating in attempts to deceive others about one's intentions, goals, or motives. In deception, the person is engaged in "controlling information to alter the target's beliefs or understanding in a way that the deceiver knows is false" (Buller & Burgoon, 1994, p. 192). People who practice deception attempt to gain something they want, which they believe they cannot obtain otherwise. Although, strictly speaking, deception is not an act of real power, it temporarily affords the deceiving person an unfair advantage over the target or victim. In the romantic/sexual arena of life there are many opportunities for deception regarding one's intentions, one's sexual history and current involvements, as well as risky sexual exploits. Deception in connection with sexual encounters may take a variety of forms, ranging from outright lying, to withholding parts of or the whole truth, to evasive manipulations that are difficult to recognize.

Because deception is usually put into action for the purpose of either gaining something of value or avoiding receiving something painful or undesirable, deception can thus become part of what has been considered by some to be a type of social-exchange process. As mentioned earlier in the discussion on raunch feminism, sex may be used in exchange for other resources or gains, such as emotional intimacy or other relationship resources (Sprecher, 1998), as women may use sex as a resource in exchange for what they desire in a relationship (Baumeister & Vohs, 2004).

For the purpose of developing a behavior-based scale about sexual deception, 267 participants associated with two universities were surveyed about their sexual deceptive behaviors (Marelich, Lundquist, Painter, & Mechanic, 2008). In the analysis of the data, three primary components of sexual deception were identified. These were labeled Blatant Lying, Self-Serving, and Avoiding Confrontation. In general, participants admitting to any of these deceptions reported more sexual partners and one-night stands. Those who admitted the use of self-serving lies or having sex to avoid confrontations were concerned about possible loss of their partners. Women were more likely to have sex in order to avoid confrontation, while men were more likely to use blatant lies to have sex.

These rather recent findings seem to confirm that many women are not yet ready to insist on enjoying sexual activities for themselves and on their own terms, despite the discussion of the Together Woman earlier in this chapter. One is reminded of Jane and Nancy, the young women who had married two brothers, who were experts in the "silent treatment," as mentioned in Chapter 3. While Nancy refused to engage in sexual activities with her husband when she was angry with him, Jane had taken the route of silently giving in to avoid confrontation and abandonment. Neither woman experienced sex as an activity that could be pleasurable to them.

Considering the working of the power dynamics within sexual relationships between men and women, one might conclude that women, who out of consideration for their perceived investment in the relationship consent to sexual intercourse with the seemingly more powerful partner, pay a high price. As a byproduct of engaging in unwanted sex, the individual over time comes to lose her own desire for it, as it takes on the flavor of a dreaded activity that one has to fulfill in order to prevent abandonment by the powerful partner (Maass, 2007).

Sadly, this type of compromise starts early, as dating relationships during adolescence are fairly common. In a survey more than 70 percent of adolescents admitted at least one serious romantic relationship involvement before the age of 18 (Collins, 2003). Why settle for compromises so early when it can easily turn into a way of life? Why try so hard and so early to wear the shoe that doesn't fit?

WOMEN'S SEXUAL ATTITUDES

Development of female sexuality; historical-cultural influences on women's sexual experiences (the double standard); searching for sexual identity; women's relationship to power; and achieving sexual assertiveness versus experiencing the anger and resentment of sexual submission are all contributors in the formation of women's sexual attitudes, and as such they have an impact on women's sexual arousal (Maass, 2007). Attitudes in subtle and not-so-subtle ways determine cognitive content during sexual activity. Cognitive distractions usually fall into the category of not-so-subtle influences during sex. Both men and women can experience cognitive distractions during sexual activity. Not surprisingly, men's cognitive distractions are performance related, while women's distractions revolve around appearance-based cognitions, such as negative body image. However, in addition to the appearance-related cognitive distractions, women are also plagued with equally strong performance-based distractions (Meana & Nunnink, 2006).

From those findings, it appears that women just have stronger impulses for worrying. Considering that the study involved college students (220 males and 237 females), participants generally being at a younger age and with fewer responsibilities to be concerned about, one can only imagine how the list of cognitive distractions during sex may increase for women in the motherhood phases of their lives.

As much of the reported research involves college students, the results may not be applicable to the general population at later ages. Research findings tend to be confirmed as long as the populations resemble the original ones. This fact was demonstrated in studies investigating the correlation between women's self-schema and their sexual behaviors. While earlier results corresponded with those obtained in later studies for college-age women, scores about self-schema and actual sexual behaviors obtained from women over 30 years of age apparently did not demonstrate a strong correlation, according to an unpublished doctoral dissertation by J. A. Volsky Rushton in 2003 (Hill, 2007).

In order to measure individuals' thoughts about their sexual self or self-schema, investigators have developed separate rating scales for men and women (Andersen & Cyranowski, 1994; Andersen, Cyranowski, & Espindle, 1999; Markus, 1977). The three main factors that emerged were characteristics such as passion/romantic, open-minded/liberal, and powerful/aggressive. Building on this work, Hill (2007) presented a modified version of the sexual self-schemas scale with the three factors of loving/warm, reserved/conservative, and direct/outspoken and presented it to 439 college students (251 females and 188 males). Statistical evaluation of the collected data showed some overall gender differences. However, these were mostly due to the fact that the female participants scored higher than the male participants on the loving/warm and the reserved/conservative factors. The direct/outspoken factor received very similar scores from both men and women.

In summary, the male college students saw their sexual selves as somewhat less loving and warm than did the female students, but not significantly so. This seems to be another indication that college students show less-pronounced gender differences in their sexual self-schemas than the same individuals might at a later age. In most people, sexual attitudes and self-concepts are not stable entities that remain rigidly the same; rather, they develop over time, with modifications as life experiences come into play. Therefore, one would expect greater variability between and even within gender at a later age.

Sandy, the young mother of two lively children looks away into space when the topic of sex is raised. Sex is just another chore for her at the end of the day.

Every weekday morning she gets up at ten minutes past five. Twenty minutes for her exercises, then quickly into the shower. While Roger, her husband, takes his shower, she gets the children up and dressed while also, step-by-step, fixing the family's breakfast. She leaves the house before Roger does because she has to drop the children off at the childcare center on her way to work. Roger is supposed to pick them up after work but there are days when he calls Sandy at work, informing her that he will be meeting a client and cannot be at the childcare center to collect the children before closing time. Consequently, Sandy has to change her after-work plans. If she had intended to do some grocery shopping, she either has to postpone this to another day or she has to take the children along—not always an easy decision, especially if the groceries are needed for this evening's meal.

At least Sandy can count on the regularity of her working hours. There is no overtime work for her. She is one of those wives who agreed to take a well-defined job with healthcare benefits for the family while Roger is developing his own business as a financial adviser. This type of security means her career wings are clipped. The dreams of her college years seem so distant now. While in college she thought she would have it all. Being away from home, she found out that she liked to spend time in passionate lovemaking with her boyfriend. And, naturally, she would have a great career, too.

When she met Roger her sexual drive was still strong and he was a great lover. Now the time for sex is late at night, after the children are tucked into bed and when she is exhausted from her busy day. The fact that she would rather sleep has turned Roger from a great lover into a complaining, sex-starved roommate. The sad thing is that Sandy does not even miss her passionate love life from the past; it's hardly worth remembering.

Popular wisdom has it that men's and women's sexual attitudes differ: As discussed earlier, men appreciate the pleasures of casual sex whereas women tend to associate sex with love and commitment. Simple comparisons by numbers would seem to confirm this idea. But sheer numbers don't tell the whole story. There are men—as well as women—who seek long-term, committed relationships and there are women who—like some men—pursue short-term or illicit affairs.

In the process of constructing a brief sexual attitude scale, researchers noted a gender difference for the subscales Permissiveness and Instrumentality, with greater endorsements from men than women on both subscales (Hendrick, Hendrick, & Reich, 2006). The Permissiveness scale included items tapping the ideas of casual sex with many different partners, as well as one-night stands and nonexclusivity of relationship. Items on the Instrumentality scale described sexual activity in terms of being primarily a bodily function that should be engaged in for one's pleasure.

Similarly, studies with young, unmarried, heterosexual undergraduate students showed that males were more likely than females to agree that casual sex with different partners was acceptable. Men reported more intercourse partners than did women during the previous year, and men also expressed the wish for more sexual partners for the next five years. Female participants had experienced more frequent difficulties with sexual arousal as well as less frequent orgasms during sexual activity with a partner (Carpenter, Janssen, Graham, Vorst, & Wicherts, 2008).

Considering the case of Sandy above, it is not surprising that the notion of enjoyment in sexual activities gets lost, even if it was existent in the beginning. Apparently, the goal of fun and joyful activities is significantly less strong in women than in men. Sadly, it is so weak that it will be pushed aside for the first somber responsibility that comes along in the woman's life. Even if it is a responsibility that the woman had looked forward to having, it may affect her attitudes about sex.

Ginny should have been ecstatically happy, she announced in her first therapy appointment. She had completed her professional education, had married the man she loved, and had given birth to the much-wanted baby daughter. Baby Tina had been born 10 months ago and progressed beautifully through the phases of her babyhood. Ginny was a staunch believer in breastfeeding Tina. She wanted her to have the best possible start in life. But she felt herself becoming irritable when her husband attempted to initiate sex. They tried to explain her lack of sexual desire with a hormonal imbalance. The combination of giving birth and breastfeeding could be expected to have an impact on her testosterone level, although many women's level tends to normalize after about six months.

While expressing her thoughts in therapy, Ginny realized that something else affected her; it seemed as though her body was not her own anymore. The baby demanded it for her needs, and when her husband touched her in a sexual way it seemed too much of an invasion. In her mind she had to repossess her body by allowing herself time for physical pampering that was meant just for her. Experiences such as Ginny's don't find explanations in most research studies done with college students.

According to some researchers, it is conceivable that in women two overlapping approaches of psychological adaptation to mating have evolved and are expressed in their sexual behaviors: those for establishing long-term cooperative partnerships for the purpose of raising children, and those for engaging in selective sexual activities with social partners to gain access to good genes for offspring (Pillsworth & Haselton, 2006).

Raising a child is a heavy burden, and according to parental investment theory, the parent with the greater investment in this burden, usually the female, should be the more selective one of the two parents. Good genes are one area for selection; material resources, cooperation, and general support are others. Men, while generally burdened less with child-raising responsibilities, may seek to increase their reproductive success by engaging in sex with additional female partners. Thus, differential investment in parenting may partly result in differences between the sexes. Men's investment in parenting is not a biological requirement, and men can engage in various strategies for minimizing their costs and increasing their reproductive output. They can even fool other males into investing in their offspring through cuckoldry (Gangestad & Simpson, 2000).

Furthermore, men can abandon their current mates and offspring if they want to pursue other mating opportunities.

For women and their offspring, material resources are a necessity. Therefore, women should be able to predict men's ability to acquire those resources. Other desirable characteristics, such as kindness or a sense of humor, are luxuries (Li, Bailey, Kenrick, & Linsenmeier, 2002). And what are the choices women make? The answer to this question has been explored in several studies involving normally ovulating women who were not using any hormone-based contraceptives (see Pillsworth & Haselton, 2006, for a review). Women were instructed to view photographs and videotapes of men and to rate them according to their attractiveness. It was found that women selected partners with facial masculinity, arrogance, dominance, and competitiveness as desirable partners for short-term relationships if the women were near ovulation in their menstrual cycle at the time of the selection.

Facial masculinity is correlated with higher testosterone levels in men, and the characteristics preferred by the women at this particular time in their menstrual cycle are indicative of "good genes" in males.

In a recent article in the magazine *Psychology Today* (Pelusi, 2009), a clinical psychologist discussed the observation that some women are attracted to "bad boys," men that exhibit a certain swagger and stride in their behavior, indicative of boldness and bravado. Again, mention is made that these men are particularly attractive for fleeting relationships, and that women seem to operate in their choices under the influence of high-testosterone-fueled masculinity that promises good-quality genes. On the other hand, these men—while good for mating—are usually not the ones to stick around long enough to raise the offspring. So, why would women want to take such risks? Psychologist Nando Pelusi has the answer: "Secretly they harbor the fantasy of turning their genetically gifted cads into loving dads who stick around long-term, long enough to help raise the kids. Think Warren Beatty and Keith Richards; fairy tales sometimes come true" (p. 59). Just a subtle reminder of the enduring power of fairy tales.

THE STORY OF HORMONES

Hormones, such as testosterone, may be differentially implicated in attraction to long-term relationships versus short-term relationships or sexual involvements. The ratings of 29 women presented with photographs of 39 men showed that the women rated men with higher testosterone levels as more attractive than lower testosterone men, but the attraction was mainly for brief involvements with the men (Roney, Hanson, Durante, & Maestripieri, 2006). In this study—as in the studies mentioned above—testosterone level and facial masculinity were found to be moderately correlated, suggesting that facial masculinity may be a cue to circulating testosterone levels in men and thus may mediate the testosterone short-term mating preference. Again, the preference for men with higher testosterone levels (via facial masculinity) for short-term relationships was viewed as a reflection of women's partiality for genetic quality.

More recently, data has been made available concerning associations between testosterone and partnering. It was shown that North American single men have higher levels of testosterone than married men, indicating that partnering is linked to lower testosterone. A study with 76 heterosexual men demonstrated that unpaired or uncommitted (single, dating, or in multiple relationships) men had higher testosterone levels than men in committed relationships (van Anders & Watson, 2006). These findings are considered to be consistent with theoretical predictions concerning male mating efforts. Partnering, such as marriage, means that men are less engaged in male-male competition for female mates, a situation characterized by lowered testosterone.

The question arises: Is it the element of competition that is correlated with testosterone levels in men, indicating that unpaired men can be viewed as still being involved in competition with other males? Or is it the men's attitudes about the level of commitment they accept in a given heterosexual relationship?

Of interest are findings concerning men in committed relationships with partners living in the same city and those who were engaged in long-distance relationships. Men in both types of relationships showed lower testosterone levels than single men (van Anders & Watson, 2007). This observation would be suggestive of the importance of the men's relationship orientation. This suggestion was confirmed in the observation that being partnered was not linked with lower testosterone in men if the partnered individuals were engaged in or expected to engage in extra-pair sexual encounters (McIntyre et al., 2006). Those observations would indicate that men's attitudes toward relationships and the likelihood of future participation in extra-pair sexual activities are more strongly associated with their testosterone levels than men's current relationship status (Gray, 2003; van Anders, Hamilton, & Watson, 2007).

Interpreting the above research findings, it would seem that when women prefer men with facial masculinity for short-term relationships, that would coincide with the men's elevated testosterone level stimulated by the pursuit of the woman in competition with other men. As the relationship develops and lasts a certain amount of time, men's testosterone levels can be expected to drop, and they may consider leaving the relationship for other pursuits. Considering that the women were selecting these men with facial masculinity primarily for short-term relationships, an amiable parting of the ways could be expected. Reality, however, does not seem to confirm this process for most couples.

It was a dreary-looking morning. Angie watched as the raindrops rolled slowly down her bedroom window. This was the second Saturday in a row that it was raining. It was also the second Saturday in a row that she was alone and had no plans for the weekend. On the previous Saturday she appreciated the extra time to catch up with all the little maintenance chores that had been put off during the hectic weeks before. Her life had really changed in the recent past. As a beautiful, single, career-oriented young woman, she had to be organized to fit all her activities into each day. She had a group of friends, casually dated several young men, and spent efforts and time on advancing her career.

After she met Bruce she found herself spending more and more time with him. He had not really been the type of man she would be easily attracted to. But his face reflected a mixture of self-assurance and masculinity that—combined with his deep and, at times, so gentle voice—resulted in a fascinating link of opposites. He was different from the other men she dated, and he pursued her ardently. Men usually complimented her on her beautiful hair and eyes or even her warm smile, but Bruce, on their first date, focused on her hands. He thought they expressed sincerity and strength as well as sensitivity, similar to what he could read in her facial expression when she felt unobserved. To emphasize his point, Bruce took her left hand into his hands, gently holding and stroking her hand down to her fingertips as he spoke, adding an almost hypnotic quality to his words.

Angie never focused much attention on her hands, except for contemplating what type and color of nail polish to use. Her hands were strong and she was grateful how fast and accurately her fingers moved along on the computer keyboard. Generally, she paid more attention to her hair, her makeup and the fitness of her body. Now, every once in a while she found herself looking at her hands and contemplating how the touch of her long slender fingers might feel to a man. Sometimes she asked herself what type of engagement ring would look best on her hand.

Another shift in Angie's consideration of Bruce came about when he inquired about her given name: Was "Angie" a shortened form of "Angela?" Responding to her confirming nod, Bruce asked permission to call her Angela. "It sounds like music and is so perfect for you," was his explanation. Angie drifted away from her friends and her previous dating partners. Bruce occupied an ever-increasing part of her life. Their lovemaking was wonderful. Bruce was a passionate but gentle lover whose primary goal seemed to be to please Angela. This blissful relationship lasted for about five months.

Almost unnoticeably at first, Bruce became more involved in his work, leaving him less time to spend with Angie. There were some meetings with old friends that he had neglected. And two weeks ago he informed her that he had to go out of town to be with his sick sister. Surely, he had not planned on staying with his sister for two whole weeks, Angie thought. He must be back by now. When she called his apartment, only the answering machine clicked on after several rings. Of course, she could call his cell phone; but that would seem that she was trying to track him down. Angie decided against it—at least, for the time being.

At about the middle of the following week, Angie called his cell phone. The sound of his voice evoked warm feelings in her until she noticed the evasiveness in his words. Apparently, Bruce was back at work; he did not give the exact date of his return but mentioned that he was extremely busy, trying to make up for the time he had spent away from his job. He could not even commit to an evening with Angie for the rest of the week. On the following Saturday, however, there was a surprise visit from Bruce and things seemed to return to normal in their lovemaking, although Bruce could not allow himself to stay through the night. He had to get up early the next day and take care of things that had piled up during his absence.

This undefined schedule in their relationship marked the beginning of a new pattern. In addition to spending less time together, Bruce did not commit to certain days and times until sometimes just a day before; he would even call Angie on a particular day asking for a date that evening. It was difficult for Angie to admit to herself her suspicions about Bruce and his behavior. She tried to make excuses for him. But when she finally confronted him about the change in their relationship, Bruce confessed that he did not feel ready to commit to a permanent and exclusive relationship.

As some studies have indicated, hormonal differences may be linked to emotional states, such as early-stage love. Among other endocrine changes, men who had recently fallen in love had lower testosterone levels while women in a new love relationship showed higher testosterone levels than control subjects engaged in long-term, exclusive relationships. At 12 to 18 months after having fallen in love, participants of the study who still remained in the relationship showed hormone levels similar to that of controls (Marazziti & Canale, 2004).

Apparently, the testosterone differences between men and women in early-stage love reflect an immediate drop in testosterone levels in men right after conquest, whereas for women the fresh love relationship results in a rise in testosterone. If we seriously consider the van Anders & Watson and McIntyre et al. studies that competition with other males raises the testosterone level in men, we could conclude that it is not the presence of a desirable woman as much as the competition with other men that is exciting to men. Furthermore, the women's increase in testosterone might well be related to a state of romantic mood at the beginning of a new relationship that seems to last a bit longer than the men's competition-related increase.

At the time of conquest, the element of competition fades, and so does the man's testosterone. In order to raise his testosterone level, the man would have to set out on a new conquest involving new competitors surrounding a new woman (or possibly the previous woman with high-level competition). In other words, by the time women in a new romantic relationship experience an increase in libido with their increased testosterone level, the men's libido is already slowly decreasing, as their testosterone level goes down in the absence of competition. What cruel timing nature has engineered.

Independent of relationship status, the fragile balance of testosterone plays an important part in human sexual desire. In women, the amount of free testosterone, which is metabolically active and influences the libido, is only 1 to 3 percent of the total testosterone, while about 95 percent of the testosterone circulating in a man's blood system is bound (on a protein molecule) and metabolically ineffective, leaving about 5 percent free testosterone to influence men's libido. There are various reasons for androgen insufficiency in women, and accurate screening for androgen deficiency is often difficult due to the significantly lower levels of free testosterone in females compared to men. In addition, the methods used for testing testosterone levels were originally developed for men, with their higher levels of circulating testosterone (Guay 2002).

In a cross-sectional, national probability sample survey of American women, 25 percent of the women reported significant distress concerning their own sexuality (Bancroft, Loftus, & Long, 2003). As Elizabeth Lee Vliet (2005), author of *The Savvy Woman's Guide to Testosterone,* explained, "female sexual desire clearly has biological components stimulated by optimal estradiol and testosterone. For women to become fully sexually aroused, it is equally or even more important to have satisfying emotional-intimacy connection" (p. 219). The scope of this book does not include in-depth discussions of female sexual desire (see Maass, 2007, for a more detailed discussion of this topic).

Women's Relationships

Mirror, mirror on the wall, who is the fairest of them all?

In fairy tales there is no room for female friendships. As discussed in Chapter 2, the question directed to the mirror represents a powerful force in isolating women by placing them in competition with each other. In patriarchies, female bonding is difficult to achieve. The voice of the looking glass sets women against each other, and in their isolated position women remain individually helpless, thus contributing in some part to their position of reduced power.

The ideology of beauty is strong enough to exert social control over women to the same degree that the myths about motherhood, domesticity, and passivity have influenced women's lives in the past. Subscribing to the beauty ideology means "assigning value to women in a vertical hierarchy according to a culturally imposed physical standard, it is an expression of power relations in which women must unnaturally compete for resources that men have appropriated for themselves" (Wolf, 2002, p. 12).

Women are said to be relational creatures. They are more emotionally expressive than men, and supposedly they are interpersonally more sophisticated and accomplished than men. Women's nature is nurturing, compassionate, and caring. Unlike men, women are socialized to sacrifice and to place the welfare of others above their own. These descriptions seem unlikely to include elements of competition. Competition is normally seen as a masculine trait and so is aggression. Cynics may say these statements are myths, idealized descriptions of women's behaviors.

Most women are not directly or physically violent, but they can be and are aggressive and competitive in indirect ways, as Chesler (2001) pointed out in her book *Women's Inhumanity to Women*. Women's competition appears less obvious than men's because the targets of female competition and aggression are not men; the targets bear the faces of other women.

In his historical explorations about women's lives in past centuries, Shorter (1982) pointed out that "women's culture was a culture of 'solace,' a place where the bodily misery of womanhood would find understanding. But the women's culture functioned also to defend women from the malignant aggression of men" (p. 293). The poor village women of the distant past turned to other women for solace and friendship because they believed that only women could understand the sufferings they experienced at the hands of men. Shorter argued that it was only at the point when women stopped accepting men's views of women's inferiority and regarded femininity in a positive light that they left the women's culture behind to form emotional bonds with men. Of course, for this to occur, men had to modify their views of women somewhat. In fact, Shorter viewed men around the time of the first wave of feminism as "new men" who had become affectionate husbands. This change in men made it possible for the surge of feminism to occur in alliance with men. However, in Shorter's view, the second wave of feminism, occurring between 1965 and 1980, seemed to have taken place in alliance against men.

Should we accept this explanation about the nature of women's bonding as confirmation of the old saying that nothing unites people as strongly as the existence of a common enemy? It would be a sad state of events if we had to have enemies in order to have friends. In addition, if we are to accept the historical data so arduously collected by Shorter as correct information about women's lives in the distant past, we are faced with a contradiction when we compare this picture to the fairy tales' descriptions of women's relationships. Whereas in Shorter's accounts the women in the popular cultures of history bonded with other women in situations of misery and hardship, the fairy tales focus not only on women suffering in isolation, but also on women harshly punishing other women.

The lessons of the fairy tales about women's mistreatment of other women, as has been so vividly described in the relationships between the heroines and stepmothers and stepsisters, have been most effective. Laura Tracy recognized this during the interviews for her book *The Secret between Us: Competition among Women*. "As a feminist, I wanted to believe that women could be more supportive than competitive, that we wanted to connect with each other far more than we wanted to hurt each other. Not so long ago, I discovered otherwise" (1991, pp. xi–xii). According to Tracy's findings, female competition involved mothers-in-law; rivals for romantic and business relationships; and even their own mothers, daughters, sisters, and friends. But it is a secret competition, one that most women refuse to admit.

Many women can join together and bond when there is a problem one of them has to face, as described by Shorter, but the difficulty arises with confronting another woman's success. From childhood on, girls know how to terrorize, ostracize, and shun other girls, and this "essentially woman-hating behavior continues into adulthood . . . it is rooted in the same fairy-tale logic that teaches us that only one female can win the day or be chosen. It is as though our knowledge that females lack value in the eyes of patriarchy means we can gain value only by competing with one another for recognition" (Hooks, 2002, p. 131).

It is not surprising, then, that women do not trust each other. They are more willing to believe the lies of a man than the lies of other women, or even an honest statement from another woman. Men tell women what they want to hear, and, instead of critically looking at the glass slipper in the man's hand, Cinderella eagerly swallows being told that she is different from all other women (Hollander, 1995). "In the face of evidence to the contrary, women often focus on the few strands that seem truthful in the incredible tapestry of fact and fantasy supplied by the man and try to weave a canvas of hope rather than reality to be able to continue believing and loving him" (Maass, 2002/2006, p. 237).

Whether justified or not, the distrust between women leads to isolation in reality as it did in the fairy tales with heroines such as Snow White, Sleeping Beauty, and Cinderella, who were basically alone, mentally and emotionally separated from and deserted by other women. Indeed, the lessons of our childhood are still powerful in our lives and seem designed to maintain the helplessness of our isolation.

MOTHER-DAUGHTER RELATIONSHIPS

Mother-daughter relationships are the most complex relationships in many women's lives. The complexity of mother-daughter connections is reflected in the wide range of relationship types, from the scenarios of mutual devotion to situations of mutual hatred. For some of those who consider motherhood the purpose of their lives, the letting go of an adolescent or young adult daughter may prove too painful, whereas others who tend to live vicariously through the achievements of their daughters may have an equally difficult time of letting their daughters break away.

Mother-daughter bonds, as well as general female interactions, are often characterized by a negative, competitive urge. What one woman lacks and the other possesses can lead to destructive impulses. Mother-daughter competitions can be understood in the adult woman's fear of aging in a patriarchal culture when compared to the youthful appearance of daughters (Hooks, 2002).

Furthermore, the hazy boundaries between mother and daughter in enmeshed families provide a scenario for great emotional turmoil and possibly the development of narcissistic character traits in the daughter. According to psychoanalyst Heinz Kohut's (1984) self-psychology constructs, narcissistic needs develop along the two lines of grandiosity and idealization. The grandiose part of the adolescent perceives itself as the powerful and entitled center of the universe. The young person, experiencing a degree of freedom and decision-making power that is beyond the person's true level of maturation, most likely will encounter difficulties in relationships outside the family circle. In interactions with both authority figures and peers the young person will insist on privileges not commensurate with the status of an adolescent but borrowed from the mother's status across the hazy boundaries of the enmeshed relationship.

The topic of mother-daughter relationships has intrigued writers and social scientists alike. Those exploring the lives of mothers and daughters from a psychoanalytic framework tend to focus on the daughters' unconscious internalization of their mothers' values and behaviors for deriving meaning for their own lives. Social learning theorists, on the other hand, emphasize the influence of reinforcement that daughters receive when they imitate the behaviors of their mothers.

Nancy Chodorow (1978), in her book *The Reproduction of Mothering,* incorporated traditional psychoanalytic concerns and social thought in her explanations on how mothers and daughters engage throughout their lives in *personal* identification, as opposed to *positional* (more characteristic of mother-son relationships) identification. In general, sons are more likely to change parts of their primary relationship with their mother as they switch to their fathers for establishing their identity. In contrast, daughters continue to identify with the care-giving mother.

And, as already mentioned, there are situations where mothers identify with their daughters. In their book *Understanding Women*, Luise Eichenbaum and Susie Orbach (1983) point to factors that define this type of mother-daughter relationship. The mother has reproduced herself in the daughter and may have difficulty differentiating herself from the daughter both in behavior and emotions. A detailed exploration of the various theories focusing on this important topic goes beyond the scope of this book. The brief discussion here is introduced in the interest of facilitating a general understanding.

"The Ballad of the Harp-Weaver" is the title of the poem Edna St. Vincent Millay dedicated to her mother. Edna was 30 years old when she wrote the poem, and was realizing the role her mother had played in her life. For Cora Buzelle Millay there was neither time nor money to pursue her musical and literary interests as a young girl. Cora's mother died early, leaving Cora with the responsibility for her younger siblings. Later, following several years of marriage, Cora raised her three daughters as a single parent. It was her goal to provide them with an atmosphere of independence and creativity as well as the opportunity to excel. And it was Cora who read in a magazine article about a poetry contest. Although Edna's poem did not win a prize, it received notice and was praised in *The New York Times*, eventually leading to Edna's admission to Vassar (Milford, 2001). Thus started the life of the first woman to win the Pulitzer Prize in poetry at the age of 31 years.

Determined to inspire the desire for accomplishment, excellence, and performance in her daughters, Cora might have pushed them too hard and too early. Edna, the oldest of the three daughters, might have felt cheated out of her childhood and tried to cling to it way into adulthood in the complicated relationship with her mother. But "Cora Millay had given her daughter a princely heritage, the will and the need to be a poet; that Edna felt her mother would have paid with her life's blood for her daughter's chance was part of the burden she had to bear" (Dash, 1988, pp. 126–127).

In poems and essays, Adrienne Rich has written about female writers who had come before her in her search to define herself. Her book *Of Woman Born* (1986) tells about her mother, who had been a young woman of remarkable talent, determination, and independence, and who had been engaged for 10 years to a young man in medical training. They got married, and, as the wife of a professor of medicine, she was expected to abandon her musical career and submit her life to her husband's professional pursuits. According to Adrienne, her mother was intimidated by her husband and felt unable to measure up to his expectations. Having produced only daughters was apparently already a major failure on her mother's part. Adrienne felt betrayed by her mother, because it seemed to her that when the mother carried out disciplinary actions that the father had ordered, her mother had chosen her father over Adrienne.

Her feelings of having been betrayed found an expression in her deep-seated competition with her mother. At the birth of her own son, Adrienne felt triumphant over her mother; the son represented Adrienne's badge of victory over her mother who had only given birth to daughters. Indulgence in this tragic and unnecessary kind of rivalry constitutes an act of pronouncing females as second-class citizen, including Adrienne and all other women. With that attitude Adrienne—although in competition with her mother—continued her mother's submission to males and invalidation of her own gender.

Sadly, Rich is not alone in her downgrading of female offspring. A survey conducted by Sanford and Donovan in 1984, interviewing a group of married women, revealed that the number of women admitting preference for giving birth to boys was twice that of women wanting daughters. Preference for producing sons may pose a problem for women, as their sex chromosomes consist of XX and they don't have the Y chromosome that is essential to produce male offspring. Whether a future husband will be a good and viable Y-chromosome donor is a question difficult to answer when making the decision to marry a man. The slipper in his hand may not reveal this genetic piece of information.

Just as Rich felt betrayed by her mother when the mother carried out disciplinary actions prescribed by Adrienne's father, so Lois in Chapter 3 felt betrayed by her mother, who refused to listen to and believe the daughter's report of having been sexually molested by the mother's father. Psychotherapists working with women hear many accounts of wonderful and healthy mother-daughter relationships. They also hear about competitive and even abusive mother-daughter scenarios. Those stories, however, the daughters relate more hesitatingly. The cultural romanticizing of motherhood to the point of sanctity leaves some daughters afraid or ashamed to reveal the lack of their mothers' love for them, because they fear that they will be judged harshly for that. There must be something wrong with the daughters if their own mothers don't love them. Similarly, at times the mothers are the targets of blame when the daughters don't meet the right prince, because mothers should teach daughters what to look for in a prospective husband. It is important not to demonize mothers, but it is equally important to treat daughters who have been victims of an unhealthy parent-child relationship with compassion and understanding.

Chesler (2001) made an interesting observation. She found that, on an unconscious level, most women expect other women to mother them. When other women fail to meet their idealized expectations they feel betrayed. The supposedly good fairy godmother becomes a dreaded evil stepmother in the mind of the disappointed woman. Interpreting this observation, one could guess that the disappointed woman's relationship with her own mother was far from being the ideal mother-daughter relationship. Why else would she need to look for the "good godmother" in the women around her? Her own biological mother may have failed the test.

And then there are situations that complicate the already difficult mother-daughter relationship even further, as might have occurred in the first half of the 20th century in the lives of the painter Vanessa Bell and her daughter Angelica. Angelica married David Garnett, a friend and former lover of Duncan Grant, her biological father and the lover and long-time companion of her mother. One is reminded of a more recent situation, Woody Allen's marriage to the girl Mia Farrow, his previous partner, had adopted. What emotional turmoil might Vanessa and Mia have experienced at their daughters' choices, and how did the daughters relate their selection of a husband to their relationships with their mothers?

The complications of mother-daughter relationships in real life are much more difficult to resolve than in the fairy tales of our childhood. The biological mothers of Cinderella, Snow White, or even Hänsel and Gretel were mute or died conveniently before problems raised their ugly heads in the thus-far harmonious setting of the tale. It was the appearance of the stepmother on the scene that added the sinister ingredients for making the story interesting. Stepmothers were mean and nasty, usually contemplating the demise or ill fortune of their predecessor's children. But stepmothers became a vital part of fairy tales because, as they could be blamed for all the evil doings, they provided the necessary tension and suspense without damaging the sacred concept of motherhood. And as we know from the Cinderella tale, stepsisters performed a similar function.

SISTERS: SIBLING RIVALRY?

Interpreting competition of sisters, Tracy (1991) suggested that Cinderella and her stepsisters were competing not for the prince, but rather for the love and protection of a fairy godmother. As Tracy explained, Cinderella wins the prince with the godmother's help. But the stepsisters, who are without the godmother's help, remain ugly no matter what they do to attract the prince. And the stepsisters' real mother, suggesting the girls cut off their toes to fit into the slipper, does not seem to match the notion of a fairy godmother.

When sisters compete like that, Tracy continued, it is for the love of a magical, idealized mother. Tracy's interpretation of the competition in the Cinderella fairy tale and Chesler's observation that women seek motherly attention from other women both point to some women's dissatisfaction with or disappointment in their relationships with their biological mothers, confirming the conflicted nature of some mother-daughter relationships.

Sibling relationships are difficult to describe because of their complexity. Susan Scarf Merrell (1995) called them "relationships without rules." Sibling relationships undergo many changes over the years of the siblings' development from young childhood to adulthood. Friends of siblings enter and exit their lives during the growth process, leaving their marks on the intimacy that is the siblings' unique bond, a bond that may last until one of them dies.

The relationship between writer Virginia Woolf and painter Vanessa Bell was by some considered to be very close, but others point to complications resulting from Vanessa's envy of Virginia's talents. Although envying Virginia, Vanessa also wanted to control her (Coates, 1998). Apparently it was Vanessa who arranged Virginia's first psychiatric hospitalization. But as two young women they were a powerful combination, according to Leonard Woolf, Virginia's husband.

He described them as beautiful, intelligent, and eccentric. They wore white dresses and large hats, and carried umbrellas to protect them from the sun. Their beauty was literally breathtaking. Looking at them, the observer stopped breathing for that moment as if stunned by the sight of a painting by Rembrandt or Velazquez in some gallery. Although they were equal in beauty, their personalities were quite different. Vanessa was passionate and vivacious, a strong contrast to Virginia's cool and more reserved nature. Whatever their differences might have been, as a mature woman, Virginia wrote to Vanessa "without a doubt, I love you more than any other person in this world" (Sello, 1994/2000, p. 30).

Then as now, the tensions below the surface experienced by same-gender siblings often take on different forms from those found in mixed-gender sibling relationships. In the struggle of establishing their individual identity and attempting to camouflage competitive strivings, siblings act out scenarios in their own characteristic ways. The bride's bouquet may have been the symbolic representation of the sisters' relationship. The guests at Annette's wedding reception noticed some unusual occurrences during the celebration. The maid of honor, Annette's sister Alice, was not dressed to match the bridesmaids' gowns. Complementing the mother of the bride's darker green gown, the bridesmaids wore dresses in a light green color, whereas Alice's gown differed significantly both in color and style. Alice appeared in an elaborate crème-colored gown with lacy puffed sleeves and a hint of a train. The color of her gown was so light that it almost looked white. She had two red roses fastened in her hair on one side of her head. She looked stunning; initially, some of the bridegroom's guests, who did not know Annette well, mistook her for the bride—and that might have been exactly what Alice had intended.

Most of the guests did not realize that the mother of the bride was embarrassed; besides, it was too late to do anything about it. Annette saved the moment by thanking her sister for the support she demonstrated in choosing a gown so similar in color to Annette's bridal gown. Their mother was not sure she could trust her ears, casting a questioning glance at her son Arthur, who had just joined his two sisters. Remembering how Alice had tried to persuade her parents to intervene in Annette's wedding plans, the mother gave Annette a big hug of relief.

In Alice's opinion, Annette was much too young to get married. But the wedding plans proceeded. Alice was away at college and too busy with her studies; she could not involve herself in the plans other than insisting on designing her own gown. Although their mother felt uneasy about it, Annette begged her to let Alice have her will. She wanted her sister to be happy at her wedding. With the condition for Alice not to choose a dark color for her gown, the mother gave in. She needn't have worried about the darkness of the color.

It was too early to relax; the show was not over yet. As father and daughter did their traditional dance, Alice crossed the dance floor, cutting in on them, telling Annette that she had had enough attention. Their father seemed surprised but Annette quickly stepped aside to let her sister take over. As the oldest of three siblings, Alice had gravitated to her father during their childhood. She had asked him to teach her to fish and to throw and catch a ball. He enjoyed her eagerness to have him for her mentor. Alice took over the place that normally would have been Arthur's position. With two older sisters, Arthur's self-confidence did not develop as well as his parents had hoped. He spent many hours in his room reading.

Luckily, the guests had not heard Alice's words to Annette and assumed that the change in the dance had been planned. When it came time for the bride and groom to leave for their honeymoon and to toss the bride's bouquet, there was yet another change. Instead of tossing the bouquet, Annette had untied it. She handed the first flower to her mother, the next one to the groom's mother, and the remaining flowers each to one of the bridesmaids. There was none left for Alice.

Had Annette counted the flowers and given the first two flowers to both mothers with the intent that none would be left for Alice? Had Annette recognized that Alice had been trying to direct the limelight away from Annette on her wedding day? If she did, she might have decided that, although she still remained the target of Alice's control attempts, she could influence the outcome to some degree and thus render Alice's goal incomplete. Perhaps her childhood memories took on a different meaning as she silently counted the flowers in the bouquet.

Alice had been two-and-a-half years old when her sister Annette was born; two years after Annette, Arthur arrived. Almost a year after Annette's birth, Alice developed asthma. A lot of the attention that would normally have been given to the baby became refocused on Alice's condition. Following Arthur's birth, Alice's condition worsened. Annette adored her older sister; she seemed mesmerized by her. Alice could be very sweet to Annette if it served her purposes. Alice enlisted Annette to turn Arthur into a "cry baby," but when their parents noticed his crying, it always looked as if Annette had been the culprit.

While their parents were around Alice was the best babysitter. She played with her younger siblings, fed them, and seemed to watch over them. As soon as the parents turned their backs, Alice became their boss and teased them. When Alice was alone with Arthur she turned the charm on him. Over the years she became quite accomplished, playing one sibling against the other. In school she excelled by sheer willpower; she had to be the best. Her parents were proud of her, although her mother had some uncomfortable moments when she overheard snippets of conversations among her children. It seemed that Alice was making all the rules in the children's play; but she tried to explain it away as being part of the particular game they were playing.

Following Annette's birth, Alice might have experienced the threat of abandonment. Up to that point she had received all her parents' attention. She had been the little princess; now she was about to be dethroned. She could not let that happen. When Arthur was born, Alice's anxiety about losing her parents' love seemed to have flared up again, resulting in a worsening of her condition. Annette, on the other hand, did not have a special position to guard. The limelight of her birth had to be shared with the concern over her sister's illness. But the admiration of her sister prevented Annette from developing strong feelings of envy and kept her from competing with Alice. Perhaps it was the possibility of competition among siblings that prompted their parents to give all three of them names that started with the first letter of the alphabet.

As a firstborn, Alice most likely experienced feelings of anger and resentment toward the newborn interlopers. She realized that her parents would be angry with her if she did anything to upset or threaten her younger siblings and cleverly found ways to make it appear that Annette had teased Arthur to the point of crying. Poor Alice could not afford to relax.

For Annette, in a way, her wedding day was saddened because she lost the sister she had adored for so many years. It would take more than time to reestablish a workable balance in their relationship. In his own way, Arthur had rendered a clever description of the wedding scene when a young female relative of the groom asked him about Alice. Without changing his tone of voice or his facial expression, Arthur calmly responded: "oh, that is my oldest sister Alice. Our parents misspelled her name; they forgot the 'M.'"

A different type of sibling relationship was experienced by Bronya and Marya Sklodovska, two sisters out of five siblings born to hard-working schoolteachers in Warsaw, Poland in the second half of the 19th century (Kerr, 1994). Marya, or Marie as she was later called, was the youngest sibling. She believed serving her country was more important than marriage. Her idea of serving was to educate the poor so that they would be less vulnerable to domination. She joined the Floating University, an underground community of Polish scholars who were dedicated to educating people beyond high school so that they could go on to teach others.

Regarding their own education the two sisters made a pact: Marie would work in a permanent job as governess to enable her older sister Bronya to attend medical school. After Bronya's graduation, the roles would be reversed, with Marie entering the university with Bronya's help. Marie's boyfriend had been too timid to marry against his parents' wishes; disappointed, Marie terminated the relationship and joined Bronya in Paris, who was now a doctor and ready to help Marie with her studies at the Sorbonne. Although determined never to marry after her first disappointment, she met the physicist Pierre Curie and eventually became known to the world as Marie Curie, a Nobel Prize winner—as discussed in Chapter 4.

What happens when sisters are too close mentally and emotionally? Amanda and Anita were just 15 months apart in age. Their parents, especially the mother, treated them as twins; their names were similar, (as in the case of Alice, Annette, and Arthur above), they were dressed alike, and they went to the same events together, from birthday parties for their little friends to sports and dancing and music lessons. Amanda, as the older one, was used to having Anita around wherever she went. Over the years the two girls came to feel like half of one person; actual identical twins could not have been any closer than Amanda and Anita. There was no sibling rivalry between them; they formed a union, somewhat separate from their other siblings and without an individual identity. Both girls were excellent students. In school, just as at home, their closeness was reinforced by their teachers' encouraging statements and by other students' snide remarks.

Amanda was the first to go away to college. Her good grades had earned her a scholarship at a prestigious school in another state. At first, her mother had hoped that both sisters would enter college together, but that would mean a waiting period for Amanda, and the scholarship was just too great an opportunity to pass up. So it was agreed that Anita would apply to the same college when her time came to graduate from high school. However, those plans never materialized. With Amanda's leaving both sisters experienced an identity crisis. Initially, Amanda had difficulties making friends in her new environment because she was so used to the comfort of being with Anita. With time she managed to adjust, but when she entered into dating relationships with young men, her involvement with them became more intense than those young men had expected. Having experienced several disappointments, Amanda decided to refrain from dating altogether—at least, until graduation.

Anita had an even harder time going on alone. The other girls in high school had formed friendships without her, remembering her close relationship with Amanda. Emotionally isolated, Anita started to date some of her male classmates. Similar to Amanda away at college, Anita searched for romantic bonding much too intense and emotionally intimate for that age. Her disappointment with the high school boys turned Anita to search for close relationships with young men beyond high-school age. Following several stormy affairs, Anita married Jeff, a mechanic with no college aspirations. Her parents were upset by this union, but Anita remained convinced that she had to lead her life in direct opposition to Amanda in order to become free of the strong bond of their past. It seemed important to get married while Amanda was still in college and planning for graduate school.

Anita's marriage turned out as disastrous as her parents and siblings had predicted. Once married, Jeff made no attempts to control his temper outbursts and his disenchantment over being married was expressed in physical abuse toward Anita. On family visits she tried to hide her bruises and made excuses for Jeff's absence on those occasions. One morning Anita failed to show up for work. A coworker, who knew a little about Anita's unhappy marriage, called her at home. After several rings Anita responded to the call in a voice that reflected her incapacitated condition. The coworker drove to Anita's home, and when she realized the need for emergency treatment she called an ambulance and contacted Anita's parents. The divorce did not take long, and soon Anita was enrolled in a college in her hometown. But her relationship to her family, and especially to Amanda, remained strained for quite some time.

In the meantime, Amanda found the man she would later marry. Within a year's time, however, her happiness seemed threatened by her clingy behavior. She didn't like it when Pete, her husband, went out to meet with friends once a week. It made her feel abandoned. Similarly, if he watched a TV show that was of special interest to him but not so to Amanda, she felt neglected. Amanda was puzzled; she had regarded herself as an independent person. Why was she so emotionally needy? Amanda had thought that she had resolved her identity crisis when she left the close relationship with Anita. But the need for emotional closeness that developed over the many years of her childhood had been strong; it was still there smoldering under the surface. Although living apart, the boundary problems were still alive in the sisters—hidden under rebellion and competition in Anita's case and engulfing Pete's life in Amanda's case. The intense intimacy of their childhood had been transferred to romantic partners. Both sisters had extreme difficulty viewing themselves as total individuals who could share with others but did not need to devour or be devoured by others.

In her therapy sessions Amanda has recognized the foundation of her "clinginess" in her marriage, and she is working on differentiating and establishing herself as a complete and unique individual, assuming her own space and releasing Pete to do the same. She is looking forward to the day when she and Anita can discuss the past and present parts of their relationship in a calm and supportive manner that will lead both of them to claim and respect their separate lives within the loving framework of their families.

WOMEN'S FRIENDSHIPS

The idealization of "sisterhood" promises deep and meaningful bonding between women and is something that many women might aspire to. But in reality, sister-sister relationships are often negatively affected by primitive hostilities and competition. Women who have not experienced the ideal sister-sister relationship may look toward other women in friendship to replace what they missed in their childhood. That is how best friendships among adult women sometimes resemble sibling relationships and can lead to similar rivalries as well as emotional closeness, as between biological siblings.

With the longing for an emotionally close friend there is also the fear of possible betrayal or abandonment by that friend. After all, as discussed in earlier chapters, the fairy tales of our childhood did not include female friendships. And even women who value their women friends sometimes put them second and their men friends first. It seems more important to respond to a call from a male than a female. This is especially true when the male friend is a romantic man friend. Thousands of female-female dates have been broken over the years when a man called and proposed to take one of them out on a date. This can occur on very short notice and it reinforces again and again the notion that, for a woman, spending time with a man is more important, more satisfying, and more enjoyable than being in the company of another woman.

As pointed out by Kolbenschlag (1979), women's priorities in relationships are determined by the conventional female role. "Friendship with a woman is sustained only when it does not conflict with or threaten the important male relationship. Every woman knows what it is to be 'ditched' on an evening by a female friend, when that significant 'One' phones and asks her out" (p. 54).

Apparently, a different type of friendship was that of writers Winifred Holtby and Vera Brittain, which began in 1920 and ended in 1937 at Winifred's death. They worked together, and they understood what it meant to place work above all else. Their friendship developed in mutual defense in each other's behalf. They encouraged each other to reserve space and time of their own. Even after Vera's marriage, Winifred helped her in the struggle to maintain herself against the traditional opinion that domesticity must be the first concern of wife and mother. For herself, Winifred "saw a conventional woman's life as a price not worth paying to indulge a passion for young men, or for the social assurance marriage offered" (Heilbrun, 1988, p. 107).

Telling a friend that she is valued like a sister is the best compliment given to the friend, and considering one's sister one's best friend is an equally complimentary statement. There are friendships that last as long as sibling relationships, and some sibling relationships are as close as the link between best friends. In general, regarding the characteristic of emotional support between female dyads, it is expected to be more prevalent in dyads of friends than in sister dyads.

Examining dyadic relationships between same-gender friends and siblings and mixed-gender friends and siblings, it was found that for female friend and female sibling dyads there was no difference along the factor of emotional support given or received. This was not true for the male dyads. Male dyads showed more practical but less emotional support than female dyads (Voorpostel & van der Lippe, 2007; Voorpostel, & Blieszner, 2008).

These studies involved a Dutch national sample of more than 6,000 participants containing various relationships with siblings and friends. In spite of the large sample size, questions arise regarding the degree to which this study can be applied to the general population. As the sections on "Sibling Rivalry" and

"Women's Friendships" demonstrate, the number of variables operating in such relationships in actuality is far greater than can be managed in a study of this scope. Nevertheless, the study is an expression of the still-active public interest in dyadic relationships of these types and their complications and rewards, which have been reported throughout history.

FEMALE RELATIONSHIPS IN THE WORKPLACE

Women have learned to compete in the workplace as much as men do, but not as much with men as with other women. Unlike their competition in beauty contests or cooking contests at the state fair, in the workplace their competition with other females is not as obvious and open. Sometimes the competition takes the form of a power struggle; at other times, it may just be the passive version expressed through lack of assistance and help from the established ones to the newcomer.

Carolyn, a woman who had been promoted to director of the department she worked in, reported how her female secretary quietly but firmly resisted her politely expressed efforts of organizing the workflow. No such resistance was evident when the secretary worked for the previous male director who had thought nothing of yelling at her; he did not request anything of her, but rather commanded her to do what he thought was needed. The secretary never once rebelled or resisted under his direction. "The same woman who will work for a man with a towering ego might sabotage his female counterpart" (Chesler, 2001, pp. 351–352).

Robin J. Ely, professor at Columbia University, wanted to find out if women in top positions would treat other women more fairly in companies or businesses where there was more room at the top for women than in those agencies that subscribed to a patriarchal system, allowing only very few women to advance (1994). To explore her hypothesis, Ely compared women's working relationships at sex-integrated law firms, which had many women partners, with male-dominated firms by interviewing subordinate women in both types of companies.

The investigator found that at the sex-integrated firms both junior women and subordinates rated the female partners in positive ways. But at the large, male-dominated law firms, subordinate women did not approve of the senior female partners and gave them negative ratings. According to Ely, male domination in the workplace and the consequent tokenism for women bring about many of the difficulties that women experience with each other at work.

Studies about female work relationships are complicated because of the tendency to deny interpersonal problems due to competition. In studying a woman-owned business, Paige Edley (2000), professor of Organizational and Interpersonal Communication at Bowling Green State University, found that women "silenced themselves" on aspects of disagreement and differences in opinion as well as in creativity. They described their relationships with each other as nurturing ones and any negative feelings they may have experienced were explained in terms of PMS (premenstrual syndrome).

Perhaps the most devastating weapons women use against other women are those of gossip, spreading rumors, and ostracism. These tactics are often hidden for a considerable period of time, and the victims are unable to defend themselves against this indirect form of aggression until it is too late. When rumors have grown sufficiently large that they become the self-evident truth in the public opinion, denying them will become an unsuccessful task.

Beverly, a registered nurse in her early 30s working at a hospital with a Christian affiliation, had applied for promotion to supervisor of nurses in her department. The hospital administration was in favor of in-house promotions, and several of her colleagues were interviewed for the same supervisory position. A few months ago Beverly had suffered a miscarriage, probably as a result of her husband's physical abuse of her. This had been her first and eagerly awaited pregnancy. She did not confide in anyone at work about her husband's violent temper. As the miscarriage initiated considerations of possible divorce in her, she hoped that a position with new responsibilities would distract her from the painful memories of the loss of her baby.

Beverly did not get the promotion. The administrators chose Rosie, another nurse among those that had applied for the supervisor position. Beverly's marriage did not improve and she filed for divorce. Only weeks after her divorce was final Beverly was called into the administrator's office. He explained to her that due to budget cuts her job, along with some others, had to be eliminated. Beverly's question about another job within the hospital was met with the administrator's expression of sincere sadness about having to let her go without a placement elsewhere in the hospital. Beverly obtained employment at another hospital some distance away.

Almost two years later she attended a conference for continuing education credits to maintain her professional certification. During the lunch break she ran into a former coworker from her previous workplace. The two women exchanged news about their own lives and those employees that Beverly still remembered. During their conversation the other nurse mentioned that she had left her job at the hospital to work for a group of physicians. But she remembered that there had been a rumor about Beverly's pregnancy. Instead of a miscarriage, the gossip suggested that it had been an abortion. "Who started that rumor?" Beverly wanted to know, but the other nurse said it was impossible to know. At the time of the promotion several of the nurses secretly had whispered about it. There had been some thoughts that Rosie, the nurse who received the promotion, might have been the source of the gossip, but nobody knew for sure. Now it was too late to do anything about it.

MENTOR—PROTÉGÉ

In 1950, at the 51st anniversary of the founding of the "Saturday Evening Girls" in Boston, 100 comfortably middle-aged, middle-class women gathered to honor the group's founder, 80-year old Edith Guerrier. The women were either immigrants themselves or children of immigrants. Guerrier, a librarian and daughter of an English immigrant, actively participated in the Americanization of individuals arriving from Eastern Europe in the second half of the 19th century. Edith, who chose to remain single, wanted to provide the immigrants with more than just survival skills. Starting as an aide in the nursery schools, supported at the time by philanthropist Pauline Agassiz Shaw, Edith later conducted meetings of girls' clubs, called the Saturday Evening Girls, in the settlement houses, maintained a reading room, and operated a Boston Public Library book delivery station (Matson, 1992).

This was the creation of a new kind of family, unconnected by ties of kinship, but instead made up of groups of women who provided economic and emotional support once supplied by traditional families. Combined with the use of the reading room and library services, it gave the women the opportunity for embarking on life-long careers, rather than just temporary jobs that would fill the time between school and marriage. When comparing these immigrant women to the general population, it was revealed that in 1910, out of the women in the 19- to 21-year age bracket in the United States, only 3.8 percent attended college; in 1920 that figure rose to 7.6 percent. But of the Saturday Evening Girls, 25 percent were enrolled in college or professional schools, and of the 48 children of Saturday Evening Girls alumnae, 40 attended college, demonstrating the legacy of Edith Guerrier's mentorship.

Mentor–protégé situations are encountered more frequently in academic settings. After retiring from her position, one female college professor remembered her observations of younger female colleagues who stumbled into traps laid for them by male faculty staff. While the young female teachers were kept busy participating in the projects of the male senior staff members, they had no research projects of their own to present when it came time for tenure considerations. The older female professor quietly and successfully avoided those pitfalls. She also avoided warning her younger female colleagues, whose contracts were not renewed (Maass, 2002/2006).

Female doctoral students who are assigned to female mentors may at times feel betrayed by them because they do not support them and their ideas as strongly and vigorously as the students might have expected. As Keller and Moglen (1987) pointed out, after years of enduring patronizing treatment and judgments from their more established male colleagues, these female mentors may not have felt powerful enough to offer stronger support to their female students. Returning to Phyllis Chesler's observation, perhaps unconsciously women might desire to be protected by a fairy godmother, which, in turn, might lead to unrealistic expectations of help and support from the female mentor. Anything that falls below those expectations could easily be interpreted as betrayal.

FIRST AND FUTURE WIVES

A special relationship between women that carries a great likelihood for hostility is that between the first and future wives of the same man. Ann Crittenden (2001), in her book *The Price of Motherhood*, discussed how easy it was for women to judge and blame other women who had been involved with and married the first women's husbands. In the "Great California Mommy War," the Coalition of Parent Support realized that fathers attempting to avoid increases in their child support payments would be less compelling and successful than if their second wives could be persuaded to argue the case. The women rose to the challenge and with tears in their eyes testified that the first wives with their children were depriving the second wives' babies of food.

Mothers took the stand against mothers. First wives regarded themselves and their children as victims of second wives when the husbands abandoned them after bearing and raising the husbands' children. They were tossed aside to make room for the new wife and her children. Similarly, second wives expressed their resentment toward first wives, complaining about the imagined luxuries the first wives enjoyed through the generous child support checks. The second wives "had married only to discover that the future was mortgaged by their husbands' prior procreations. They were taking out their rage and frustration not on their husbands but on a safer target, the other woman" (Crittenden, 2001, p. 173).

Nancy, an embittered, divorced woman, demanded babysitting money from her ex-husband's second wife, arguing that when Nancy's 16-year-old daughter visited her father and stepmother on weekends, she was left to baby-sit her young stepbrother while the father and second wife went out for several hours. Rita, the second wife, protested and claimed that Nancy was bleeding them mercilessly and left the new family hardly enough money to live on. If Nancy wanted money for the little time that her daughter was playing with her stepbrother, then Rita could charge her for the food Nancy's daughter consumed while at the second wife's home. After all, the child support checks from her husband were supposed to already take care of all the daughter's needs.

A different relationship developed between Ruth and Melanie, first and second wives of Larry. It began with Ruth's visit to Melanie's home after she had adjusted to the reality of being a divorced woman and mother of a very young daughter, Annabel. Ruth's intent was not to befriend Melanie; rather she wanted to personally know the woman in whose home her daughter would spend time on a more or less regular basis when visiting Larry. Ruth refrained from expressing any hostility toward Larry's second wife, and Melanie, highly pregnant with her first child, was able to understand Ruth's reason for the visit. In fact, she told Ruth that her baby would also be a little girl, and she hoped that Annabel and Rebecca, her expected daughter, would get along well during visitations. The two women were able to remain respectful of each other's position. As Ruth admitted, she had made that first step mainly to prevent additional hardships for Annabel.

Almost four years later, Larry had become involved in another extramarital affair and his new love was pregnant with a little boy. Whether it was the novelty of getting a son after having two daughters or the excitement over his new relationship, Larry divorced Melanie to marry her successor. During the divorce Ruth managed to support Melanie emotionally. She did not treat Melanie in a way that would imply Melanie deserved what she got because of what she did to Ruth. Ruth had progressed over blaming the "other woman" because she had made the attempt to get to know her. It was at this point that the two women developed a friendship, and, because their two daughters had formed a close sisterly bond, Ruth and Melanie insisted that Larry's visits with his daughters would occur on the same weekends. In other words, the two stepsisters would be less traumatized if their visits to their father and stepmother were scheduled as conjoint visits.

Discussing their adjustment to the divorces, the women came to compare the characteristics that had made Larry attractive to them. They both had liked Larry's easy-going attitude about life until they became victims of it. His decision-making skills had impressed both of them until they realized that most decisions were made in Larry's favor; that's why he could decide so swiftly. With the assistance of the therapist Ruth had consulted when Larry first brought up the divorce, the two women constructed something of a personality profile. They outlined those of Larry's features and characteristics that had contained elements of the "dangerous attraction" for them. That profile should help them in recognizing these elements in future dating prospects. As they reasoned, they both fell for a prince who did not act princely. The same could happen again if they did not learn from their past experiences.

Sadly, this story is a description of a rare occurrence. As pointed out by Crittenden, women are often too ready to blame other women for some of the betrayals that their husbands committed. Although the "other woman" may not be completely innocent in the betrayal of the erstwhile wife, the main responsibility belongs to the man who makes the decision to trade his wife for a (usually) younger model.

MOTHERS—STAYING AT HOME OR WORKING OUTSIDE THE HOME?

Hostility also exists between mothers in relation to each other even without ranking them into first, second, and other future wives. There is ample room for tension between two main categories of mothers, those that work and those that are stay-at-home mothers. Sometimes they feel sorry for each other, at other times they feel animosity for each other because each feels threatened by the very existence of the other.

Working mothers may feel judged for choosing work over the welfare of their children. Mothers who devote all their time to the care of their children may fear to be negatively compared to those who divide their time between motherhood and participating in the workforce. They might imagine working mothers and the rest of the world pointing the finger at them and what they might conceive of as their "laziness."

Confirmation of this animosity could be seen in Sarah Palin's Republican candidacy for vice president. There were women in the general public who criticized her strongly for what they interpreted as placing her career before her motherhood duties, in particular pointing out that her youngest is a "special needs" child.

Women have plenty of practice in valuing the approval of others. They do a lot for their mother's smile, their girlfriends' acceptance, and their boyfriends' attention. The image of their person is reflected in the behaviors of those around them. Women are trained in reading the faces of others like they would search for perceptions in a mirror. If the reflection in someone's face is not outright approval, it must mean something is wrong with them. Setting their own standards for themselves is difficult to do for many women. They are more used to reading their relative standing in society's opinion by comparing themselves to other women and their accomplishments. This comparison is especially painful in the area of motherhood. And the comparisons about one's mothering qualities do not stop between sisters or even between mothers and daughters.

Laura's mother had been a registered nurse who worked all the years of her two daughters' childhood. Laura's father had been severely injured in an accident and his wife had to deliver him to and from his workplace so that he could perform his job duties while safely seated in a wheelchair. Megan, Laura's older sister, admired their mother. She was proud of her mother's profession and, according to Laura, often bragged about it in school or with their friends. Not surprisingly, Megan followed in her mother's footsteps professionally. Laura felt neglected at home. Her mother was too busy to embark on special projects just with her, so Laura gravitated toward her maternal grandmother, who took her to her home during summer breaks from school. Megan remained with her parents during those times, except for briefer visits to the grandmother.

As expected, Megan became a registered nurse just like her mother. In due course she married and gave birth to three children. Her son Raymond was followed by a set of twin daughters, Rachel and Regina. Laura—although younger than Megan—married and gave birth to her first child, a daughter named Hannah, shortly before Megan's wedding. Laura did not pursue a profession but spent the few years prior to her marriage working as a secretary. She stopped working six months into her first pregnancy and devoted her time to preparing herself and her home for the arrival of little Hannah. Over the next three years Hannah was joined by two sisters—Eileen and Amber. A year and a half after the birth of Megan's twin daughters, Laura gave birth to her son, Alfred, junior.

Although financially not required, Megan returned to work—first on a part-time basis, and later full time; Laura remained a full-time mom. In terms of motherhood, Laura had outdone both her mother and her sister with the number of children she gave birth to. At first, Laura's mother thought that Laura might want to take care of Megan's children while Megan was at work, but Laura did not want to shortchange her own children by making the home a "daycare center" for her sister or anyone else. However, when Megan's children visited, they never left Laura's home without a generous package of home-baked cookies or home-made jellies and jams. She even sewed little decorative pillows for Rachel and Regina similar to the pillows she had made for her own daughters.

On family get-togethers Laura became the center of attraction due to the loads of homemade goodies she brought along. Laura basked in everyone's praise. Megan and Laura's parents were considering preparing for their retirement by purchasing a home in Florida. They were going to try it out for the summer months before actually moving there in a couple of years. They thought it would be a great opportunity for Megan and Laura to come down with their families and spend as much time as they could manage, with their jobs, living as one big family. Although grateful for their parents' generosity, Megan pointed out that the two sisters should take turns bringing their families down because it would definitely be too much for their parents to accommodate both families at the same time.

The mother was surprised by the firmness in Megan's voice and decided to probe deeper into Megan's reasons for her statement. In a mother-daughter talk somewhat later, Megan admitted that she was hesitant to expose her daughters to her sister's beliefs and opinions for an extended period of time. Megan herself would not be able to spend more than perhaps two weeks in Florida, and if she left her children behind, Laura's presence might distract her daughters from their determination to explore suitable careers for themselves. Megan added that she had overheard Laura's remarks about her opinion on motherhood. Laura believed that a mother needed to care for her children on a full-time basis until they had developed their own lives.

Megan felt judged by those remarks because she chose to divide her time between motherhood and her profession. Her mother understood because she had made a very similar decision in the past, although her continuing to work outside the home had been more of a necessity due to her husband's impairment. Megan's mother confided in her that at the time her own mother had frowned upon her decision, saying that if she had to drive her disabled husband to his job, that was enough time spent away from her children. If her husband's income was not sufficient for the family to live on, then they could all move in with Megan's grandparents. That's what family was for. However, Megan's mother did not want to give up her independence. She added that it seemed as though in every generation a daughter would choose for herself just about the opposite of what the mother had done. Nevertheless, Megan and Laura needed to respect each other's right to their own opinion.

Julia, a young woman and first-time mother, described her experiences when, reluctantly but also with a little bit of relief, she had located a respectable childcare center and returned to her full-time job after the birth of her son. Her husband worked full-time and studied law in the evenings. Julia realized that this was not a workable situation, and she negotiated for a part-time job with her employer. With this arrangement, Julia found herself living in two worlds. In the mornings at her job she was in contact with other women who worked full-time and left their children in the care of others, whereas in the afternoons she interacted with full-time mothers at playgrounds or in the neighborhood (Koenig, 2004).

In her contacts at her job with full-time working mothers, Julia detected some stereotyping, as some of these working mothers assessed the lives of stay-at-home mothers in terms of watching soap operas and being concerned with body weight issues while not producing much else. On the other hand, the full-time mothers Julia encountered in the afternoons seemed to regard the decisions of full-time working mothers to leave their children in the hands of strangers as tragic and insensitive to their children's needs.

Following the birth of her second child, Julia decided to give up her career and stay home full-time for the benefit of the family. At a point four years later, when her second child started to spend a few mornings in preschool, she reflected on her experiences, being grateful for the opportunities to exercise different choices along the way. No matter what choices women make in relation to work and motherhood, it would be best for all to respect the individual differences and share in the common bond of motherhood. Julia's sentiments found an echo in Leslie Morgan Steiner's introduction to her 2006 book *Mommy Wars*: "The two groups misunderstand and envy each other in the corrosive, fake-smiling way we women have perfected over the eons . . . Motherhood in America is fraught with defensiveness, infighting, ignorance and judgment about what's best for kids, family, and women—a true catfight among women who'd be far better off if we accepted and supported all good, if disparate, mothering choices" (p. x).

Leading a Self- or Other-Determined Life?

Historically, women have been defined within families, living and working within the parameters of family life, especially with emphasis on motherhood— implying that if they were not mothers or future mothers, they were nothing (Hoare, 1967). In contemporary society, women fulfill other social roles in addition to being a mother, but many regard the mother role as their primary role. In a study interviewing 1,200 parents, women identified themselves as mothers more often than identifying themselves by their occupation or by their marital status. Men, on the other hand, identified themselves not by their father role but by their occupation or marital status (Rogers & White, 1998).

THE "AMERICAN GIRL" ROLE MODEL

For countless generations, toy manufacturers have supplied many teaching devices instructing children about their future roles. Girls especially seem to be willing targets, as demonstrated by the long-lasting popularity of certain types of dolls. Barbie was the role model of yesterday, and her influence still lingers on. However, a new doll in a somewhat chubbier version, the American Girl, has made her appearance on the American scene with the suggestion to "follow your inner star"—as announced on the title page of the American Girl catalog (2008). Pictures and suggestions about how to do that are provided inside the catalog.

The catalog offers dolls from different historical periods and different cultural backgrounds, all supplied with appropriate wardrobe and accessory items. Little booklets telling the stories of the particular doll round out the package. In addition to the historical characters, there are dolls available that promise to be just like the little girl customer—or is it the other way around when the customer girls are encouraged to dress like the dolls?

The American Girl is quite active. She engages in sports, such as playing volleyball, tennis, golf, and soccer. She can become a cheerleader and she can skate and become a skating star as well as a singing star. Other activities include running a concession stand or perhaps thinking of being a reporter, supplied with appropriate outfits and informational booklets—all for a price, of course. Housewifely duties, such as cooking, baking, and doing laundry are not neglected by any means. As the dolls perform the function of role models for young girls, the culmination is the category of babies, with accessories and information on how to bring up a baby, or even twins. A changing table for the baby can be purchased for just $40, but additional items for comfort and convenience, such as a pad for the table and a storage cube, cost another $20.

Strangely enough, the American Girl did not have a wedding before becoming a mother, an oversight the manufacturers will surely remedy in time. The temptation for providing new booklets, fabulous outfits, and accessories for brides of various cultural backgrounds is too great to pass up. Besides, wouldn't it set a less than wholesome example for little girls to become mothers without experiencing the glory of having been a beautiful bride first?

TRANSITION FROM PREADOLESCENCE TO ADULTHOOD: A TIME OF LOSSES

Discussing this topic in a more serious vein, if motherhood is to be women's destination, how can girls make the transition from childhood to adulthood when they do not know what or who they are until motherhood? During adolescence young girls run the risk of losing or abandoning the selves that served them through childhood. It can be a time of disconnection or even dissociation, as girls at the edge of adolescence lose their vitality and resilience and become prone to mood swings and depression (Brown & Gilligan, 1992). With the cultural influences of the time, young girls who as children had been courageous and outspoken become reluctant to express their feelings, thoughts, and even their knowledge.

Young girls' experience of emerging adulthood has undergone some modifications. In recent decades, demographic changes in the timing of marriage and motherhood have had an impact on emerging adulthood. The average age of women entering marriage is now about four years older than it was in the 1950s (Arnett, 2000), demonstrating the existence of a link between adolescent future aspirations and their expected role timing, the time when they can be expected to assume the roles of wives and mothers. Young females with high aspirations for education and career plan the birth of their first children at a considerably later age than girls with less ambitious career aspirations.

One could argue that with postponement of marriage and motherhood until their late 20s, females have more time and greater opportunities for explorations of different life directions and therefore are in a position to make better choices for themselves. The question then arises as to how they put the additional time to use. If the overall societal influences about deferring their own wishes to those of others is still strongly embedded in their beliefs and value systems, are the young females really able to make the best choices for themselves?

According to psychologist Mary Pipher (1994), for many girls the period from preadolescence to adulthood constitutes a transition marked by the loss of precious traits, such as curiosity, resiliency, and optimism. They seem to trade in their previous energetic exuberance for submissive and moody rebelliousness, which results in a condition of uncertainty, hesitancy, and concern about what to do to please others. Despite the expanded time available for exploration of directions, for many females the concern about pleasing others lingers on through significant parts of their adulthood; it impacts career-making decisions and becomes a significant part of their role in life.

This situation was illustrated by female students ranging in age from 18 to 36 years who approached the university counseling center with complaints of depression and anxiety connected with their career decisions (Lucas, Skokowski, & Ancis, 2000). The problems reported by these young women ranged from wanting to please their parents by continuing in a major area of study that their parents had suggested (but that did not hold strong interest for the female students themselves) to difficulties in setting limits they experienced in their relationships with controlling boyfriends.

Transition periods are periods of unpredictability, uncertainty, turmoil, and lack of control when experienced without plans or appropriate guidance. This is especially true for the transition from adolescence to young adulthood. When young girls lose their curiosity, exuberance, and optimism they give up the very qualities necessary for exploring and determining their future. Their worldview becomes restricted to what little is right in front of them. The situation can be compared to a group of people living in a small ethnic neighborhood who restrict themselves to the limited culinary options available in the neighborhood restaurants, instead of venturing out and tasting the different foods at the tables of the world.

ADULTHOOD: A TIME OF CHAOS?

In discussing adaptations of a model based on chaos theory for life-transition counseling, psychologists Cori Bussolari and Judith Goodell (2009) related the case history of a 35-year-old woman (referred to here as Karen), who could have been one of the young women described by Pipher.

Following high school graduation, Karen was ready to study interior design at the local community college. Instead, she got married to Ted because she was pregnant. She did not feel ready to have a child and contemplated having an abortion. Ted, however, threatened to leave her if she got an abortion, and Karen gave in to his demands. Ted's future plans included college and law school, which he steadfastly pursued. Financially, the young couple was dependent on Ted's parents. But it was Karen who had to ask for money needed for their household. Ted could not be bothered with things like that.

Ted was no help with the household or the children because he needed all the time to make it through law school as fast as possible. In the meantime, Karen became increasingly more dependent on her mother for emotional support and on his parents for the money she needed for the family, which now included two children. Her friends from high school had gone off to college or taken interesting jobs. They did not have much in common with a homebound young woman with two children. Karen remained at home, bored and lonely.

After graduation from law school, Ted's excellent grades got him in with a prestigious law firm. He spent a lot of time in the office—one way to be noticed by his bosses for his dependability and hard work. Karen saw very little of him. Her vague ideas of taking night classes to see if she could slowly work on something related to her initial dreams fell by the wayside, because she could not count on Ted to be home with the children in the evenings.

As Karen described the next crisis in her life, one evening Ted came home and told her that he was divorcing her because they had nothing in common. Karen was stunned. She felt helpless, not knowing how she could go on alone with her two children. She decided to move in with her mother, who had just retired from her job.

As mentioned, the authors conceptualized the above case history within an adaptation to chaos theory. The theory was popular in the 1960s and 1970s and posits that events do not always occur in predictable ways. As a meaning-making model, chaos theory considers unpredictability, disorder, and lack of control as normal parts of the transition process. Individuals are viewed as potentially resilient and adaptive systems that are embedded in and interact with their environment in a way that promotes growth. As these systems develop new ways of behaving within a complex network of feedback loops, there is no possibility of determining cause and effect (Skar, 2004). Certainty and determinism in human behaviors constitute questionable elements in this framework.

Based on those formulations, chaos theory could lead to misinterpretations. It could be understood by some to let things happen, rather than to plan, and then adapt to events as they come along. This way of reasoning would be closer in meaning to other-determinism than most known theories. Furthermore, some events are difficult to adapt to, and true resilience might have been better expressed in avoiding involvement in the event. Cinderella and other fairy tales might seem closer to chaos theory than would be comfortable.

Long ago, what course of action would a good fairy godmother have suggested when Karen's prince presented his proposal? Perhaps he sincerely believed that abortion is a crime that he did not want to consent to. Although he had the right to his beliefs, he did not force Karen to marry him. And because Karen had considered the possibility of an abortion, her beliefs apparently were not the same as Ted's. On that basis she could have determined what would be best for her future: living within her own beliefs, or submitting to Ted's beliefs. Apparently, she chose Ted over her future professional plans, and with that she handed the determination of her fate over to Ted.

The fairy godmother might have encouraged Karen to look closer at Ted's proposal and what it entailed. There was no negotiation, just his demands—this might have been a very tight slipper, indeed. As the years went on, from Karen's report, it seemed that Ted was pursuing his plans without any consideration to her desires. The fairy godmother might have cautioned about conceiving another child by such a disinterested father and husband. With just one child, she could possibly have asked her mother to baby-sit while Karen could take classes or do something to improve her situation. With two children, however, she was ever-more dependent upon Ted and his decisions for her.

Perhaps chaos theory could be applicable in some part of women's lives, such as involving the general transition to motherhood. When it occurs, women in their resiliency are expected to adapt to it. The rules and standards for that condition are not for the young women to determine. Because children are thought to be sacred and immeasurably valuable, standards for mothering are socially prescribed (Hays, 1996). Thus, it is not left to the individuals who fulfill the mothering role to determine the standards for the care they are providing. They cannot be entrusted with this sacred responsibility; society determines what the role of mother consists of.

Children are so fragile that they need continuous mothering (Blair-Loy, 2003), which means that mothers need to be emotionally available and attuned to their children's needs (Belsky & Pasco Fearon, 2002). To comply with the criteria for social construction's ideal of motherhood, which Hays (1996) called *intensive mothering,* mothers must become self-sacrificing and cease to be persons with their own needs and interests. The implication of this ideology is that only women who stay home should be mothers (Bassin, Honey, & Kaplan, 1994).

For the purposes of this book, the issue about criteria for what constitutes good mothering is not the primary concern; valuable and detailed information regarding this topic is available in the relevant literature. It is, however, important—as the authors above pointed out—to realize that the standards for mothering are prescribed by society. If even the mother role is not determined by the woman, she may generalize this experience of not being allowed to decide her actions in this important sphere onto the rest of her life and refrain from seriously defining it the way she would want to.

Transition to parenthood constitutes a drastic change in people's lifestyles, and various emotional responses would be expected to accompany such events. Indeed, studies have revealed that parents, in general, were more depressed than childless people (Evenson & Simon, 2005). Although other studies found mixed results, it was noted that the parenthood studies neglected to address the experience of anger. Further investigation with a large, cross-sectional probability sample of participants, aged 18 to 90, confirmed that anger was an important issue. Mothers expressed significantly more anger than fathers or childless women and men (Ross

& Van Willigen, 1996). The researchers concluded that the psychological costs of parenthood apparently overshadowed the rewards—at least for women.

More recently, this finding was confirmed in a study tracking 577 university graduates for a period of seven years (Galambos & Krahn, 2008). The transition to parenthood was associated with anger for the participating individuals, but especially so for women. The reasons for the connection of anger and motherhood were stated as gender inequalities, such as economic strain and childcare responsibilities, which typically affect women more than men. These findings may indicate that the women entered into marriage without fully knowing the ranges of commitment to marriage and parenthood their husbands were agreeing to.

Expressing expectations and negotiating terms are prerequisites to marriage, as we have learned from Karen's story above. Saying "yes" to an unknown situation would be equal to accepting a shoe without knowing whether it fits, and it might invite a fair amount of chaos when the woman realizes the "mis"-fit.

THE FORGOTTEN SENSE OF SELF

While struggling with the stressors of adolescence, some of childhood's dreams and wishes may get pushed into the back of girls' memories. As these dreams don't fit in with the demands of current life situations, they become faint and fade into oblivion in the process of adopting conformity in response to cultural pressures. They become displaced by the more urgent demands for matching criteria of female attractiveness or attending to others. Later, after a period of abandonment of the self, they may awaken to a confession like the following:

"I had naively confused recognition of my youth and beauty with recognition of me . . . Like Sleeping Beauty, I had fallen into a trance around the age of fifteen from which I had spent my life perfecting the game of pleasing and attracting others (particularly men) and relying on my youth and looks to do this much more than I had realized or cared to admit" (Melamed 1983, p. 12).

Even when the trance lifts, for many girls it is a temporary arousal, as their wedding day and transition to motherhood offer additional opportunities for abandoning themselves. On her wedding day Lisa White becomes Mrs. Robert Black, and somewhat later she will be known as little Lisa and Robert Black Junior's mother. But there are moments for some women to regain their forgotten sense of self. Lost voices can return decades later, after dormant periods spent in detours and transformations while attempting to succeed at living the conventional life.

Many times this afternoon Susan walked back and forth the distance from their front door to a window at the other end of their house. She did not want to miss the first signs of her nephew's arrival. Her older brother's only child, Mathew, had married early and raised two children. Now that the children were away at college, Mathew and his wife Linda decided to visit friends and relatives on an extended trip through several states from Phoenix, Arizona to Allentown, Pennsylvania. Susan was ready for them, the guest bedroom and bathroom all freshly made up, and a special welcome meal prepared. But instead of the expected car, a motor home turned into her wide driveway and proceeded to park next to the garage.

"Dad used to tell me about the family vacations when you and he were children," Mathew explained after all the hugs and kisses were exchanged. "He remembered the fun when the whole family got packed into the car and you used to say that you wanted them to have a motor home and just keep on going wherever they wanted to. Grandfather teased you that you would need to find a husband with more money than he made because motor homes were expensive. Dad told me that he called you the 'family gypsy'—do you remember?" Mathew asked as he continued the story. "I thought that was a great idea and Linda and I are trying it out as our children are safely stashed away at college. While we are following a path from one set of relatives or friends to the next, we also allow for detours in between to explore sites that we are interested in or that catch our fancy as we go along."

Susan felt surprise, followed by sadness. Her childhood dreams had remained alive within the family, while in her own memory they had been pushed way back into the darkest corner. The dreams had not fit the lifestyle when she married Tom, whose goal it was to build his own business. It also did not seem appropriate for raising their children; they needed stability. Susan's children had left the house and settled in cities several hundred miles away—why hadn't she remembered her dream before Mathew and Linda arrived? Was it because Tom was still deeply involved in his business? How could she have let go of what once seemed so exciting and promising to her?

Childhood recollections can be understood and interpreted within the psychology of life stories, as proposed by McAdams (2001). Those recollections reflecting particular past situations that occurred at a particular time and place become self-defining or personal event memories. As they are later remembered, they evoke sensory images that contribute to the sensation of "reliving" the events and linking the details to particular moments of phenomenal experience within the one remembering.

Among the many types of event memories, some are influential in self-determination and carry symbolic messages that the individual interprets as generating or affirming a particular interest. At the time of encoding when the original event occurred, the memory selection was established according to the goals inherent in the interest or "dream." The original events may remain dormant for many years or decades, until suddenly a turning-point episode in the individual's life stirs up the self-defining memory (Pillemer, 2001).

Personal event memories often originate early in individuals' childhood years. Those years are characterized by the ability to develop passions with less distraction than later on in life. It is a time favorable for individuals to fall in love with an idea, a concept first introduced by researcher Paul Torrance at the University of Georgia to explain the process by which creative individuals select and focus on their life's work. Falling in love with an idea is not just the ability to identify an idea or subject that is personally exciting. It can be a lasting, absorbing interest that might ultimately lead to an expansion of that idea, unless it becomes buried in a distant corner of the individual's memory. Falling in love with an idea is not the exclusive domain of a creative genius; most individuals with an open mind and lively curiosity can experience those intense, passionate involvements with an idea or a dream. However, many peoples' lives are over-stuffed with television, with the Internet, and with information about many public spectacles, making it difficult for these personal event memories to surface.

Mathew's appearance with the motor home, and his reflection of Susan's childhood dream, created just such a turning-point episode, which triggered personal event memories in her. The notion of turning-point episodes and personal event memories fits in well with the idea of the individual being engaged in a process of becoming that has been outlined by humanist psychologists and envisioned with particular significance for women by Simone de Beauvoir, as expressed in her words at the beginning of Chapter 4. Thus, the awakening of the forgotten sense of self refers to a type of past impression that can be extremely useful to women for adjusting to the present and planning for the future of their lives.

At times it can be beneficial for the exploration of significant, personal event memories that have been pushed into the darkest corner to examine photographs taken at different occasions in the past. Searching a once-familiar face for cues about the thoughts and dreams expressed in those pictures can bring back memories not only on a cognitive level, but on an emotional basis as well. It is especially helpful to have several photographs from different times for comparison. For instance in Susan's case, she was able to study her facial expressions in several family photos and pictures of special events, such as graduation, birthday parties, her own wedding, and so on.

It was quite a surprise to observe the change in her facial expressions from the days of the little family gypsy to the young bride and proud and loving mother. Susan experienced a sadness looking at the different pictures—how much had she lost of herself, she wondered. But is it really too late to fulfill her childhood dream now? Her children are grown and her husband's retirement is soon becoming a reality. This might be the time for Susan to determine the next phase of her life, which is to begin with her husband's retirement.

TOO BUSY TO PLAN FOR A WOMAN'S LIFE

"Why does being a bride feel like going through a second adolescence? And why, over the last decade, has the wedding industry exploded into a hundred billion-dollar industry that sends increasing numbers of newly married couples into debt?" Those are questions asked by Kamy Wicoff in her 2006 book *I Do but I Don't: Walking Down the Aisle without Losing Your Mind*. The author used the event of her own wedding as basis for her inquiry. In the introduction to the book she realized that "a bride is not an individual woman, but an icon of womanhood;

a bride is not a person, but a thing" (p. ix). It took almost 300 pages to describe the process of getting the icon or thing to walk down the aisle to express her 'I do.'

The author's statement might be the answer to the title question of this chapter, whether women's attitudes about life are self-determined or other-determined. An icon or a "thing" does not determine anything—it just is. And, as discussed in earlier chapters, many young girls exist and wait for the prince to come by and notice them. Others may plan something such as a career, but they most often do so with wifehood and motherhood in mind. Fewer will focus on themselves and their interests from an early age on and continue the focus.

When Cinderella is chosen by the prince she automatically becomes his wife, a princess by marriage. Her behavior and her activities will be observed and evaluated within the framework of the role that is assigned to her—not only by the prince, but by everyone around her. Certain activities are expected of her as part of her role; some behaviors will be more or less sharply criticized, depending on how much they deviate from those prescribed for a person occupying this particular role. In fact, the role becomes the measuring stick against which all of Cinderella's behaviors are considered. As discussed earlier regarding the ideology of intensive mothering, the role defines the person—often without the young woman's full awareness.

THE VACUUM BETWEEN THE DIFFERENT ROLES IN A WOMAN'S LIFE

As stated before, young women's career choices are not always entirely focused on what their real professional interests may be; often, they are influenced to some degree by their future lives as mothers. Young women may sacrifice strong professional ambitions in favor of a particular job's ease of transitioning into part-time employment or taking a prolonged leave of absence as may be desirable for the fulfillment of motherhood responsibilities. When making that choice, the young women are probably convinced that their decision is the best for themselves and their families. Only years later does the earlier decision take on the resemblance of a sacrifice.

After graduating from high school, Sandra entered college as her parents suggested. She had enjoyed her acting performances in high school and thought about majoring in drama and literature, but, growing up in a family of pharmacists, pharmacology was a more appropriate choice in her parents' view. They wanted their two children to continue with the family business, and Sandra went along with her parents' wishes, although she was not excited about this choice. During her freshman year she met Peter, who was a senior with a major in business administration. Peter was a handsome young man, full of energy, who quickly won Sandra's parents' approval. They loved his friendly and helpful nature and somewhat reluctantly agreed to let Sandra drop out of college and obtain an office job in order to make some money to ease the financial burdens of marriage to a college graduate looking for his first job.

Everybody thought Sandra had made an excellent choice; Peter was success-ful in business and an excellent provider for Sandra and their two children. The business required frequent short travel, and Sandra quit her job after the birth of her first daughter. She took her roles as wife and mother seriously in the way she conceived of them. Sometimes she thought it would be easier to raise a daughter and a son instead of two daughters. With two girls the element of competition was an ever-present possibility, and she saw it as her responsibility to raise happy, well-adjusted children and provide a harmonious family atmosphere.

Peter loved his family; he was a devoted father and the two girls adored him and the fun activities he arranged for them. Despite his frequent travels, he man-aged to be at home for the weekends, holidays, and most evenings during the week. But there were also opportunities for sexual escapades with people in the towns his business took him to. His notion of the role of a husband was not affected by these adventures; after all, he provided well for Sandra and the girls and he was always there when they needed him. However, Sandra's conception of a husband's role included more than Peter was ready to supply: she expected hon-esty and fidelity. When she realized that those expectations were not fulfilled, she withdrew emotionally from Peter.

Sandra did not confide in her friends but learned from their discussions regarding other marriages that the general consensus about straying husbands focused on the possibility that their wives might not be attractive or interesting enough as sex partners for their husbands. Sandra was attractive, she worked hard to keep her slim figure, and she was interested in sex. What was missing in her? Finally, she approached Aunt Meredith, her father's sister, for advice. Meredith had been married twice but both marriages remained childless. Her first husband had died suddenly in an accident after just three years of marriage, and her sec-ond husband, after 20 years of marriage, succumbed to a long battle with cancer. Since then Meredith had been working part-time in her brother's pharmacy. Sandra felt especially close to this aunt and trusted her to have more experience with husbands and marriages than she herself had.

Meredith was sad for her niece's disappointment and left her with the advice that one had to make some allowances for straying husbands if they were otherwise acceptable, especially when there were children involved. Did Aunt Meredith experience betrayal from her husbands? Sandra wondered, but before she could manage enough courage to ask her, Meredith, who was quite a bit older than Sandra's father, died.

Aunt Meredith's statement left Sandra to wonder which of her roles was the most important one. It seemed obvious that she had failed as a wife because Peter went outside the marriage for some of his needs, and she herself did not feel ful-filled in that role either. However, if she left Peter, she would deprive her daugh-ters of the daily presence of their father. With that she would also fail in her role as mother. Sandra decided to remain married to Peter. On the outside her life was picture perfect: With her charming and successful husband and two pretty young daughters, she lived in a beautiful, grand house, tastefully furnished and supplied with all conceivable conveniences. The family played a prominent part in the community. In due course, the daughters graduated from college, married acceptable young men, and moved away, too far for daily visits but reachable during weekend trips.

Sandra felt lonely and empty inside. She had been hiding her depression from friends and neighbors, but in those solitary hours alone in her house and garden she was confronted with what felt like a different person, a stranger that looked vaguely familiar but seemed so disconnected from the vivacious girl from long ago. Where had that girl disappeared to? Would she ever come back and move into the vacuum Sandra felt within herself? Although on the surface Sandra's daily life seemed harmonious, without great upheavals interrupting the flow, her dreams became more vivid and somewhat unsettling. She experienced very detailed scenarios in her dreams, filled with colors and shapes and movements that seemed to spin out after a while and leave everything flat, colorless, and empty at the end. There were people in her dreams, but before she could recognize them they, too, faded away. Usually she woke up from these dreams feeling that she had been in friendly environments that became deserted, and that she had lost something precious.

Like most people, Sandra believed in the symbolic meaning of her dreams. However, the harder she tried to describe her dream experiences and to put the details of the content into words, the more it became nebulous and blurry in her memory. The harder she tried to decipher the symbolism, the more elusive it became.

A rather recent contemplation of dream theories, which seems to be a departure from the traditional views of disguised meaning and symbolic language in dreams, suggests that dream images are difficult to understand because we are looking for symbolic metaphors when indeed they are self-evident (Jennings, 2007). The *self-evident dream theory* proposes that the dream's details are expressions of the dreamer's experiences and psychological issues, the direct embodiment of the dreamer's personality. As such, the embodied meaning includes three aspects: the cognitive/semantic aspect, the visual image aspect, and the sensual/emotive aspect. In other words, searching for the symbolic meaning, as Sandra attempted to do, made her focus on the cognitive/semantic aspects of the dream's image, which pushed the other two aspects of the embodied meaning— the visual image and its sensual/emotive qualities—into the background.

In Sandra's dreams, the colorful, moving images filled with people she did not recognize presented her life as a young girl turning into womanhood with the activities she engaged in while fulfilling various roles in her life. With passing time these roles were shrinking and fading away—along with the people that had been associated with them. The sphere of her existence had turned into a colorless vacuum as the different roles disintegrated. The vacuum was the space where her own role for herself, defined by herself, was supposed to be. Being busy with performing according to the roles defined for her by others in her environment, she never recognized the need for setting up criteria and goals that pertained only to her.

Using a quote from Eleanor Roosevelt: "The future belongs to those who believe in the beauty of their dreams," Nancy Pelosi, Speaker of the House, addressed America's daughters regarding the beauty of dreams without limits and the power within each of us. Upon her election to the Democratic leadership, she received many congratulatory messages from women and girls around the world but also many from fathers of daughters, who perceived her success as opening new opportunities for girls. It is the recognition of the power within us that provides us with choices, and when we know our power, others will know it, too, according to Pelosi (2008).

FOLLOWING HER OWN SENSE OF DESTINY

Losing one's self-determining dreams is not a genetically determined condition, linked to women's double-X chromosomes; it is more of an environmental condition, a learned effect. There are women who—from childhood on—have a sense of themselves and their future goals that will give meaning and direction to their lives, and they hold on to that sense.

For Joyce Treiman, identity development started in early childhood. She realized as a child that her destiny was to be an artist (Pomeroy, 1999). Her revelation came when she tried to draw items she saw in her environment and her drawings looked a lot like those items. At the time it seemed like a miracle to her. With her parents' and her teacher's encouragement she followed her destiny. Her life was devoted to her paintings—her own and those of others.

In her own works she developed a particular way of placing art and artists from the past in a contemporary context, making her paintings into philosophical and psychological commentaries on the nature of human existence. Her creations did not fit into any particular art movement. She considered her work to be her life as well as her autobiography, asking only that it should be meaningful.

The European art world of the 19th century distinguished between "painting" (professionally done, and mostly by men) and "feminine visual culture" (middle-class women's artwork of amateur status), which tended to be submerged in a marginal area on the periphery of a dominant patriarchal culture (Higonnet, 1992). The difference between these categories "made the difference between entering and becoming part of art history and being ignored by it. It made the difference between Berthe and Edma Morisot's careers" (p. 58).

The two sisters studied and painted together as amateur painters for 12 years. Their parents provided instruction from the same painters and mentors for both of them and they worked side-by-side. At the end of those 12 years, Edma believed she had to choose between marriage and art. She decided to marry and stopped painting almost immediately. According to biographical evidence, Berthe Morisot was distraught by the contrast between her own choice to continue to paint and her sister's decision to abandon art in favor of marriage and children.

Berthe Morisot became an important member of the Impressionist movement, a painter among Monet, Cassat, Degas, Renoir, Manet, and others. When she married Eugene Manet in 1874 she combined marriage—and later motherhood—with her profession as painter, although at the time it was believed impossible for a professional artist to be a good mother. An easy explanation for the different paths of the two sisters would be to think that Edma's talent did not approach the level of her sister's. However, some critics of the time actually considered Edma's talents to be greater than Berthe's.

From her adolescence to her death, Berthe Morisot's training and commitment reflect a pattern of the dedicated professional, as she left the amateur artist tradition of her girlhood and transitioned into the world of professional male painters. Throughout she maintained her personal authority, the power to determine the pattern of her life. With that, she chose the most fundamental form of power for herself, the power to be self-determining.

SELF-ACTUALIZATION OR OTHER-ACTUALIZATION?

Abraham Maslow, in one of his most enduring contributions to the field of psychology (his originally constructed motivational scheme), proposed that human needs constitute a hierarchy ranging from physiological or survival needs, through affiliation and esteem needs, to the need for self-actualization. He described his concept of self-actualization as referring "to the [person's] desire for self-fulfillment, namely, to the tendency for him to become actualized in what he is potentially" (Maslow, 1943, p. 382).

The concept, as viewed by Maslow (1968), assumes the existence of inherent creative abilities, which are often weak and subtle and easily defeated by habit, cultural pressure, and erroneous attitudes toward them. Recognizing their fragility, Maslow raised the question: How can the development of these inherent capacities be facilitated? It is an important question, considering the enduring scholarly and research attention into our times. Searching for the answer, we tend to look at individuals who possess and are recognized for great talents. But, as discussed in Chapter 3, for every celebrated artist there are several who did not succeed despite their talents. Not all seem to be truly self-actualizers.

Furthermore, how do the many who do not possess a great, recognizable talent achieve the goal of self-actualization? As stated by Sidney Jourard in 1968 at a seminar entitled Art and Civilization: "It has seemed to me that artists in society embody and disclose possibilities of experiencing that are available to everyone, but are generally stifled" (Jourard, 1968, p. 173).

If these "possibilities of experiencing" are available to everyone, what are the reasons that determine whether or not an individual will achieve self-actualization? It has been suggested that creativity requires a decision by the individual to be creative (Sternberg, 2001), and, instead of an unfolding of inborn potentialities pushing for expression, self-actualization is a product of self-awareness, assertiveness, and authenticity in the individual's process of becoming (DeCarvalho, 2000).

Following those suggestions, does that mean that those female artists who at times seem to have buried their talents in favor of their husbands' accomplishments decided not to be creative themselves? When Mary Shepherd Greene, who had become a well-recognized artist, as discussed in Chapter 4, moved from painting to jewelry-making, she suppressed her talents to avoid competition with her husband, Ernest Blumenschein, a highly competitive man and painter. Similarly, as mentioned in Chapter 3, Russian artist Sonia Terk turned her talents toward decorative arts to make money that enabled her husband, Robert Delaunay, to devote himself to his painting; and Marjorie Organ Henri, in her transition from painter to being her husband's "muse," put her husband's career before her own. Similarly, Lee Krasner devoted her energy to furthering Jackson Pollock's career at the expense of her own work. Surrealist painter Kay Sage, as described in Chapter 4, used her financial resources to further the career of Ives Tanguy and abandoned her own work.

Did these female artists see the meaning of their lives in serving their husbands' talents rather than their own? As Maslow (1943) explained, the needs in his concept of a need hierarchy take on different forms from one person to another. Whereas in one individual it may be expressed as athletic ability, and in another as inventing new machines or products, in still others it may be the desire to be an ideal wife or mother. If being an ideal wife to their husbands had been the goal of these female artists, why weren't they happy in self-actualization when their husbands' careers reached the heights of fame and popularity? None of the women seemed to have been happy or at peace; perhaps peace finally came for Kay Sage when her second suicide attempt was successful in January of 1963.

Marianne Werefkin's parents, a Russian general and his artist wife, recognized and nurtured their daughter's talent early. While living in Moscow, her father built a studio for her in their garden and arranged for lessons from well-known artists. When the family moved to Petersburg, Marianne became a private student of Ilja Repin, the most famous Russian painter of that time. In her youth she was regarded as the "Russian Rembrandt." It was in Repin's studio that Marriane met Alexej Jawlensky, a lieutenant and part-time student of painting at the Petersburg academy. He remembered her as an intelligent and fantastically talented woman. They lived and worked together for 30 years, first in Petersburg and later in München, Germany, in 1896, where Marianne continued to promote his work (Sello, 1994/2000).

Although she refused to marry him, she provided him with a studio and the opportunity to create without having to worry about finances. Her purpose in life at that time was to transform him into a great artist, while she neglected her own work. Later she asked herself whether it was possible that, while she created with others' hands (Jawlensky's), there was a true artist in herself, the artist she neglected to recognize. The question she put to herself received an answer in her association with artists such as Kandinsky, Franz Marc, and Paul Klee, who admired her work and were inspired by it. Eventually, Marianne became the intellectual center of a circle of artists known as "Der blaue Reiter" (the blue rider). Following a trip to Paris in 1907, she finally returned to her own creations that placed her among the significant artists of the 20th century. Her question also indicates that she experienced at least some doubt about the option she chose some 30 years earlier.

Employed women carrying the responsibility for their family's health insurance (such as Marcia in Chapter 1 and Nadine, Laverne, and Anne in Chapter 2), because their husbands do not provide it, are supporting their husbands' interests or careers just like the better-known female artists mentioned above. While the husbands are following their dreams of running their own business instead of engaging in employment that carries such benefits, the wives' own dreams and goals are curtailed by the necessity of steady employment with good benefits for the family. Are they any happier than the artists? It does not seem so. Did they trade self-actualization for other-actualization as they chose the slipper with insufficient space for growth?

It has been argued that the motivational theory that survived for more than three decades in psychology textbooks is inaccurate or incomplete. In his later and mostly unpublished writings, adding another level beyond self-actualization to his motivational hierarchy, Maslow identified a construct of self-transcendence. "At the level of self-actualization, the individual works to actualize the individual's own potential . . . At the level of self-transcendence, the individual's own needs are put aside, to a great extent, in favor of service to others and to some higher force or cause conceived as being outside the personal self" (Koltko-Rivera, 2006, pp. 306–307).

Could one say that the women described above, by putting someone else's welfare—their husbands' and families'—above their own, reached the level of self-transcendence, sidestepping the self-actualization level? Perhaps they had not been aware of the various options. In the humanistic view, increased self-awareness and exercising choices are prerequisites for becoming self-actualizing. Making wise choices means making well-examined choices, which requires considering the alternatives and the consequences of each alternative. "Meaning, then, is that alternative which the individual affirms from among several possible choices inevitably available as ways of conceiving a situation. Given a particular situation the human individual is always able to conceive of some other way in which it might be—for better or worse. People are not bound in their conception to that with which they are presented" (Jenkins, 2000, p. 83).

THE SELFHOOD MODEL

To determine one's life, first of all, requires expanding the thought and energy to examine the self and its possibilities, a task that women are poorly trained for. Being instructed to favorably respond to the needs of others diminishes the importance one may assign to oneself. Also, some individuals may shy away from deciding their life's path out of fear of making mistakes. If they let others decide for them, they cannot be blamed for erroneous decisions. However, in the overall scheme it may be trivial to determine where to direct the blame compared to decisions of major consequences to one's life.

The importance of the self can be conceptualized as occupying steps or degrees along a continuum ranging from selflessness to selfishness. Although the concept of self or selfhood is linked to the construct of personality, it has been argued that the two are not synonymous. Rather, selfhood is just one important aspect of personality (L'Abate, 2005). Selfhood relates to individuals' being and doing within important relationships and encompasses the aspects of selflessness, no self, selffulness, and selfishness. Relating his model to the characteristic of limit-setting as an example, L'Abate described selfish (externalizing) individuals as pushing limits, selfless (internalizing) individuals as unable to set limits, no-self persons as inconsistent and contradictory, approaching extremes, and selffulness persons as firm, clear, and flexible in limit-setting.

In this model, selffulness represents a higher level of functionality than selfishness and selflessness, which occupy intermediate levels in dysfunctionality. The lowest level of functionality is found in the psychopathology of no-self individuals. Gender differences within this model can be observed to the degree that selfishness predicts a higher ratio of men over women, whereas selflessness contains a reverse ratio, more women than men. In selffulness, intimacy and negotiation are possible, but they are impossible in no-self situations. In selfish and selfless relationships, development of intimacy is risky and full of conflict.

Viewing selffulness as a maturational process, it includes the capacities of differentiating oneself from family of origin and from significant others, thinking and deciding by oneself, acknowledging one's value and the value of others, awareness of one's feelings as well as sharing them appropriately, flexibility in stressful situations, adapting without losing a sense of self, and learning from experiences, among others. "In this propensity, importance of self is exchanged democratically with intimate others, where 'Everybody wins'" (L'Abate, 2005, p. 264).

THE SELFHOOD MODEL'S APPLICATION IN THE DEVELOPMENT OF SELF-DETERMINATION

Samantha, the divorced mother of two sons and a daughter, found herself stuck in a no-win situation. Her ex-husband Jeff, a physician, insisted that Samantha bring and pick up the children from their visitation with their father. Due to his profession, he claimed, he could not make long-range plans regarding the visitation, and Samantha needed to be ready for his call. Initially, she went along with his demands but she soon realized that this would leave her at his beck and call and she could not plan her own activities, not even for the time that the children were with their father. At times Jeff called her soon after she had delivered the children, requesting she pick them up again, explaining that he had to respond to a medical emergency. Recently Samantha had complained about his unreasonableness, only to have Jeff inform her that because she had initiated the divorce, the whole situation was her fault and now she had to face the consequences of her actions.

It was true Samantha had been the one filing for divorce. Twelve years into their marriage, Jeff had purchased a condominium near the hospital he worked at—to be close while on emergency duty, he explained. Jeff's family did not occupy the condominium at those times; they stayed in their regular home. After some time, Samantha found out that at various times there were other occupants—Jeff's girlfriends. When she confronted Jeff with her observations, he at first denied it and then made light of the situation; it was meaningless and Samantha was exaggerating.

At first, when Samantha decided to discuss the unfairness of the visitation schedule with Jeff, she was convinced that she was doing the right thing. She felt abused. Jeff was taking advantage of her good nature, she reassured herself. However, when he blamed her for the situation that made it necessary that the children had to come to visit with him instead of all of them living together like a real family, Samantha lost her conviction of being right. Jeff had a way of turning things around, so that he was blameless. Samantha was confused. She started to stammer and collected her children to return home.

What made her situation worse was that her own parents did not approve of her divorcing Jeff. In his profession, Jeff was an important man; one needed to make allowances for him. Besides, it was not beneficial for the children to have their father separated from them. It had been Samantha's responsibility to provide a happy home for her family.

Considering Samantha's situation within L'Abate's selfhood model, it is apparent that their relationship is a selfish-selfless arrangement, with Jeff pushing the limits and Samantha being unable to set and maintain limits. This framework had been operating throughout their marriage and even before. Jeff set the limits that suited him, and Samantha caved in when it came to confrontations.

Jeff and Samantha had met in college; Jeff was a medical student, and Samantha was enrolled in the nursing program. They dated for a while and made plans for a joint future. Samantha was impressed by Jeff's self-assuredness. The beginning of Jeff's internship threatened to postpone their intimate relationship, as Jeff was ready to move to another state. This was a prestigious setting for any medical student's internship; rejecting it would be a sacrifice to his future. His suggestion was to get married so that Samantha could move with him. But Samantha was not finished with her training; she had at least another year to go. Jeff brushed her concerns aside with the argument that it made sense for their future to make the move together. She could get a job in their new environment, which would help them with their finances. Later, after Jeff was established, Samantha could return to school to finish her nursing degree if she wanted to.

As could be expected, Samantha gave in. They got married, she obtained a full-time job with health benefits in the state they moved to, and their first child was born. There was another move for Jeff's current position, and two more children arrived. Samantha never returned to school. Thus, from the beginning of their relationship Jeff determined Samantha's life by establishing the parameters of his goals, and Samantha accepted his demands. Even now as they were leading separate lives, Jeff still determined Samantha's activities and goals by making it impossible for her to plan anything with any assurance that she could adhere to her plans. At this point Samantha sought the help of a psychotherapist. The shoe in Jeff's hand that she had eagerly tried to fit into at the time of her infatuation with Jeff had been constraining, and it was still pinching her toes, even though she thought she had slipped out of it. Mentally, she was still confined in it.

With the help of her therapist Samantha explored her options. She could take Jeff to court to have a judge determine Jeff's responsibilities as a father. This was not a promising path for at least two reasons. Samantha did not have the money to hire an attorney, and it would aggravate the situation to the point that Jeff would be even more aggressive and the children might suffer. Another option would be to approach Jeff again with the hope that he would be more agreeable. Samantha admitted that this option had a very slim chance to succeed, unless her new approach included something of benefit to Jeff. An appeal to his selfish nature had a better probability for success.

Samantha knew some of Jeff's ambitions. He wanted to look good professionally and in the community because he was entertaining the possibility of running for a political office some day. He did not want to be thought of as a bad father. That was one of his reasons for being against the divorce. With that in mind, Samantha worked on another proposal to Jeff. She was willing to share the transportation of the children for their visits with Jeff. Considering the consequences of either delivering the children to Jeff's house or picking them up, she decided it would be in her best interest to have Jeff pick up the children at her house and agree to collect them from his house. Furthermore, to reduce the stress on the children—who waited for unspecified periods of time for their father—Samantha suggested that Jeff would determine the time and she would allow for reasonable delays (one hour).

As her therapist reminded her, there was no guarantee that Jeff would agree to this suggestion because he had been so disagreeable before. But if Samantha was able to maintain her limits, she could prepare for several possible consequences. In response to Samantha's proposal, Jeff declared it to be ridiculous and refused to discuss the issue. Before Samantha exited the discussion she left a written statement of her proposal, a copy of which she retained for her own files. When the day of the next visitation weekend came around Samantha and the children were ready. An hour later they left to visit with a friend of Samantha's who had two children of her own about the age of Samantha's two oldest boys. There had not been any sight or message of Jeff. Although Samantha was a bit anxious, they managed to have a good time and stayed until it was time to return home for the children's bedtime.

The telephone answering machine blinked; there were three calls. They were calls from Jeff, his voice expressing increasing degrees of anger as he informed them that he had come to pick up his children and found the house empty. He was furious, and on the third call he threatened to sue for full custody of the children. Over the years of her marriage Samantha had learned to fear Jeff's anger and disapproval. She needed time to calm down and prepare herself for her next communication with him.

Samantha called him the next day, reminding him of their conversation and her suggestion for sharing the transportation aspect of the visitation. She also mentioned calmly that she had kept a journal recording the biweekly visitation activities as they occurred. It took one more weekend for Jeff to learn that Samantha kept the limits she had established for this situation. Finally Jeff enlisted the help of his mother in taking care of the children when he was not able to do so. Samantha had previously considered recruiting the help of her former mother-in-law in order to cope with Jeff's resistance, but she had dismissed the idea. The children had a good relationship with their grandmother. Samantha did not want to put the older woman in the middle of the struggle between her son and her grandchildren.

In due time, Samantha reorganized her life. Her former mother-in-law was happy to be a regular part of her grandchildren's life again. She created learning activities for them that they enjoyed, which in turn allowed Samantha time to return to school and embark upon her interrupted career again. After years of letting others determine her life, she assumed the responsibility for her own plans and goals, realizing that others would hardly be able or willing to make the best decisions for her well-being. According to L'Abate's theory, Samantha had started developing her selfhood toward increased selfulness.

Whether one considers theories of self-actualization or selfhood or any other psychological-developmental theory, (such as Alfred Adler's motivational construct of overcompensation for a particular deficiency or inferiority, which has often been called "striving for superiority"—a construct that was later modified by Adler to mean fulfilling innate potentialities), women can start determining their life at any time. Adler's shift in emphasis from overcoming to fulfilling defines the person in a more powerful or active way. The person, or the self, moves the mental life and determines the direction of the move (Rychlak, 1973). This move can be undertaken at any time that the person becomes aware of its desirability and benefits. Thus, if—as in Samantha's case—women don't recognize in their youth the need for self-determination, they can make that decision at any time in their lives.

Returning to Lynn, the divorced mother of two children introduced in Chapter 4, she saw marriage as her only choice when her parents did not support her wish to go to college. At the time she finally filled out her college application, her husband had abandoned her and their two children after a few years of marriage. In the small town she grew up in there were no job opportunities beyond part-time work at the local café, and there was no public transportation. The money she made at the café was not sufficient for her small family, not even with the leftover food she received as payment for working as a maid in her parents' house when her mother needed her. Lynn had to apply for public assistance, a fact her mother was ashamed of—but not ashamed enough to offer more substantial help.

Fortunately, the public library was within walking distance from the little apartment above the café that Lynn occupied with her children. The librarian had once mentioned the mental-health agency in the next town, which had a sliding fee scale and where Lynn might be able to get advice for her seemingly hopeless situation. However, Lynn had no chances of getting there. One day, on her frequent visits to the library, Lynn ran into a former classmate. Becky had been the envy of all the other girls when she married Martin, a popular member of the high school football team.

Becky and Lynn had not been close friends back in school, but they started talking as they met at the library. Becky was widowed now; she and her young daughter lived with her parents-in-law. Her marriage had not been happy, but she did not complain. Her parents had died many years ago, and even her grandparents, who had raised her, were long gone. Her husband, an alcoholic by that time, had died in an accident that left Becky and her daughter penniless. Her parents-in-law offered room and board in exchange for help with the household chores and assistance in the care for her ailing father-in-law.

The two poverty-stricken young women sat together and exchanged notes about their hopeless life situations. They became friends, and Lynn mentioned the mental-health agency she had heard about from the librarian. Becky was able to borrow her in-laws' car for needed shopping trips, and she thought they might allow her the use of the car to find out about this agency in the next town. Even with the sliding fee scale, the two women did not have enough money to spend on individual sessions. But they reasoned that if married couples and families could be seen in conjoint sessions, couldn't that work for them? Their situations were similar and their need for assistance was equally great—why not ask for conjoint sessions? For once they got what they asked for; the therapist agreed to the "two for the price of one" deal.

Becky had not realized the degree of her depression. As a young girl she had an even temperament that seemed to be able to cope with anything. She was talented in arts and crafts and had used her talents to cheer up those around her. Since she and her daughter moved in with her parents-in-law, it seemed she had lost her talents. She made no attempt to put a brighter aspect to her environment. Lynn, on the other hand, had difficulty controlling the strong anger she felt for her parents, and in particular for her mother and the unfair treatment she had received from her mother all her life. Yet, she had to admit that the food packages left over from her parents' holiday dinners helped provide special treats for her children. It was especially problematic when she served the food to her parents, her brothers and their wives, and the children's table like a hired maid. Cleaning her mother's house was easier by comparison.

As they worked on anger and depression issues, the therapist encouraged Becky and Lynn to express wishes and dreams they may have had at some time. Becky's wishes had always been for a loving family, something she had once thought she was in the process of getting. And she had enjoyed her arts and crafts projects in the past. Apparently, she had no other ambitions for herself. Lynn, however, had wanted to go to college to learn more about the world. Since her frequent visits to the public library, she thought being a librarian would be great. This was the turning point in the two women's history. They conquered their negative feelings and set about exploring options to improve their current lifestyles.

While continuing with their usual tasks, Becky turned to her crafts projects and found ways to advertise and sell them on the Internet, even though she did not own a computer. Lynn, with the help of the librarian, worked on setting Becky up in the online business while she searched for studying materials to successfully take the college entrance examination. Among the available information about scholarships, Lynn selected those that appeared appropriate for her situation. Every extra penny was set aside to cover the cost of those applications. Her efforts paid off; Lynn passed the exam with flying colors and was awarded a scholarship that enabled her to move with her children to the other side of the state to start on her college career. She found a part-time job and a childcare facility in her new environment.

Both Becky and the librarian of her hometown attended Lynn's graduation. Their therapist had moved away, but both Becky and Lynn kept up the contact. Lynn went on to graduate school and became a librarian. She also became active in the local politics and ran for public office. She wanted to improve the living conditions of single women who were in need of help. Several years later she tried marriage again; she had met a man who understood and supported her ideas. Becky remained in their hometown. Her business grew, and she was able to invest in a computer of her own. As her depression dissipated, she made life much more pleasant for her daughter and her parents-in-law, who transferred the title for their house to Becky.

Becky, too, remarried. The local high school teacher, whose wife had left him for a man with a more flamboyant career, recognized Becky's caring nature, and, to his delight, Becky's parents-in-law gave their blessing. Becky and Lynn remained close friends and visited as frequently as they could. Finally, both women had been able to select a path of their own desires, and they continued their movement along that path, fulfilling their very different innate potentialities.

The case histories of these three women demonstrate that there are opportunities throughout life for changing one's course and determining a new direction, even after having followed the directions of others for some time. A necessary first step is to gain the awareness of what the real benefits and deficits are in holding on to myths and influences from the past that serve to lead women onto paths that have not been chosen by them with their own best interest in mind. Although it may relieve one of responsibility for the decision, it is implausible that one person would really know what is best for another individual and, furthermore, that this person would actually decide in the best interest of the other. As people have the responsibility for themselves, they practice making the best decisions for themselves first, and perhaps secondly for another person they care for.

Women, when confronted with past influences or an old myth, might want to ask the question, "Who is standing to gain from this directive?" before following its path. For instance, when confronted with appeals to their nurturing nature and requests for putting the interests of others before their own, women can examine whether or not these requests are expressed in the pursuit of acquiescing women's complaints of unfairness or gender inequality. Or when societal voices just want to make sure that women adhere to their "feminine duties," it would be appropriate to remember that in her book *The Myth of Women's Masochism,* psychologist Paula Caplan cited a statement made in 1966 by Dr. Hendrik Ruitenbeck, in *Psychoanalysis and Female Sexuality,* that too many women wanted to do or get something for themselves instead of just reflecting the achievements of their husbands.

Apparently in Dr. Ruitenbeck's opinion, the determination for women's destiny should be to live and act for their husbands' aggrandizement—along with raising the children and keeping the household functioning smoothly. Considering this statement objectively, was Dr. Ruitenbeck primarily thinking of the welfare of women, or of the welfare of the women's husbands? Smart Cinderellas will not want that shoe to fit.

References

American Girl, (2008). December 2008 Catalog, T80D08. Middleton, WI and at americangirl.com/stores.

American Society of Plastic Surgeons (2007). *National clearinghouse of plastic surgery statistics: Procedural statistics trends 1992–2006.* Retrieved April 30, 2007 from *http://www.plasticsurgery.org/meda/statistics/2006-Statistics.cfm.*

Andersen, B. L., & Cyranowski, J. M. (1994). Women's sexual self-schema. *Journal of Personality and Social Psychology, 67,* 1079–1100.

Andersen, B. L., Cyranowski, J. M., & Espindle, D. (1999). Men's sexual self-schema. *Journal of Personality and Social Psychology, 76,* 645–661.

Arnett, J. J. (2000). Emerging adulthood: A theory of development from the late teens through the twenties. *American Psychologist, 55,* 469–480.

Bancroft, J., Loftus, J., & Long, J. (2003). Distress about sex: A national survey of women in heterosexual relationships. *Archives of Sexual Behavior, 32,* 193–209.

Bassin, D., Honey, M., & Kaplan, M. M. (1994). Introduction. In D. Bassin, M. Honey, & M. M. Kaplan (Eds.), *Representations of motherhood* (pp. 1–25). New Haven, CT: Yale University Press.

Baumeister, R. F., & Tice, D. M. (2000). *The social dimension of sex.* New York: Allyn & Bacon.

Baumeister, R. F., & Twenge, J. M. (2002). Cultural suppression of female sexuality. *Review of General Psychology, 6,* 166–203.

Baumeister, R. F., & Vohs, K. D. (2004). Sexual economics: Sex as female resource for social exchange in heterosexual interactions. *Personality and Social Psychology Review, 8,* 339–363.

Bay-Cheng, L. Y., & Eliseo-Arras, R. K. (2008). The making of unwanted sex: Gendered and neoliberal norms in college women's unwanted sexual experiences. *Journal of Sex Research, 45,* 386–397.

Bellas, M. L. (1992). The effects of marital status and wives' employment on the salaries of faculty men: The (house) wife bonus. *Gender & Society, 6,* 609–622.

Belsky, J., & Pasco Fearon, R. M. (2002). Early attachment security, subsequent maternal sensitivity, and later child development: Does continuity in development depend upon continuity of care-giving? *Attachment & Human Development, 4,* 361–387.

Benstock, B. (1993). Non-negotiable bonds: Lillian Hellman & Dashiell Hammett. In W. Chadwick & I. de Courtivron (Eds.) Significant others: Creativity & intimate partnership (pp. 173–187). New York: Thames and Hudson, Inc.

Bentler, P. M., & Newcomb, M. D. (1978). Longitudinal study of marital success and failure. *Journal of Consulting and Clinical Psychology, 46,* 1053–1070. Berkeley, CA: University of California Press.

Blair-Loy, M. (2003). *Competing devotions: Career and family among women executives.* Cambridge, MA: Harvard University Press.

Blumberg, E. S. (2003). The lives and voices of highly sexual women. *Journal of Sex Research, 40,* 146–157.

Bogguss, S. (1993). Hey Cinderella. Album: *Something up my sleeve.* Liberty Records. http://www.cowboylyrics.com/lyrics/bogguss-suzy/hey-cinderella-4714.html. Retrieved 04/05/08.

Bond, S. B., & Mosher, D. L. (1986). Guided images of rape: Fantasy, reality, and the willing victim myth. *Journal of Sex Research, 22,* 162–183.

Bottigheimer, R. B. (1987). *Grimms' bad girls & bold boys.* New Haven, CT: Yale University Press.

Brown, L. M., & Gilligan, C. (1992). *Meeting at the crossroads: Women's psychology and girls' development.* Cambridge, MA: Harvard University Press.

Buller, D. B., & Burgoon, J. K. (1994). Deception: Strategic and non-strategic communication. In J. A. Daly & J. M. Wiemann (Eds.) Strategic interpersonal communication (pp. 191–224). Hillsdale, NJ: Erlbaum.

Bussolari, C. J., & Goodell, J. A. (2009). Chaos theory as a model for life transitions counseling: Nonlinear dynamics and life's changes. *Journal of Counseling & Development, 87,* 98–107.

Caplan, P. J. (1985). *The myth of women's masochism.* New York: E. P. Dutton.

Caplan, P. J. (1992). Gender issues in the diagnosis of mental disorder. *Women & Therapy, 12,* 71–82.

Carpenter, D., Janssen, E., Graham, C., Vorst, H., & Wicherts, J. (2008). Women's scores on the Sexual Inhibition/Sexual Excitation Scales (SIS/SES): Gender similarities and differences. *Journal of Sex Research, 45,* 36–48.

Cassel, C. (1984). *Swept away.* New York: Simon and Schuster.

Centers for Disease Control and Prevention (2007). Sexually transmitted diseases surveillance 2007 – STDs in adolescents and young adults. http://www.cdc.gov/std/stats07/adol.htm. Retrieved 04/08/09.

Chadwick, W. (1990). *Women, art, and society.* London: Thames and Hudson Ltd. Repr., 1992.

Chancer, L. S. (1998). *Reconcilable differences: Confronting beauty, pornography, and the future of feminism.* Berkeley, CA: University of California Press.

Chesler, P. (1997). *Women and madness.* New York: Four Walls Eight Windows.

Chesler, P. (2001). *Woman's inhumanity to woman.* New York: Thunder's Mouth Press/Nation Books.

Chesler, P. (2005). *The death of feminism: What's next in the struggle for women's freedom*. New York: Palgrave Macmillan.

Chodorow, N. (1978). *The reproduction of mothering*. Berkeley: University of California Press.

Clarke, S. C. (1995). Advance report of final divorce statistics, 1998 and 1990. *Monthly Vital Statistics Report, 43* (Suppl. no. 9). Hyattsville, MD: National Center for Health Statistics.

CNN.com/health (2008). "Study: 1 in 4 teen girls has an STD." http://www.cnn.com/2008/HEALTH/conditions/03/11/teen.std.ap/index.html.

Coates, I. (1998). *Who's afraid of Leonard Woolf? A case for the sanity of Virginia Woolf*. New York: Soho Press.

Collier, M. J. (1961). "The Psychological Appeal in the Cinderella Theme," *American Imago, 18* (Spring), 399–406, 408.

Collins, W. A. (2003). More than myth: The developmental significance of romantic relationships during adolescence. *Journal of Research on Adolescence, 13*, 1–24.

Critelli, J. W., & Bivona, J. M. (2008). Women's erotic rape fantasies: An evaluation of theory and research. *Journal of Sex Research, 45*, 57–70.

Crittenden, A. (2001). *The price of motherhood*. New York: Henry Holt and Company.

Daniluk, J. (1998). *Women's sexuality across the life span: Challenging myths, creating meanings*. New York: Guilford Press.

Dash, J. (1988). *A life of one's own: Three gifted women and the men they married*. New York: Paragon House.

de Beauvoir, S. (1952). *The second sex*. Trans. and ed. H. M. Parshley. Repr., New York: Vintage, 1974. (1)

de Beauvoir, S. (1970). *The second sex*. Repr., New York: Bantam Books, Inc., 1970, pp. 271–272. (2)

DeCarvalho, R. J. (2000). The growth hypothesis and self-actualization: An existential alternative. *The Humanistic Psychologist, 28*, 59–66.

Deutsch, H. (1944). *The psychology of women*. Vol. I. New York: Grune & Stratton.

Disney Enterprises (1995). *Walt Disney's Cinderella*. (First American ed.) Grolier Books.

Dowling, C. (1981). *The Cinderella Complex: Women's hidden fear of independence*. New York: Pocket Books.

Edley, P. P. (2000). Discursive essentializing in a woman-owned business: Gendered stereotypes and strategic subordination. *Management Communication Quarterly, 14*, 211–306.

Eichenbaum, L., & Orbach, S. (1983). *Understanding women*. New York: Basic Books.

Ellis, A. (1973). *Humanistic psychotherapy: The Rational-Emotive approach*. New York: The Julian Press, Inc.

Ellis, A. (1979). *The intelligent woman's guide to dating & mating*. Secaucus, NJ: Lyle Stuart, Inc.

Ellis, H. (1920). *On life and sex*. Garden City, NY: Garden City Publishing.

Ely, R. (1994). The effects of organizational demographics and social identity on relationships among professional women. *Administrative Science Quarterly, 39*.

Eriksen, K., & Kress, V. E. (2008). Gender and diagnosis: Struggles and suggestions for counselors. *Journal of Counseling & Development, 86*, 152–162.

Evenson, R. J., & Simon, R. W. (2005). Clarifying the relationship between parenthood and depression. *Journal of Health and Social Behavior, 46*, 341–358.

Fein, E., & Schneider, S. (2007). *All the Rules: Time-tested secrets for capturing the heart of Mr. Right*. (First Compilation Edition: January 2007) New York: Warner Books.

Fine, M., & McClelland, S. I. (2007). The politics of teen women's sexuality: Public policy and the adolescent female body. *Emory Law Journal, 56*, 993–1038.

Finer, L., & Henshaw, S. K. (2006). Disparities in rates of unintended pregnancy in the United States, 1994 and 2001. *Perspectives on Sexual and Reproductive Health, 38*(2), 90–96.

Fisher, H. (1999). *The first sex*. New York: Random House.

Forbes, G. B., Jobe, R. L., & Revak, J. A. (2006). Relationships between dissatisfaction with specific body characteristics and the Sociocultural Attitudes toward Appearance Questionnaire-3 and Objectified Body Consciousness Scale. *Body Image, 3*, 295–300.

Frederick, D. A., Peplau, A., & Lever, J. (2008). The Barbie mystique: Satisfaction with breast size and shape across the lifespan. *International Journal of Sexual Health, 20*, 200–211.

Freud, S. (1965). *New introductory lectures on psychoanalysis*. Trans. and ed. J. Strachey. New York: W. W. Norton. (Orig. pub. 1933).

Frey, J. N. (2000). *The key: How to write damn good fiction using the power of myth*. New York: St. Martin's Press.

Galambos, N. L., & Krahn, H. J. (2008). Depression and anger trajectories during the transition to adulthood. *Journal of Marriage and Family, 70*, 15–27.

Gangestad, S. W., & Simpson, J. A. (2000). The evolution of human mating: Trade-offs and strategic pluralism. *Behavioral and Brain Sciences, 23*, 573–644.

Gaze, D., ed. (1997). *Dictionary of women artists*. Vol. I. Chicago: Fitzroy Dearborn Publishers.

Geller, J. (2001). *Here comes the bride: Women, weddings, and the marriage mystique*. New York: Four Walls Eight Windows.

Gilbert, L. A. (1987). Female and male emotional dependency and its implications for the therapist-client relationship. *Professional Psychology: Theory, Research, and Practice, 18*, 555–561.

Gilbert, L. A., & Walker, S. J. (1999). Dominant discourse in heterosexual relationships: Inhibitors or facilitators of interpersonal commitment and relationship stability? In J. M. Adams & W. H. Jones (Eds.) Handbook of interpersonal commitment and relationship stability (pp. 393–406). New York: Kluwer Academic/Plenum.

Glick, P., & Fiske, S. T. (2001). An ambivalent alliance: Hostile and benevolent sexism as complementary justifications for gender inequality. *American Psychologist, 56*, 100–118.

Goldberg, J. (2008). Cinderella vs. the Barracuda. *The Indianapolis Star*, December 21. Conversations/National Voices, E2.

Graves, R. (1955). *The Greek myths*. Vol. I. New York: Penguin Books, Inc.

Gray, P. B. (2003). Marriage, parenting and testosterone variation among Kenyan Swahili men. *American Journal of Physical Anthropology, 122*, 279–286.

Guay, A. T. (2002). Screening for androgen deficiency in women: Methodological and interpretive issues. *Fertility and Sterility, 77* (Suppl. no. 4), 83-88.

Guerin, B. (2003). Language use as social strategy: A review and an analytic framework for the social sciences. *Review of General Psychology, 7*, 251–298.

Harrison, K. (2003). Television viewers' ideal body proportions: The case of the curvaceously thin women. *Sex Roles, 48*, 255–264.

Hays, S. (1996). *The cultural contradictions of motherhood.* New Haven, CT: Yale University Press.

Heilbrun, C. G. (1988). *Writing a woman's life.* New York: Ballantine Books.

Hendrick, C., Hendrick, S. S., & Reich, D. A. (2006). The brief sexual attitude scale. *Journal of Sex Research, 43,* 76–86.

Henning, Jr., W. T. (1978). *Ernest L. Blumenschein Retrospective.* Colorado Springs: Colorado Springs Fine Arts Center Catalog.

Heyn, D. (1992). *The erotic silence of the American wife.* New York: Turtle Bay Books, a Division of Random House.

Heyn, D. (1997). *Marriage shock: The transformation of women into wives.* New York: Villard Books.

Higonnet, A. (1992). *Berthe Morisot's images of woman.* Cambridge, MA: Harvard University Press.

Hill, D. B. (2007). Differences and similarities in men's and women's sexual self-schemas. *Journal of Sex Research, 44,* 135–144.

Hoare, Q. (1967). On women: The longest revolution. *New Left Review, 41,* 78–81.

Hollander, D. (1995). *101 lies men tell women: And only women believe them.* New York: HarperCollins.

Holtby, W. (1992). Feminism divided. In M. Humm (Ed.) Modern Feminisms. New York: Columbia University Press.

Hooks, B. (2002). *Communion: The female search for love.* New York: William Morrow, an Imprint of HarperCollins Publishers.

Hopper, J. (2001). The symbolic origins of conflict in divorce. *Journal of Marriage and Family, 63,* 430–445.

Horsfall, J. (2001). Gender and mental illness: An Australian overview. *Issues in Mental Health Nursing, 22,* 421–438.

Hull, T.H. (2008). Sexual pleasure and wellbeing. *International Journal of Sexual Health, 20,* 133–145.

Hyde, J. S., & DeLamater, J. (1997). *Understanding human sexuality* (6th ed.). Boston: McGraw-Hill.

Impett, E. A., & Peplau, L. A. (2002). Why some women consent to unwanted sex with a dating partner: Insights from attachment theory. *Psychology of Women Quarterly, 26,* 360–370.

Impett, E. A., & Peplau, L. A. (2003). Sexual compliance: Gender, motivational, and relationship perspectives. *Journal of Sex Research, 40,* 81–100.

Janssen, E., Carpenter, D., & Graham, C. A. (2003). Selecting films for sex research: Gender differences in erotic film preference. *Archives of Sexual Behavior, 32,* 243–251.

Jenkins, A. H. (2000). The liberating value of constructionism for minorities. *The Humanistic Psychologist, 28,* 79–87.

Jennings, J. L. (2007). Dreams without disguise: The self-evident nature of dreams. *The Humanistic Psychologist, 35,* 253–274.

Jourard, S. M. (1968). *Disclosing man to himself.* New York: Van Nostrand Reinhold Company.

Kamen, P. (2000). *Her way: Young women remake the sexual revolution.* New York: New York University.

Katz, J., Kuffel, S. W., & Brown, F. A. (2006). Leaving a sexually coercive dating partner: A prospective application of the investment model. *Psychology of Women Quarterly, 30,* 267–275.

Keller, E. F., & Moglen, H. (1987). Competition: A problem for academic women. In V. Miner and H. E. Longino (Eds.) Competition: A Feminist taboo? New York: The Feminist Press.

Kerr, B. A. (1994). *Smart girls: A new psychology of girls, women, and giftedness.* (Revised edition). Scottsdale, AZ: Gifted Psychology Press.

Kimmel, M. S. (2000). *The gendered society.* New York: Oxford University Press.

Kipnis, L. (2006). *The female thing: Dirt, sex, envy, vulnerability.* New York: Pantheon Books.

Kirby, D. (2007). Abstinence, sex, and STD/HIV education programs for teens: Their impact on sexual behavior, pregnancy, and sexually transmitted disease. *Annual Review of Sex Research, 18,* 143–177.

Kirby, P. (2008, Spring). Cinderella . . . probably lost her slipper because her feet hurt! *Radius Magazine,* Pitter from Pat (column).

Knafo, D., & Jaffe, Y. (1984). Sexual fantasizing in males and females. *Journal of Research in Personality, 18,* 451–462.

Koenig, J. S. (2004). The common bond of motherhood. *The Indianapolis Star,* May 9, Opinion/My View, E3.

Kohut, H. (1984). *How does analysis cure?* Chicago: University of Chicago Press.

Kolbenschlag, M. (1979). *Kiss Sleeping Beauty good-bye: Breaking the spell of feminine myths and models.* Garden City: Doubleday.

Koltko-Rivera, M. E. (2006). Rediscovering the later version of Maslow's Hierarchy of Needs: Self-transcendence and opportunities for theory, research, and unification. *Review of General Psychology, 10,* 302–317.

Konau, B. (1999). Georgia O'Keeffe's black maple trunk-yellow leaves. *Women in the Arts, 17,* 14–16.

L'Abate, L. (2005). *Personality in intimate relationships: Socialization and psychopathology.* New York: Springer Science + Business Media, LLC.

Ladurie, Emmanuel Le Roy (1979). *Montaillou: the promised land of error.* Trans. Barbara Bray. New York: Random House/Vintage, chs. 10–12.

Langer, C. L. (1996). *A feminist critique: How feminism has changed American society, culture, and how we live from the 1940s to the present.* New York: Icon Editions, an imprint of HarperCollins Publishers.

Laumann, E. O., Gagnon, J. H., Michael, R. T., & Michaels, S. (1994). *The social organization of sexuality: Sexual practices in the United States.* Chicago: University of Chicago Press.

Lawrence, K., & Byers, E. S. (1995). Sexual satisfaction in long-term heterosexual relationships: The Interpersonal Exchange Model of Sexual Satisfaction. *Personal Relationships, 2,* 267–285.

Lederer, W. (1968). *The fear of women.* New York: Harcourt Brace Jovanovich, Inc.

Levy, A. (2005). *Female chauvinist pigs: Women and the rise of raunch culture.* New York: Free Press, a Division of Simon & Schuster, Inc.

Li, N. P., Bailey, J. M., Kenrick, D. T., & Linsenmeier, J. A. W. (2002). The necessities and luxuries of mate preferences: Testing the trade-offs. *Journal of Personality and Social Psychology, 82,* 947–955.

Liebau, C. P. (2007). *Prude: How the sex-obsessed culture damages girls (and America, too).* New York: Center Street, a division of Hachette Book Group USA, Inc.

Lieberman, M. K. (1986). Some day my prince will come: Female acculturation through the fairy tale. In J. Zipes (Ed.) Don't bet on the prince. (pp. 185–200). New York: Methuen, Inc.

Liz Claiborne Inc. (2008) *Love is not abuse.* Study on teen dating abuse conducted by Teenage Research Unlimited. http://www.loveisnotabuse.com/statistics.htm retrieved 4/10/09.

Lo, V., & Wei, R. (2002). Third-person effect, gender, and pornography on the Internet. *Journal of Broadcasting and Electronic Media, 46,* 13–33.

Lucas, M. S., Skokowski, C. T., & Ancis, J. R. (2000). Contextual themes in career decision making of female clients who indicate depression. *Journal of Counseling & Development, 78,* 316–325.

Maass, V. S. (2002/2006). *Women's group therapy: Creative challenges and options.* New York: Springer Publishing Company.

Maass, V. S. (2007) *Facing the complexities of women's sexual desire.* New York: Springer Science + Business Media, LLC.

Maass, V. S. (2008). *Lifestyle changes: A clinician's guide to common events, challenges, and options.* New York: Routledge/Taylor & Francis Group.

Mahoney, S., & Zarate, Jr., C. (2007). Persistent sexual arousal syndrome: A case report and review of the literature. *Journal of Sex & Marital Therapy, 33,* 65–71.

Malamuth, N. M. (1996). Sexually explicit media, gender differences, and evolutionary theory. *Journal of Communication, 46*(3), 8–31.

Marazziti, D., & Canale, D. (2004). Hormonal changes when falling in love. *Psychoneuroendocrinology, 29,* 931–936.

Marelich, W. D., Lundquist, J., Painter, K., & Mechanic, M. B. (2008). Sexual deception as a social-exchange process: Development of a behavior-based sexual deception scale. *Journal of Sex Research, 45,* 27–35.

Markus, H. (1977). Self-schemata and processing information about the self. *Journal of Personality and Social Psychology, 35,* 63–78.

Maslow, A. H. (1943). A theory of human motivation. *Psychological Review, 50,* 370–396.

Maslow, A. H. (1968). *Toward a psychology of being.* (2nd ed.). New York: Van Norstrand Reinhold Company.

Mathewes-Green, F. (2002). *Gender: Men, women, sex, feminism.* Ben Lomond, CA: Conciliar Press.

Matson, M., ed. (1992). *An independent woman: The autobiography of Edith Guerrier.* Amherst, MA: The University of Massachusetts Press.

McAdams, D. P. (2001). The psychology of life stories. *Review of General Psychology, 5,* 100–122.

McDonald, D. (2004, April). Conrad wanted more. *Vanity Fair,* 290–339.

McGinty, S. M. (2001). *Power talk: Using language to build authority and influence.* New York: Warner Books.

McIntyre, M. H., Gangestad, S. W., Gray, P. B., Chapman, J. F., Burnham, T. C., O'Rourke, M. T., et al. (2006). Romantic involvement often reduces men's testosterone levels—but not always: The moderating role of extrapair sexual interest. *Journal of Personality and Social Psychology, 91,* 642–651.

Meana, M., & Nunnink, S. E. (2006). Gender differences in the content of cognitive distraction during sex. *Journal of Sex Research, 43,* 59–67.

Melamed, E. (1983). *Mirror, mirror: The terror of not being young.* New York: Linden Press/Simon & Schuster.

Merrell, S. S. (1995). *The accidental bond: The power of sibling relationships.* New York: Times Books.

Meyers, L. (2007). Sexual harassers target women who violate gender norms. *Monitor on Psychology, 38*(5), 12.

Milford, N. (2001). *Savage beauty: A biography of Edna St. Vincent Millay.* New York: Random House.

Millsted, R., & Frith, H. (2003). Being large-breasted: Women negotiating embodiment. *Women's Studies International Forum, 26,* 455–465.

Moran, J. P. (2000). *Teaching sex: The shaping of adolescence in the 20th century.* Cambridge, MA: Harvard University Press.

Morton, C. (2006). *How to walk in high heels: The girl's guide to everything.* New York: Hyperion Books.

Muller, H. J. (1954). *The uses of the past.* New York: New American Library.

Murray, J. (2000). *But I love him.* New York: Regan Books, an imprint of HarperCollins Publishers.

National Campaign to Prevent Teen Pregnancy (2006). *How is the 3 in 10 statistic calculated?* Washington, DC: Author.

National Museum of Women in the Arts (Holiday 2007). Washington, DC: *Women in the Arts, 25,* Museum Shop.

Osman, S. L. (2007). Predicting perceptions of sexual harassment based on type of resistance and belief in token resistance. *Journal of Sex Research, 44,* 340–346.

O'Sullivan, L. F., & Allgeier, E. R. (1998). Feigning sexual desire: Consenting to unwanted sexual activity in heterosexual dating relationships. *Journal of Sex Research, 35,* 234–243.

Otnes, C. C., & Pleck, E. H. (2003). *Cinderella dreams: the allure of the lavish wedding.*

Paul, B., & Shim, J. W. (2008). Gender, sexual affect, and motivations for Internet pornography use. *International Journal of Sexual Health, 20,* 187–199.

Pelosi, N. (2008). *Know your power: A message to America's daughters.* New York: Doubleday.

Pelusi, N. (2009). The appeal of the bad boy. *Psychology Today, 42,* 58–59.

Peters, M. (1977). *Unquiet soul: A biography of Charlotte Brontë.* London: Futura.

Phillips, L. M. (2000). *Flirting with danger: Young women's reflections on sexuality and domination.* New York: NYU Press.

Pillemer, D. B. (2001). Momentous events and the life story. *Review of General Psychology, 5,* 125–134.

Pillsworth, E. G., & Haselton, M. G. (2006). Women's sexual strategies: The evolution of long-term bonds and extrapair sex. *Annual Review of Sex Research, 17,* 59–100.

Pipher, M. (1994). *Reviving Ophelia.* New York: Ballantine Books.

Pitino, R. (1997). *Success is a choice.* With Bill Reynolds. New York: Broadway Books.

Polhemus, R. M. (2005). *Lot's daughters: Sex, redemption, and women's quest for authority.* Stanford, CA: Stanford University Press.

Pomeroy, J. (1999). Painting in a lonely arena: Joyce Treiman & the old masters. *Women in the Arts, 17,* 14–15.

Purdum, T. S. (2008, July). The comeback kid. *Vanity Fair,* 76–82, 127–131.

Rich, A. (1986). *Of woman born: Motherhood as experience and institution.* (10th anniversary ed.) New York: W. W. Norton.

Rich, E. (2005). Young women, feminist identities and neoliberalism. *Women's Studies International Forum, 28,* 495–508.

Rogers, S. J., & White, L. K. (1998). Satisfaction with parenting: The role of marital happiness, family structure, and parents' gender. *Journal of Marriage and the Family, 60,* 293–308.

Roney, J. R., Hanson, K. N., Durante, K. M., & Maestripieri, E. (2006). Reading men's faces: Women's mate attractiveness judgments track men's testosterone and interest in infants. *Proceedings of the Royal Academy of London, Series B, 273,* 2169–2175.

Ross, C. E., & Van Willigen, M. (1996). Gender, parenthood, and anger. *Journal of Marriage and the Family, 58,* 572–584.

Roundtree, C. (2000). *On women turning 30: Making choices, finding meaning.* San Francisco: Jossey-Bass Publishers.

Rowe, K. E. (1986). Feminism and fairy tales. In J. Zipes (Ed.) Don't bet on the prince (pp. 209–226). New York: Methuen, Inc.

Rubinstein, C. S. (1982). *American women artists from early times to the present.* Boston: Hall.

Rudd, E., Morrison, E., Sadrozinski, R., Nerad, M., & Cerny, J. (2008). Equality and illusion: Gender and tenure in art history careers. *Journal of Marriage and Family, 70,* 228–238.

Ruggles, S. (1997). The rise of divorce and separation in the United States, 1880–1990. *Demography, 34,* 455–466.

Rychlak, J. F. (1973). *Introduction to personality and psychotherapy.* Boston: Houghton Mifflin.

Salmon, C., & Symons, D. (2003). *Warrior lovers: Erotic fiction, evolution, and female sexuality.* New Haven, CT: Yale University Press.

Sarwer, D. B., Nordmann, J. E., & Herbert, J. D. (2000). Cosmetic breast augmentation surgery: A critical overview. *Journal of Women's Health and Gender-Based Medicine, 9,* 843–856.

Sattel, J. W. (1983). Men, inexpressiveness, and power. In B. Thorne, C. Kramarae, & N. Henley (Eds.) Language, gender and society (pp. 118–124). New York: Newbury House Publishers. A Division of Harper & Row, Publishers, Inc.

Schooler, D., Ward, L. M., Merriwether, A., & Caruthers, A. S. (2005). Cycles of shame: Menstrual shame, body shame, and sexual decision making. *Journal of Sex Research, 42,* 324–334.

Scovell, J. (1998). *Oona: Living in the shadows.* New York: Warner Books, Inc.

Seifert, T. (2005). Anthropomorphic characteristics of centerfold models: Trends towards slender figures over time. *International Journal of Eating Disorders, 37,* 271–274.

Sello, G. (1994). *Malerinnen des 20. Jahrhunderts* (4. Auflage 2000) [female painter of the 20th century] (4th ed.). Hamburg: Ellert & Richter Verlag GmbH.

Shainess, N. (1984) *Sweet suffering: Woman as victim.* Indianapolis/New York: Bobbs-Merrill.

Sheehy, G. (2008, August). Hillaryland at war. *Vanity Fair,* 74–86.

Shields, S. A. (2005). The politics of emotion in everyday life: "Appropriate" emotion and claims on identity. *Review of General Psychology, 9,* 3–15.

Shorter, E. (1982). *A history of women's bodies.* New York: Basic Books, Inc., Publishers.

Showalter, E., ed. (1988). *Alternative Alcott.* New Brunswick, NJ: Rutgers University Press.

Shulman, J. L., & Horne, S. G. (2006). Guilty or not? A path model of women's sexual force fantasies. *Journal of Sex Research, 43,* 368–377.

SIECUS, 2005. *http//en.wikipedia.org/wiki/.*

Skar, P. (2004). Chaos and self-organization: Emergent patterns at critical life transitions. *Journal of Analytical Psychology, 49,* 243–263.

Slatkin, W., ed. (1993). *The voices of women artists.* Englewood Cliffs, NJ: Prentice Hall.

Smith, W. (2008). Room at the top: Women land more high-ranking jobs in the arts but big-money posts still go to men. *Indianapolis Star/INDY Sunday,* February 10. Arts + Entertainment, 6–10.

Sommers, C. H. (1994). *Who stole feminism: How women have betrayed women.* New York: Simon & Schuster.

Solé, Jacques (1976). *L'amour en Ocident à l'epoque moderne.* Paris: Michel, pp. 87–92.

Speer, S. A. (2005). *Gender talk: Feminism, discourse and conversation analysis.* London: Routledge/Taylor & Francis Group.

Spender, D. (1980). *Man made language.* London: Routledge and Kegan Paul.

Sprecher, S. (1998). Social exchange theories and sexuality. *Journal of Sex Research, 35,* 32–43.

Steiner, L. M., ed. (2006). *Mommy wars: Stay-at-home and career moms face off on their choices, their lives, their families.* New York: Random House.

Sterling, S. F. (1995). *Women artists: The National Museum of Women in the Arts.* New York: Abbeville Press.

Sternberg, R. J. (2001). Teaching psychology students that creativity is a decision. *The General Psychologist, 36,* 8–11.

Sue, D. (1979). Erotic fantasies of college students during coitus. *Journal of Sex Research, 15,* 299–305.

Suleiman, S. R. (1993). The bird superior meets the bride of the wind: Leonora Carrington & Max Ernst. In W. Chadwick & I. de Courtivron (Eds.) Significant others: Creativity & intimate partnership (pp. 97–117). New York: Thames and Hudson Inc.

Suther, J. D. (1993). Separate studios: Kay Sage & Ives Tanguy. In W. Chadwick & I. de Courtivron (Eds.) Significant others: Creativity & intimate partnership (pp. 137–153). New York: Thames and Hudson Inc.

Tracy, L. (1991). *The secret between us: Competition among women.* Boston: Little, Brown and Company.

Travis, C. B., & White, J. W., eds. (2000). *Sexuality, society, and feminism.* Washington, DC: American Psychological Association.

Tuchman, B. (1978). *A distant mirror.* New York: Alfred Knopf.

Ussher, J. (1991/1992). *Women's madness.* Amherst, MA: University of Massachusetts Press.

Valenti, J. (2007). *Full frontal feminism: A young woman's guide to why feminism matters.* Emeryville, CA: Seal Press, Imprint of Avalon Publishing Group, Incorporated.

van Anders, S. M., Hamilton, L. D., & Watson, N. V. (2007). Multiple partners are associated with higher testosterone in North American men and women. *Hormones and Behavior, 51,* 477–482.

van Anders, S. M., & Watson, N. V. (2006). Relationship status and testosterone in North American heterosexual and nonheterosexual men and women: Cross-sectional and longitudinal data. *Psychoneuroendocrinology, 31,* 715–723.

van Anders, S. M., & Watson, N. V. (2007). Testosterone levels in women and men who are single, in long-distance relationships, or same-city relationships. *Hormones and Behavior, 51,* 286–291.

Viorst, J. (1998). *Imperfect Control: Our lifelong struggle with power and surrender.* New York: Simon & Schuster.

Vliet, E. L. (2005). *The savvy woman's guide to testosterone.* Tucson, AZ: HER Place Press.

Voorpostel, M., & Blieszner, R. (2008). Interpersonal solidarity and support between adult siblings. *Journal of Marriage and Family, 70,* 157–167.

Voorpostel, M., & van der Lippe, T. (2007). Support between siblings and between friends: Two worlds apart? *Journal of Marriage and Family, 69,* 1271–1282.

Wagner, A. M. (1993). Fictions: Krasner's presence, Pollock's absence. In W. Chadwick & I. de Courtivron (Eds.) Significant others: Creativity & intimate partnership (pp. 223–243). London: Thames and Hudson, Ltd.

Walker, B. G. (1983). *The women's encyclopedia of myths and secrets.* New York: Harper & Row.

Webber, R. (2008). In sickness and in health. *Psychology Today, 41*(6), 88–94.

Whitehead, B. D. (2003). *Why there are no good men left: The romantic plight of the new single woman.* New York: Broadway Books.

Wickham, R. A. (2008). *You may kiss the bride! (Now what?): The essential plan for the marriage of your dreams.* New York: Morgan James Publishing, LLC.

Wicoff, K. (2006). *I do but I don't: Walking down the aisle without losing your mind.* Cambridge, MA: Da Capo Press (member of the Perseus Books Group).

Wikipedia (2008). *The Bachelor.* http://en.wikipedia.org/wiki/The_Bachelor_(TV_series).

Winn, D. (2000). *The manipulated mind: Brainwashing, conditioning, and indoctrination.* Cambridge, MA: Malor Books.

Wohlberg, J. W. (1999). Treatment subsequent to abuse by a mental health professional: The victim's perspective of what works and what doesn't. *Journal of Sex Education and Therapy, 24,* 252–261.

Wolf, N. (2002). *The beauty myth: How images of beauty are used against women.* New York: Perennial, an imprint of HarperCollinsPublishers.

Wollstonecraft, M. (1792). *The vindication of the rights of women.* Boston: Peter Edes/Thomas & Andrews.

Woolf, V. (1929). *A room of one's own.* New York: Harcourt Brace Jovanovich.

Yalom, I. D. (1980). *Existential psychotherapy.* New York: Basic Books.

Yolen, J. (1977). America's Cinderella. *Children's Literature in Education, 8,* 21–29. [This essay has also been reprinted in Alan Dundes, ed., *Cinderella: A Casebook.* New York: Wildman, 1983, pp. 294–306.]

Zipes, J. (1986). *Don't bet on the prince.* New York: Methuen, Inc.

Zipes, J. (1997). *Happily ever after: Fairy tales, children, and the culture industry.* New York: Routledge.

Zipes. J. (2003). *The Brothers Grimm: From enchanted forests to the modern world.* New York: Palgrave Macmillon.

Index

About the Author

VERA SONJA MAASS, Ph.D, is a licensed clinical psychologist, marriage and family therapist, sex therapist, mental health counselor, and co-owner of Living Skills Institute, Inc., a private practice agency. She has more than 30 years experience working in mental health agencies and in private practice. Through her work and her teaching experience as adjunct faculty at local colleges, she has become intimately acquainted with women's dreams, hopes, and aspirations, their disappointments and heartbreaks, as well as with the thoughts and feelings of the men who shared these women's lives. Maass is serving as president of the National League of American Pen Women's Indianapolis and Indiana chapters. She is the author of four earlier books for professionals, *Counseling Single Parents: A Cognitive Behavioral Approach* (2000), *Women's Group Therapy: Creative Challenges and Options* (2002/2006), *Facing the Complexities of Women's Sexual Desire* (2007), and *Lifestyle Changes: A Clinician's Guide to Common Events, Challenges, and Options* (2008).